D0850332

WITHDRAWN

Shakespeare in his Context: the Constellated Globe

Shakespeare in his Context: the Constellated Globe

The Collected Papers of Muriel Bradbrook
Volume IV

M.C. BRADBROOK

Professor of English Emerita,
University of Cambridge, and Fellow of
Girton College

BARNES & NOBLE BOOKS
TOTOWA, NEW JERSEY

First published in the United States of America 1989 by
BARNES & NOBLE BOOKS
81 Adams Drive, Totowa, N.J. 07512

ISBN 0 – 389 – 20877 – 9

Library of Congress Cataloging in Publication Data
are available from the publisher.

Printed in Great Britain

Contents

A Note on the Cover Illustration

Sometime between 1666 and 1669 that inveterate collector, Samuel Pepys, acquired an engraving which he termed 'A Dutch kermis', modifying the title from one engraved on the work itself. This very large plate (436 × 695mm) he bound into a folio volume; it had to be folded at the outer edge; in the catalogue of the Pepys Library compiled by A.W. Aspinall, ed. R.W. Latham (1980) it appears in Vol. 3 as No. 38–9. It is ascribed to Nicholas de Bruyn after David Vinckeboons; the same subject was also engraved by Boetius Adams Bolswart. De Bruyn (1571–1656), Vinckeboons (1578–1629) and Bolswart (1580–1633) work in the tradition that had been seen in Breughel's well-known picture of a booth stage at a fair, and which was to descend to Hogarth, in such compositions as his 'Strolling actresses dressing in a barn'. The upper quadrant of Vinckeboons' scene and the Hogarth are both reproduced in Bamber Gascoyne, *World Theatre* (London, Ebury Press 1968). He states that the original oil painting of Vinckeboons is in the Herzog Anton Ulrich Museum, Braunscheig, and dates it 1608. This would put it in the same year as Greene's visit to Styria, where several English troops were in the Netherlands.

The stage from de Bruyn bears the same relation to the inn behind it as did the stage in the yard of the Boar's Head; one of its interesting features is the netting inclined outwards at an angle from the stage, to prevent climbing from the yard. It is like the perimeter fences of modern defence establishments; a man who has attempted the climb has slipped underneath the stage, another with his hands on the boards is being lashed by the clown. The stage, which has no trap, is supported on barrels and extends behind the curtain, with access to the inn through a window. At the side, a man is urinating through a pipe on to the head of a woman below – a Hogarthian idea. Two flags are displayed and a drummer beats to attract the crowd. In the foreground (not shown here), a group of grand visitors progress: a young lady with a boned starched ruff opening on to a V-shaped bodice, with hanging sleeves, inner sleeves puffed and slashed below the elbow, and her hair in two little curled horns in the Venetian style; an older woman wearing a cartwheel ruff, a gentleman in knee breeches, doublet and cartwheel ruff. Thieves are being chased from the inn by a woman and a man with a sword. All the levels of society are here.

The Boar's Head stage perhaps had such a perimeter defence, for rubbish had to be cleared from underneath it by the builders when carrying out improvements.

Foreword

Muriel Bradbrook is a human institution. Her first book on the Elizabethan theatre appeared in 1932. Since then the famous books on Elizabethan tragedy, Elizabethan comedy, Shakespearean poetry, and the Elizabethan player have been supplemented by other books and four collections of essays. This collection of her essays marks her eightieth birthday, and testifies yet again to the durability of those qualities she has brought to the study of the Shakespearean context. It is a durability apparent not only in the fifty-seven years which her publications on the subject have covered, but in the lasting strength of the principles of secure factual evidence and delicate analysis of implications which she has brought to it all.

The length of the time through which her books have dominated the study of Elizabethan theatre is enough to have made her an institution, but more importantly she has humanised her subject too. In that first book, published fifty-seven years ago, she gave the first clear demonstration of the qualities which have marked her work ever since, above all the control of a mass of disparate and elusive material evidence about Shakespearean theatre, the history and above all the human sociology of the writers, the players and the subjects of that time. The Shakespearean industry is huge, and very few scholars can claim to have mastered more than a small expanse of the broad fields which supply its factories. It is a subject which all too easily can seduce its workers into floating away from the factual grounding on clouds of fantastic industrial pollution. Professor Bradbrook has herself covered more of the ground than any other scholar this century. In the process she has done more to keep scholarly feet fixed to that ground than anyone since E.K. Chambers, whose own territory (the theatre and the London of Shakespeare's lifetime) has always been her main interest. She has amplified and extended, and, perhaps most substantially, has humanised our understanding of that huge and difficult territory.

Her grasp of the vast array of material evidence, and her capacity for drawing significant inferences from it all, has been unrivalled for several decades now. That same rich suggestiveness is evident in the essays in this volume, whether she is reassessing Shakespeare's early comedies (in the first part of the book), or calling attention to the citizen associations of Shakespeare's fellow-playwrights (in the second and third parts). The same delicate sensitivity is at work when applied to the human relations between the individuals of the playing companies in part III as is applied to analysis of the texts in part I. She is adept at the throwaway line which gives the subject a revealing new aspect, like the tiny parenthesis in her comments about Michael Bogdanov's production of *Romeo and Juliet*. That parenthesis, besides its visual and verbal pun, precisely identifies the reductiveness of an extravagantly modernised Shakespeare which has Tybalt entering noisily in a red sports car: '(his Triumph?)'.

Her own throwaway statement in the introduction to this book, that she has now retired from being retired, is difficult to relate to her scholarship because the flow of these invaluable books on Shakespeare's context has if anything increased through the last fifteen years. The claim that this is the last of her Shakespearean essays should perhaps be taken no more seriously than her original retirement. The investment of such a lifetime surely cannot be set aside so easily.

Professor Andrew Gurr

Preface

The fourth and valedictory volume of my *Collected Papers* appears in my eightieth year. Although I do not command the energy to offer a further full-length study, I hope this collection, all of it written in the last ten years, may continue the lines of enquiry found in Volumes I and III, and in my earlier works on Shakespeare and his theatre. The aim here is to display the many and conflicting forms of theatrical life which Shakespeare's London exposed him to, and which produced the variety and flexibility of his own style.

I have begun with studies of particular earlier works, and surveys, written for various parts of the world. For a second aim is to show the degree of cultural adjustment needed in talking of the Elizabethan theatre in Asia, Africa, America and Europe in these years when the study of International Shakespeare is developing in conferences and through visits. (A periodical on the subject was begun in 1974 in Tokyo by T. Oyama and is now being continued by Yoshiko Kawachi (Yushodo Shoten Co).) After my release from duty at Cambridge University I was able to visit other places more easily; now I am retired from being retired, I hope still on their visits to this country to meet friends who gave me such insights. The fellowship of scholars, the happiest international society that really adheres, is held together by Shakespeare.

These very different approaches, after the first group, in the second part of the book, look at various forms of entertainment in London. I discuss the indoor theatres and there is some consideration of Ben Jonson. I brought in Marlowe and Webster in Volumes I and III, and Heywood in Volume III. I had thought of including here John Lyly, but my study of him is appearing in a collection, to be published by Macmillan, from the University of Warwick, where I now hold a visiting professorship (see p. 211). The third part deals with the popular theatres of London. In the piece on 'The Brownes, the

Greenes, and the Red Bull' I gained much help from Mary Edmond's knowledge of the London archives. The three pieces on Popular theatre give Shakespeare's usual context, those on *The Two Gentlemen of Verona* and *The Phoenix and Turtle* his nobler affiliations.

The two writers in the Epilogue reflect the Shakespearean play that speaks most deeply for our time, *King Lear*. Guy Butler, President of the Shakespeare Society of Southern Africa, has studied and written on this tragedy and has himself written and produced many plays in the Eastern Cape across racial divides. Empson, perhaps the first to write on the fool in modern terms, sometimes liked to play that kind of rôle! So we see in Butler something like the view from Dover Cliff; in Empson, the combination of Yorkshire scenes and the galaxies.

Essays which did not fit into this general scheme, and are not included, are listed on pp. 209–11.

All the Shakespearean essays from those earlier volumes were collected in *Muriel Bradbrook on Shakespeare* (Harvester Press, 1984) and my new collection may also be seen as its sequel, to complete my essays on Shakespeare.

This volume is dedicated to The Shakespeare Society of Southern Africa.

M.C. Bradbrook
Cambridge

Shakespeare's Works

I.

What is 'Shakespeare'? (Tokyo)

'Shakespeare' being now heavy industry, a headline name for newspapers and television, speculation on the writer and the works engages many who have never opened a copy of his plays or poems. They are invited to judge as they may do on any other question, so that he provides an expeditious means for gaining attention for the army of the academically ambitious, who now compete with actors for publicity. The most rapid route is by discovering some new item attributable to 'the Bard', as the media, for reasons of economy in printing, tend to name him. In order to be new the discovery must necessarily be obscure, but this is irrelevant to its market value; a bibliophile will value a modern book for its dust jacket.

In the last two months of 1985 and the early months of 1986, three examples of such finds came to my notice. The first, Gary Taylor's claim for a nine stanza lyric, opening 'Shall I die?' is to be included in the Oxford Shakespeare; Eric Sams's claim for the anonymous MS play *Edmund Ironside* produced his very elaborate edition.[1] A claim for the integration of 'A lover's Complaint' with Shakespeare's Sonnets, with which it was published in the Quarto of 1609, appeared in an edition of the Sonnets for the New Penguin series, edited by John Kerrigan. The *Sunday Times* of 24 November 1985 flaunted the headline: 'How Gary discovered the Bard's "lost poem" '. His first step after reading nine stanzas of a lyric with the name William Shakespeare appended in a Bodleian manuscript (MS Rawlinson 160) was to subject them to a computer check against Spevack's *Concordance*, for, as the newspaper observed 'Shakespearean analysis is now a scientific art which relies on computers to crosscheck text'. The mere suggestion of irrefutable scientific data suffices to awe the general public, although in this case neither a science nor an art.

Professional interests provoked a debate in the *Times Literary*

Supplements, which lasted for three months. Early intemperate views became modified – the Oxford editors at first claimed that the onus was on dissenters to prove the lines were *not* by Shakespeare. Neither positive nor negative proof can be established; while various experts presented paleographic, bibliographic, formalist and musi-cological evidence, majority opinion did not favour the ascription. Another version of the lines was found in a manuscript at Yale. The verses, which I have recorded in the Appendix, deteriorate as they proceed; one may assume either they were sung in a play by Shakespeare without being of his authorship or that he knew how bad they were and, contrary to his practice of 'never blotting a line', he suppressed them!

From the works found in it, MS Rawlinson 160 is dateable in the mid 1630s, or twenty years after Shakespeare's death; poetic miscel-lenanies have been much utilised in editing such poets as Ralegh, Donne and Marvell and a single late ascription carries only limited weight. The long lapse between composition and recording would invite contamination, and a degree of textual corruption is evident. My own contribution concerned the topoi, arguing that the first four stanzas represented a current songform, a love plea found in verses by Downland, whilst the verse form survives as late as Purcell. The last five stanzas, a blazon of the lady's beauties given as a dream vision, seem to belong to a different tradition, are much more corrupt, and may have been added. [This letter appeared, along with Taylor's reply to the objectors, in the issue of 17th February 1986.]

The question arises why the attribution of such feeble lines should be of any consequence (a set of mocking verses that circulated in a northern university ascribed them to Francis Bacon!) The market-able value of a painting depends upon its being the traceable work of a great master and neither a copy nor a forgery; archaeological objects vary similarly in price, although sometimes the forgeries represent quite considerable skill and are of interest in their own right. Since Shakespearean investigation now produces over 3,000 items every year, it is not surprising that the Oxford editors have seized on any chances to present new versions of the text. The 'two-text theory' for *Troilus and Cressida* and *King Lear*, the alternative title of *All is True* for *King Henry VIII* and the revival of the name 'Oldcastle' for Falstaff in *King Henry IV* should in my view remain where they now are in previous editions – in the footnotes; for the established text is intended for general use. In former times, each generation regarded itself as the guardian of its inherited masterpieces, with a prime duty to transmit and not to tinker; although on the principles which the great classical scholar and poet A.E. Housman laid down in his preface to Manilius, the editor's duty is always to make a clear choice among alternatives – at his own risk.

The original writer of these works achieved universal appeal by transforming his life and opinions into his writings, leaving himself invisible. He presents conflicting issues 'which he did not choose to simplify, codify, reconcile or resolve' as Germaine Greer has recently observed.[2] He is almost as inscrutable as his brother Richard of whom we know only that he was cited before the church court and fined twelve pence. In 1898 Sidney Lee, Shakespeare's biographer, conceded that biographical studies were of little more relevance to the works than a public statue. Shakespeare remains anonymous, speaking for and through his fellow actors and his popular audience; this invisibility evokes a passionate identification which in the nineteenth century generated speculations about the plays' secret authorship, Francis Bacon, Christopher Marlowe and various noblemen being credited with their authorship by American amateurs, by French and German scholars.[3] The psychology of such fantasy lies close to the surface – the great unknown and unrecognised genius is already famous under another title! This dream is surpassed by the number of the mentally afflicted who claim themselves to be the author.

The late Allardyce Nicoll told me a badly wounded naval officer with this belief became sufficiently recovered to return to duty but only as a convinced Baconian! An Air Force officer who believed Christopher Marlowe to be the author sent me elaborate calculations; and when I said they reminded me of counting down aeroplanes, he wrote with gratification 'How did you guess?'

The cryptographers who verify the author by extracting code messages were conclusively exposed by the great cryptologists William and Elizabeth S. Friedman,[4] who established the principle that no code allowed any extensions, small deviations or additions – which disposed of many claimants. Following the rules themselves exactly they produced far more lengthy and coherent messages, such as: 'Dear Reader; Theodore Roosevelt is the true author of this play, but I, Bacon, stole it from him and have the credit. Friedman can prove that this is so by this cockeyed cypher invented by Dr C!'

Cryptograms are now replaced by claims for other forms of counting, including the computer. Computer scientists are among the first to refute excessive claims. 'Shall I die?' was reported on by Gina Kolack in *Science*, Vol. 231, 9 February 1986. Two scientists carrying their analysis against Spevack's *Concordance* to words used 100 times reported 'There is no convincing evidence for rejecting the hypothesis that Shakespeare wrote it' whilst stressing that they cannot prove that Shakespeare wrote it. Another computer scientist observed that when he read the verses they didn't sound convincing 'but after the reading of the analysis I'm as convinced as I would be by any other authenticity check'. Such modesty will not be deemed excessive. The method was based on a count evolved ten years ago to compute the number of butterfly species in Malaysia. A biologist after collecting and recording over a long period was asked how many species he had *not* seen, and, on the assumption that the selection had been random, the computer undertook such a calculation!

The very unit employed, the word, is open to varied interpretation. The opening line contains 'die,' whose permutations and varieties of meaning, its use as noun, verb and interjection indicate some of the difficulties. Nils Bohr's theory of complementaries permits alternative descriptive techniques to be simultaneously valid for different purposes; for Shakespeare and his contemporaries, the oxymoron was a tool of thinking as well as of rhetoric. Any scientist worth his salt will regard any hypothesis as no more than the most plausible explanation of observed data, will constantly test it against the strongest objections and will leave it to the further judgment of time. Shakespeareans act rather as advocates, determined to advance their own cause and their client's. An episode in the well known TV series *The Paper Chase* shows a battle at Harvard between the law students and the engineers – the lawyers in the end beating the computer by asking a hypothetical question which its system is not programmed to deal with.

Eric Sams at first (1982) made use of a part of Spevack's *Concordance* in claims for the Shakespearean authorship of *Edmund Ironside*, but he has not pursued them in his edition *Shakespeare's Lost Play* (Fourth Estate, 1986). The manuscript, now in the British Library, like Rawlinson 160 dates from Caroline times and can be traced to the latest of the London Caroline theatres, Salisbury Court. The play was first connected with Shakespeare by an American, R.B. Everitt, in 1954. The text is known generally through the Malone Society Reprint edited by Eleanore Boswell in 1928; it deals with the wars between King Canute and Edmund Ironside as leaders of the Danes and English. A series of combats are interspersed by atrocities, the comments of a chorus and dumb shows. It is nearest to the plays on early English history which were a feature of the Admiral's Men at the Rose, and Sams thinks it was written for Edward Alleyn. The best known in this genre are *Locrine* and Haughton's *Grim the Collier of Croydon*. The atrocities include a stage trick to cut off the noses and hands of two young hostages; but to counteract such spectacle the Chorus at one point enters in black and proclaims:

> The fight is hot but Canutus is o'er come
> and Edmund hunts him out from place to place.

He flies to Worcester, Edmund follows him.
The way is long and I am waxen faint.
I fain would have you understand the truth
and see the battles acted on the stage
but that their length will be too tedious.
Then in dumb shows I will explain at large
their fights, their flights, and Edmund's victory
for as they strived to conquer and to kill
even so we strive to purchase your good will.

(III.iii.964–74)

Such dramaturgy might make the Nine Worthies think again and Peter Quince blush. Whilst Sams made some use of computer – reader analysis, he relies in his lengthy Commentary, 153 pages to 60 pages of text, on image clusters, single words, etc., to relate this 'abominably bad play' (Kenneth Muir's words) to the early Shakespeare of *Henry VI* and *Titus Andronicus*.

One British national daily paper asked me for a review and, faced with the need to express views on such technical matters in a popular paper, I decided that a jesting role was the only one possible; so I wrote a burlesque.[5] Sams had advanced the view that the play, like *Sir Thomas More*, was witheld by censorship, because of clerical opposition to the invective between the Archbishops of Canterbury and York, followers respectively of Canute and of Edmund Ironside. Noting that the Princely Pleasures of Kenilworth, where Queen Elizabeth had been entertained in July 1575, included a play by Coventry tradesmen on the wars between the English and the Danes – which had been banned by the clerics of Coventry – and that Shakespeare as a boy is often credited with attendance at these neighbouring festivities and with having then gained hints from some plays for *A Midsummer Night's Dream*, I suggested that at the age of eleven this play of *Edmund Ironside* was written to celebrate his move from the petty school to the upper school at Stratford – then as now, eleven is the age for such a move. Moreover, his schoolmaster, Simon Hunt, was about to leave England and to join the Catholic order of Jesuits, if indeed his father also were not a secret Catholic; so that disrespectful scenes between the Archbishops might have been a suitable offering. I contrived to remember one image common to this play and the popular account of the Coventry play known as *Laneham's Letter*.

A teacher in the local training college said he wasn't sure if I meant this seriously. If it is lese-majesty to be less than reverential to Shakespeare, it was even more heinous to question the supreme importance of the examination then known as 'the eleven-plus'.

John Kerrigan, the young editor of *Love's Labours Lost* for the Penguin series, indulged in some fantasy in a piece for the *London*

Review of Books and was sharply taken up by Sams in a subsequent issue. Kerrigan has also prepared for the Penguin series an edition of the *Sonnets* putting forward a theory that the Quarto of 1609 included by design 'A Lover's Complaint', forming a sequel in the manner of other such volumes published earlier, in the 1590s. The lament of the forsaken girl, enclosing her recollection of the hypocritical complaint by which her seducer won her, is told to an old man; the pastoral scene distances the more fervent story of the Sonnets – some of which Kerrigan puts as late as 1604 – and relates to the willow song in *Othello*, performed that year. I do not find 'A Lover's Complaint' much more resonant than 'Can I fly?' yet this claim serves as yet another illustration of the impulse to find something new for yet another edition. The argument from genre form as book form is original, but in my view Hallett Smith comments fairly in *The Riverside Shakespeare* that if 'A Lover's Complaint' is by Shakespeare it neither detracts from achievement nor adds to it. None commented at the time and few have commented since. Rare is the restraint which could confine a newdiscovered sonnet by William Earl of Pembroke (a candidate for the role of Fair Youth and false lover) to an appendix in the poems of his forsaken mistress. The sonnet protests his constancy.[6] In April 1988 Peter Levi of Oxford, claimed for Shakespeare some verses added to Marston's *Ashby Entertainment* of 1606. His claim was demolished by James Knowles in the *Times Literary Supplement* of 29 April 1988.

Through centuries the works of Shakespeare have been emended. As editor Lewis Theobald produced the line on Falstaff's death 'A babled o' green fields' in 1726; Wilson Knight recovered the significance of *Pericles* in 1930, awarding not only a safe but an honoured place to the play excluded from the First Folio and mocked by Ben Jonson. Yet the end was for many years banished from *King Lear* and a happy ending supplied by Tate in 1681 was retained; current movements to break down the First Folio include the two-text versions of *Troilus and Cressida*, *King Lear* and *Hamlet*, the attribution of parts of *Macbeth* and *Timon* to Thomas Middleton, advanced by R.V. Holdsworth, and the new additions here considered. As early as 1726 Theobald claimed to have seen the lost *Cardenio* and to have incorporated parts in his own play, *The Double Falsehood*; while in 1795 the seventeen year old William Ireland produced not only domestic papers but an entire play *Vortigern and Rowena*, creating even in those days quite a stir, till unmasked by Edmund Malone.

The urge to emend, add or conjoin is a consequence of that appeal for collaboration which Shakespeare made by the stage audiences in his comedies and in *Hamlet*, in the choruses in *King Henry V* and in his prologues and epilogues. There is no objection to including in the record everything relating to an author who has become the victim of his own spellbinding. He has been much enriched and is now

> an honour longing to our house,
> Bequeathed down from many ancestors,
> Which were the greatest obloquy i' th' world
> In me to lose.
>
> (*All's Well*, IV.ii.42–5)

But there is complementary need to distinguish the power of those greatest works, the radiant core, from the mass of accretions. The late Professor Quiller-Couch would declare roundly by way of definition 'Tragedy is the *Agamemnon, Hamlet* and things like that!' To say that 'Shakespeare is *King Henry IV, Hamlet* and things like that!' seems to me good Platonism and good sense.

Appendix: 'Shall I Fly?'

1

Shall I die? Shall I fly
Lover's baits and deceits,
            sorrow breeding?
Shall I tend? Shall I send?
Shall I sue, and not rue
            my proceeding?
In all duty her beauty
Binds me her servant for ever.
If she scorn, I mourn,
I retire to despair, joying never.

2

Yet I must vent my lust
And explain inward pain
            by my love breeding.
If she smiles, she exiles
All my moan; if she frown,
            all my hopes deceiving —
Suspicious doubt, O keep out,
For thou art my tormentor.
Fly away, pack away;
I will love, for hope bids me venter.

3

'Twere abuse to accuse
My fair love, ere I prove
            her affection.

Therefore try! Her reply
Gives thee joy — or annoy,
            or affliction.
Yet howe'er, I will bear
Her pleasure with patience, for
            beauty
Sure will not seem to blot
Her deserts, wronging him doth
            her duty.

4

In a dream it did seem —
But alas, dreams do pass
            as do shadows —
I did walk, I did talk
With my love, with my dove,
            through fair meadows.
Still we passed till at last
We sat to repose us for pleasure.
Being set, lips met.
Arms twined, and did bind my
            heart's treasure.

5

Gentle wind sport did find
Wantonly to make fly
            her gold tresses.
As they shook I did look,

But her fair did impair
                    all my senses.
As amazed, I gazed
On more than a mortal
                    complexion.
Them that love can prove
Such force in beauty's inflection.

6

Next her hair, forehead fair,
Smooth and high; next doth lie,
                    without winkle,
Her fair brows; under those,
Star-like eyes win live's prize
                    when they twinkle.
In her cheeks who seeks
Shall find there display'd beauty's
                    banner;
Oh admiring desiring
Breeds, as I look still upon her.

7

Thin lips red, fancy's fed
With all sweets when he meets,
                    and is granted
There to trade, and is made
Happy, sure, to endure
                    still undaunted.
Pretty chin doth win

Of all the world commendations;
Fairest neck, no speck;
All her parts merit high admirations.

8

A pretty bare, past compare,
Parts those plots which besots
                    still asunder.
It is meet naught but sweet
Should come near that so rare
                    'tis a wonder.
No mishap, no scape
Inferior to nature's perfection;
No blot, no spot;
She's beauty's queen in election.

9

Whilst I dreamt. I, exempt
From all care, seemed to share
                    pleasures in plenty;
But awake, care take —
For I find to my mind
                    pleasures scanty.
Therefore I will try
To compass my heart's chief
                    contenting.
To delay, some say,
In such a case causeth repenting.

William Shakespeare

Notes

1 Eric Sams (ed.), *Shakespeare's Lost Play* (London, Fourth Estate, 1986).
2 Germaine Greer, *Shakespeare* (Oxford University Press, 1986), p. 17.
3 Samuel Schoenbaum, *Shakespeare's Lives* (Oxford, Oxford University Press, 1970) chronicles these claims.
4 *The Shakespeare Cyphers Examined* (Cambridge, Cambridge University Press, 1957).
5 *The Guardian*, 13 February, 1986.
6 Josephine A. Roberts (ed.), *The Poems of Lady Mary Wroth* (Baton Rouge and London, Louisiana University Press, 1983). Pembroke is Kerrigan's candidate for the role of betrayer.

II.

'The Cause of Wit in Other Men' (Grahamstown)

The popular game of 'Who wrote Shakespeare's plays?' was played very entertainingly a year ago by the Nigerian dramatist Wole Soyinka when he elaborated the idea that *Antony and Cleopatra* could only have been written by an Arab, because of its intense feeling for the people of the Nile, its sense of the Kingdom of the Dead, so deeply Egyptian. He puts his case with all the elegance of a poet playing a farce, identifying the dramatist as Shayk el Subair, his wife as Hanna Hattawa.

I have a new suggestion: that the plays of Shakespeare are being written all the time by H.C. Earwicker or Here Comes Everybody, king of the dream world in *Finnegans Wake*. You and I, John Milton, S.T. Coleridge, Mr Krige, David Garrick and Laurence Olivier have built up the rich deposit which grows and grows every year. Some contributions drop off very fast; but the weightier ones, attracted by this great magnetic star, fall into it, as the lighter stuff drifts away in gradation out to sheer lunacy. Because each one of us contributes from the depth of our being, we often guard our versions more jealously than Shakespeare himself seems to have done. At gatherings of scholars after an evening's performance, each furiously attacks that particular intonation or gesture which has contradicted something he or she cherishes deeply. Actors, of course, hope to provoke discussion; in the seventies they used to insult the playwright or the spectator or both, in order to awake them from torpor; although I think this mood is passing.

The printing of his plays did not interest Shakespeare, it seems. He wrote a scenario, handed it over and took a supportive role. The latest textual studies explore the theory that where we have more than one early textual version of a play (as in *Hamlet, King Lear* and *Troilus and Cressida*) these represent successive forms evolved in the playhouse – the later ones perhaps containing new elements by

Shakespeare, or signifying his acquiescence in what stage experience evolved. There were special performances with insertions, we may be sure; at the beginning and the end of his career, Shakespeare also collaborated. He wrote a speech for the play of *Sir Thomas More* about 1592, joining four other collaborators. Others seized speeches or favourite lines from his works, whether in print or not. His friend Thomas Heywood had included such play-stoppers as 'I'll kiss thee ere I kill thee' in *The Golden Age* (1611).

In the eighteenth century Sheridan shows Mr Puff, playwright hero of *The Critic* opening his tragedy on *The Spanish Armada* with its audible echoes of the opening scene of *Hamlet*, and introducing a mysterious Yeoman of the Guard with the line 'Perdition catch my soul but I do love thee!' The author at first denies that this has anything to do with Shakespeare but when the persistent enquirer mentions *Othello*, says 'Two people happened to hit upon the same thought, and Shakespeare made use of it first, that's all!'

That practised filcher, T.S. Eliot, who remarked 'Bad poets imitate; good poets steal!' found it necessary to get away from Shakespeare's pervading presence and took *Everyman* as his first dramatic model. But his most perfect poem is close to Shakespeare, *Marina*.

It was urged at the World Conference on Shakespeare in 1981 that Shakespeare is understood in subtle ways by those for whom English is not their mother tongue; they pick up nuances not clearly visible to careless native speakers. That question was wittily explored by Soyinka. The process of adding to Shakespeare, like the equally significant one of 'cutting' may date from Shakespeare's own day, as the textual innovators suggest. Ben Jonson remarked 'He flowed with such facility that sometimes it was *necessary* he should be stopped' – and the line he quotes from *Julius Caesar* 'Caesar did never wrong but with just cause' was changed; although the original makes devastating, if paradoxical sense. And he heads his comment 'On *our* Shakespeare'. He thereafter said Shakespeare was incomparable; and Dryden, a most persistent adaptor, wrote in the prologue to his version of *The Tempest*:

> Shakespeare's magic could not copied be:
> Within that circle none durst walk but he.

Drama is not a form of minstrelsy; Shakespeare's relation to his texts is not identical, though something very distantly related, to Burns's relation to Scottish lyric.

I am proposing to look first at some historic adaptations; in the modern field of cultural adaptation, I come to learn of you. I must first distinguish between Shakespeare's effect on his auditory and the 'manipulator' of modern times. By way of coming down to brass tacks I shall take a look at *A Midsummer Night's Dream*, which I shall suggest is the comedy for our time, as *King Lear* is the tragedy for our time. Behind will loom one or two general questions that I hope you may debate; for I too aspire to be the cause of wit in other men.

W.B. Yeats once wrote to a friend that 'A poem comes right with a click like a closing box'; Eliot also wrote of poems where 'every word is right' and 'the complete consort dancing together'. In 'O Mistress Mine' or 'Full Fadom Five' Shakespeare surrendered to the musicians (whom he inspires as Donne, for example, does not). In the influences of stage performance, audience, actors, designers change the rhythms, the colour, by their contributions; they will cut and shape, adding a character or a name here or taking one out there; in Shakespeare's day the audience might call for what they wanted to see, or dismiss what they did not.

The Shakespearian textual theories of the eighties, to which I've already alluded, imply that the 1604 *Hamlet* versus the 1623 First Folio of Collected Plays, the 1609 *Lear* or *Troilus* versus the Folio, represent Shakespeare's first submissions; and the later Jacobean form, one he may have 'authorised'. Philip Edwards, who is editing *Hamlet* for the New Cambridge, accepts, as he wrote (1984):

Twentieth century editors of Shakespeare have for a long time been tied to the concept of a single authoritative text, and have been unwilling to listen to what centuries of theatre history make plain, namely that texts written for the stage are unfixed and fluid.

Only recently have they begun to explore again the possibility that the wide divergencies in the extant texts of many of Shakespeare's plays may represent successive stages in the play's life in the theatre.[1]

Edwards maintains that the cuts at the end of the closet scene and the omission of the fourth soliloquy 'How all occasions do inform against me' in the 1623 Folio *strengthen* the play as drama. He admits that 'There's letters sealed ...' is superb theatre, full of muscle; but Hamlet's plans should not be so definite here. So an impulse to destroy Rosencrantz and Guildenstern later comes in a flash; a line is added 'Why, man they did make love to this employment' to meet the demur of Horatio 'So, Rosencrantz and Guildenstern go to't'. The nerveless Hamlet of the fourth soliloquy not only contradicts the closet scene, but seems to belong to an early stratum of the play. Edwards prefers the eloquent silence left by these cuts. Shakespeare (he thinks) was being curbed – just as Jonson had said he was. He improved because his team, including the bookkeeper, jabbed him into it.

Of course these scholars do not dispute the unique authority of the early text, but only ask what sort of authority it is. I find myself nearer to Kenneth Muir; this dramatic tightening can be seen in Beaumont and Fletcher and goes with the 'hamming' they practised. Jonson himself introduced primacy of literacy texts, cutting out his collaborators. The later seventeenth-century improvements of Shakespeare were in the interests of such drama. For instance, Davenant's *Law Against Lovers* (1662) puts Benedick and Beatrice as heroic comic relief into *Measure for Measure*, Benedick being made Angelo's brother, Beatrice his ward — much more eloquent than Pompey. Isabella married Angelo, Shakespeare's invention of Mariana being discarded; their debate is sharpened by couplets.

Angelo: You must by yielding teach me to relent,
             Make haste! the mourner's tears are almost spent . . .

Isabel: And with the mornings wings your cruel doom
             He shall convey where you must shortly come,
             Before the judge, whose power you use so ill,
             As if, like law, t'were subject to your will.
             The cruel there shall wish they had been just,
             And that their seeming love had not been lust.

Angelo: These useless sayings were from cloisters brought;
             You cannot teach as soon as you are taught.
             You must example for my mercy give
             First save my life, and then let Claudio live.[2]

The antagonists are making a stand on principles of love and honour; the play asks to be judged by its own convention, which shows the conflict of law rigorously enforced for general good and the essentially antisocial attitude of a ruling clique. It should be looked upon as a Restoration version, in the language of the stable by Shakespeare out of Corneille.

Dryden's *Troilus and Cressida*, built on the same model, drew from an enthusiast praise for excelling Shakespeare.

             As with Ennius Vergil did of old,
             You found it dross and you have left it gold.

The problem plays (so first classed at the beginning of this century) have acquired great popularity because they are taken to be disturbing, questioning, iconoclastic; history plays are similarly treated, allowing all kinds of modern reflections; the last plays now range from colonialism to space travel in Directors' Shakespeare.

Shakespeare begged the audience to 'work, work your thoughts'. If the audience would 'piece out your imperfections with your thoughts', if the players could 'on your imaginary forces work' the 'mutual act of all our souls' might merit applause. He addressed his audience through his fellows in intimate and complex interplay that does not sink to manipulation. The man who penned Antony's speech in the forum, and created Iago and Iachimo was not unaware of such powers. But the man who showed the manipulation by Oberon was aware of its risks as between mortals and spirits.

When it comes to interpreting a four-hundred-year-old dramatist in modern terms the audience is doing partly what Shakespeare asked, and partly what in his own day he feared – insults or libels, as when the Virgin Queen said of an early play on matrimony 'this is all written against me'. In France today Coriolanus is taken as a hero of unquestioned principle, not in England. T.S. Eliot, always aware of this extra-dimension, said 'Its meaning to others is as much a part of it as what it means to oneself' and later he allowed that 'the reader's interpretation may not only differ from the author's and be equally valid – it may even be better. There may be much more in a poem than the author was aware of'.

Lately, studies in America have tended to talk of Shakespeare's manipulation of his audience. Modern plays, written in an age when subliminal pressure through advertisements follows market research by means of public images, may consciously engineer a passive audience – passive because it does not realise what is being done to it, and cannot contribute. This resembles the coercion of electoral campaigns. Images that can be manipulated are addressed to 'the Public' – not to the collective imagination defined as 'that power by which we apprehend living beings and living creatures in their individuality, as they live and move and not as ideas or categories'.[3] This definition by my friend Edwin Muir continues:

'Imagination is therefore never exact knowledge – exact knowledge is only a fragment of the knowledge we need in order to live . . . Perhaps the best way to regard 'the Public' is as a mental stage shared by all of us for the smaller or greater part of our lives rather than as the multitude of human beings summoned up by the imagination with all the thoughts and feelings and difficulties and joys and griefs to which human beings are subject. In its sphere, it has no need to encounter the intimate aspects of things and it has no technique for doing so'.

If the hours in our lives which we give up idly or seriously to public and general things have increased with growth of the media, this may

'Give our minds and feelings a certain predilection for the abstract and the cliché and the cliché is the popular expression of the abstract. It tends to make us view life impersonally, as third parties and onlookers'.

The engagement of the imagination protects us by requiring us also to share in an alien point of view, historically speaking. We have to gain other perspectives, such as the doctrine of wifely obedience that underlies *The Taming of the Shrew*.

The audience are not asked to forgo their own beliefs. 'The poet never affirmith and therefore never lieth' Philip Sidney said; and Samuel Johnson of Shakespeare 'He shows us human nature, not only as it acts in real exigencies, but as it would be found in trials to which it cannot be exposed'. In the words of Coleridge, the audience must 'entertain that willing suspension of disbelief that constitutes poetic faith'.

Culturally, Shakespeare may luckily match quite alien material, as in the Japanese film, *Throne of Blood*, on Macbeth which locks on to their own medieval blood feuds. I am trying to distinguish the audience from that public castigated by R.S. Thomas:

> It was a time when wise men
> were not silent but stifled
> by vast noise. They took refuge
> in books that were not read.
>
> Two consellors had the ear
> Of the public. One cried 'Buy'
> Day and night, the other
> More plausibly 'Sell your repose'.

(*Later Poems*, London, Macmillan, 1972, p. 16)

Modern Elizabethan actors are very good scholars in many cases. They have no need of A.L. Rowse's recent attempt to render Shakespeare intelligible in *The Contemporary English Shakespeare* by substituting 'you' and 'yours' for 'thou' and 'thine' which really should cause no one any difficulty. The attempt roused the editor of the *Shakespeare Quarterly*, John F. Andrews, and they met on TV in the McNeill Lehrer Report, where Rowse called Andrews a nitwit talking third rate rubbish. But what is gained by Juliet's saying:

> You know the mask of night is on my face
> Else would a maiden blush bepaint my cheek
> For that which you have heard me speak tonight.
>
> (II.ii.75–76)

Thomas Otway wrote in 1680:

> Thou knowest the mask of night is on my face
> Else should I blush for what thou heard'st me speak.
> (*Works of Otway*, 1757, vol. III, p. 145, II.i.)

This was in his *History and Fall of Caius Marius*, which also included such stunners as

> O Marius, Marius! wherefore art thou Marius?

Deny thy Family, renounce thy name:
Or if thou wilt not, be but sworn my love,
And I'll no longer call Metellus Parent.

I should like to add a footnote on contemporary playing abroad of his plays in his own lifetime, not by his own company, but the rival group led by Robert Browne the elder, who had belonged to Ned Alleyn's company and was indeed quite possibly Alleyn's step-brother. Browne went to Arnhem in 1592, again in 1593 and there-after quite regularly till his death. In the plague year 1603 he toured in Germany. Robert Browne the younger explored as far as Austria, Poland and even Russia until the outbreak of the Thirty Years' War. I think he was a nephew and he played, not in English, but in German. The first Robert Browne was known both as a clown and as a musician, the younger as musician and swordsman (see Chapter XI).

Farce and tragic violence are easier to convey in an unknown tongue. Of Shakespeare's plays, *Titus Andronicus* and *Hamlet, The Taming of the Shrew, The Merchant of Venice, The Merry Wives of Windsor*, 'Pyramus and Thisbe', *Twelfth Night* are recorded. The route to Germany lay through the Netherlands; in Utrecht and Leiden, Munster and Augsburg actors regularly appeared, and at the great fair in Frankfurt in spring and August, and also in the courts of princes – Maurice of Orange-Nassau, Julian Duke of Brunswick, both of whom wrote plays. The latter included in his plays the English clown, Pickle Herring, a gross comedian.

King James VI was brother-in-law to the King of Denmark, the Duke of Brunswick and the Duke of Saxony. English players visited all three; some players enroled at the courts of foreign princes, others settled down as merchants in the great trade centres. This inter-course, which has not been sufficiently recognised, was centred on the Boar's Head in Whitechapel, close to where ships berthed downstream from London Bridge. Henslowe became involved at one point, and a later clown in Shakespeare's company named Shanks.

Shakespeare did not go abroad, but every summer returned to the county where he was born. I shall turn to that most delicately balanced complex comedy of city and country which I shall term the 'Creation of a New World' – *A Midsummer Night's Dream*.

In the New Cambridge Edition, R.A. Foakes describes 'two main acting traditions, one emphasising charm and innocence; the other stressing darker suggestions of violence and sexuality, showing that both are necessary for a full understanding of the play'.[4] With respect, I must dissent. 'Night and silence; who is here?' may be eerie, but it is not sinister. The modern tendency in Director's Theatre stems from Jan Kott's notorious version, based on some misreadings, and on the middle European tradition of the sinister fairies. I cannot accept the 'dark' version. Today the element of the numinous has faded because the supernatural in our urban life is now channelled into science fiction and star wars. The *frisson* lies in the encounter of two levels of being, the elemental and the dreamy mortals. For a marriage night, that eerie sense of encounter with the other is perfectly appropriate and the implication of the natural unity between the union of individuals and the whole rhythm of nature, a theme of poets as, in Spenser's *Epithalamion* published at this time.

The spirits of this comedy arrive to bless the bridal and expressly to drive away all dark and menacing forces with which the modern view would associate them. They are 'spirits of another sort', from churchyard ghosts or from evil witchlike powers. They are morning spirits, not evening spirits. It is here I think that from Africa special insights might come. Much of what I have learned about elemental beings came from my dear friend Monica Wilson, the anthropologist of Rhodes and Cape Town universities. The shades and their powers are better understood today in Africa than in Europe or America.

But you will say these are local spirits, and how can 'the nodding violet' convey its perfume to the Karoo. If 'I know a bank whereon the wild thyme blows' may need translating, the Paradise Garden is known in every land. The way in for members of alien cultures is, I would think, through the intricate conclusion where all strands of the play are woven together. Begin with Act V and the play of 'Pyramus and Thisbe' — the play Elizabethan actors took abroad. Notice that Athens had no special features — it contains a temple, a hall and a bedchamber; none of which are described.

If today the strong individuality of *Hamlet* is yielding to the relatedness of *King Lear*, perhaps *A Midsummer Night's Dream* is the comedy for our time, as *King Lear* is the tragedy. The problem of how relationships can be reached is the subject of the play itself, and this involves the relation of the imagination to the knotted events by which the play works upon groups. It is the two activities that most involved Shakespeare — human lovemaking and play-acting, that are subject to disabling praise and affectionate mockery. Great security alone would permit this comic transformation. The fairies, hailed from the beginning as Shakespeare's most original creation, have inspired lyric, opera, ballet, painting, but above all perhaps, musicians.

The illustrations of Blake and Fuseli are famous; the two greatest English composers, Henry Purcell and Benjamin Britten, both made operas, the one in 1692, the other in 1960, from this play. Sixty years after Purcell, Garrick wrote *The Fairies* which omits the Athenian workman, but adds songs from *Love's Labours' Lost, Much Ado,*

The Tempest, King Henry VIII, as well as from *L'Allegro, Comus* and various minor poets. In the nineteenth century Mendelssohn supplied a musical setting of which the wedding march has become a near universal feature of marriage services.

The tradesmen on the other hand, have proved irresistible to actors. Their play reflects earlier and quite serious drama on the theme of tragic love, including Shakespeare's own *Romeo and Juliet* with its orchard wall and tragic death scene. The tradesmen's play is a mirror of a magic greater than Puck's – Shakespeare's own. It reflects the interplay between actors and audiences which generates the energy of performance – a kind of marriage rite, a harmonious discord.

Like *Macbeth*, the play is built on a series of triads – the contrast between daylight and Athens, the woodland kingdom of fairies and dream, and their conjunction in the last act; between the court, the city workmen, the fairy realm. The plots as such end with Act IV and the pairing off of the lovers, the reconciliation of Fairy King and Queen. The lovers come from Latin comedy with their cross-wooings; they are there to provide the continuity and action. The two men swivel, the two women remain constant; the pattern is that of a dance. The fairies and the tradesmen provide the actual dance measures in another triad: the first dance of reconciliation of Oberon and Titania, the absurd and farcical bergomask which ends the play-within-the-play, and the final dance by the spirits to bless the bridal.

The three worlds interweave constantly; not for nothing is the most fully individualised character Bottom the weaver. He is supremely the cause of wit in other men – Shakespeare's good-natured parody of his own profession. Compare him with Falstaff in his power of imaginative improvisation.

His play of *Pyramus and Thisbe* is derived from Ovid who supplied the whole idea of transformation, that lay behind Shakespeare's woodland poem *Venus and Adonis*; but the story of Pyramus and Thisbe entertainingly mocks Golding's translation of Ovid's *Metamorphoses*, in which lovers thank the courteous Wall:

But yet, thou shalt not find us churles; we think ourselves in debt
For this same piece of courtesy in vouching safe to let
Our sayings to our friendly ears thus freely come and go.

We learn from another play, Sharpham's *Fleire*, 'Like Thisbe in his play has almost killed himself with the scabbard'. But Golding's couplet is too monstrous to be forgotten:

This said, she took the sword yet warm with slaughter of her love
And setting it beneath her breast did to her heart it shove.

Other plays had been given at festive occasions only – Christmas, May or Whitsun, Corpus Christi, or Harvest, or, of course, a wedding. Midsummer Eve was the time in which traditionally maids dreamed of the young men they would marry; herbs gathered on Midsummer Eve were of special power. Within these special church festivities, the Reformation had banished much of the world of angelic and demonic spirits – the hierarchies of the nine spheres of planets. Shakespeare revived, reincarnated this triple world in new form with his woodland spirits. This was familiar from Ovid and English poetry from Chaucer to Spenser, whose *Epithalamion* had for chorus the line in which the woods answer till the echoes ring. It was to fascinate Milton who celebrated how:

> Sweetest Shakespeare, Fancy's child,
> Warbles his native woodnotes wild.

Comus is filled with reminiscences of this play and of *The Tempest*, where Shakespeare once more invents elemental spirits who fascinated his contemporaries.

Oberon has a distinguished ancestry; his servant is a blend of Puck, the shape changer, and Robin Goodfellow, the folk goblin, the 'lubber fiend' who sweeps the house for the maids and expects a bowl of cream to be set out by the fire as payment. These two roles played in and out of each other and blend with classical roles; for Puck is also Cupid, and the presiding goddess, in her highest form, is Diana, one of whose names was Titania, as Noel Purdon showed in his excellent study.[5] In Act V the climatic joining of the triads opens with Theseus, the ruler's, great speech on Imagination, rewritten, as Dover Wilson first showed, to include with the lunatic and the lover, the poet who is 'of imagination all compact'. His 'shaping fantasies' apprehend 'more than cool reason ever comprehends',

> And as imagination bodies forth
> The forms of things unknown, the poet's pen
> Turns them to shapes and gives to airy nothing
> The local habitation and a name.
>
> (V.i.14–17)

The lunatic's imagination applies only for himself, the lover's to a universe of two, but the poet's imagination functions for and awakens everyone, but awakens them as individuals in a social context. This is the justification of the arts. Theseus dismisses the story of the lovers which they themselves had wondered at, but his bride feels that the 'story of the night' holds 'something of great constancy'. In the world of his theatre, on the other hand, Theseus is sympathetic to Bottom and Quince while Hippolyta is at first bored

– though eventually joining in, 'Well shone, Moon'. The debate on the concrete representation of Lion, Wall and Moonshine, which has so preoccupied the actors, broadens out into a second world of enchantment for them in the glorious splendor of playing before their ruler. The artificial diction of the lovers in Act I is far outdone by Pyramus and Thisbe, and the presiding Moon becomes Starveling the tailor. Did the woodland scenes belong equally to the lunatic, the lover and the poet? Love is certainly shown as a kind of lunacy, but it masquerades as cool reason. When Lysander had been enchanted by Oberon's magical herb he proclaimed to his new love that the change is due to reason, 'Reason says you are the worthier maid' – while his deserted Hermia dreams within the dream of being attacked by a serpent. Lysander is indeed a false being created by Puck, like Spenser's Snowy Forimell. The distinction between dreams and visions, which are dreams understood or interpreted was fully explained by Chaucer and earlier playwrights such as Lyly, and Puck also explains in the epilogue.

The lovers marvel at the events of the night. In its wonder and humility, the dream reaches towards, and ends with that of Bottom who had taken his own metamorphosis and the love of the Fairy Queen so prosaically. He is moved to quote scripture: 'Eye of man hath not seen, Ear hath not heard, neither have entered into the heart of man, the things which God hath prepared for him that love him' (I Corinthians 2.9); it becomes

> The eye of man hath not heard, the ear of man hath not seen, man's hand is not able to taste, his tongue to conceive or his heart to report what my dream was.
>
> (IV.i.205–7)

Literally true, they can't.

The new dreams of the wedding night include that special dream, a play: and it is generally thought that this play was designed for a wedding (the favourite choice of Foakes is the wedding of the Lord Chamberlain's granddaughter in January 1595). The Queen herself might have been present, as the very direct compliment to the 'Fair vestal throned by the west' suggests.

It has been customary to blame the lovers for their reception of the workmen's play, but audience and players are all well wined and well dined, the young men want to display their wit, and Theseus their lord commends the play. The players certainly take the banter as complimentary and showing attention. With 'lovers to bed; 'tis almost fairy time' Theseus abdicates and the kingdom of dreams returns with the banishment of more sinister supernatural worlds and hungry lions, not stage lions, wolves and screech owls.

The true lovers are united; and, as in this play, a modern poet whom I have already quoted, began the last poem he wrote: 'I have been fed by dreams and fantasies', Edwin Muir ends it in the faith

> That Plato is the truest poesy
> And that these shadows
> Are cast by the true.

Puck ends 'If we shadows have offended . . . Think you have but slumbered here while these visions did appear'. He hopes to 'scape the serpent's tongue' – the theatrical hiss of course, but something more too. Like Bottom's, his play is commended by dispraise.

It will be clear that I regard the dark readings of this play as a serpent's hiss. It is not necessary to be phallic in order to be comprehensive; Freud himself did not limit himself to the phallic which he thought less mature than the genital impulse. Not only would I be prepared to endorse Bottom rather than Theseus on dreams; I would go further. The censorship in later years did not so much as permit the name of God to be mentioned on stage, but Shakespeare turned disabilities into opportunities and has here set his imagination free, which generates other men's. Another spirit is invoked in his jumbled but far from pagan ecstasy.

> The multitudes came together and were confounded because that every man heard them speak in their own language. And they were all amazed and marvelled, saying one to another . . . 'How hear we every man in our own tongue wherein we were born . . . we hear them speak in our tongues the wonderful works of God (Acts 2, 6–11).

This play echoed in Shakespeare's latest work. *The Two Noble Kinsmen* has been termed '*A Midsummer Night's Dream, Part II*' by Glynne Wickham; and in the final blessing of bridal which crowns *The Tempest*, Prospero-Oberon looks far ahead:

> We are such stuff
> As dreams are made on; and our little life
> Is rounded with a sleep.
>
> (IV.i.156–58)

Notes

1 'Shakespeare's alterations in *Hamlet*', in *Literature and Learning in Medieval and Renaissance England* ed. John Scattergood, Dublin, Irish Academic Press, 1984, p. 175. From a lecture at Aberdeen, 1980. See also p. 180.

2 Sir W. Davenant, *Works* (1673), Folio part II, pp. 272–324, see p. 314, ll. 17–18. 25–31.

3 Edwin Muir, *The Estate of Poetry* (Cambridge Mass., Harvard University Press, 1962), p. 81.
4 Cambridge, Cambridge University Press, 1982, pp. 1–4.
5 Noel Purdon, *The Words of Mercury* (Salzburg, Studies in English Literature, University of Salzburg, 1974).

III.

The Building of Tragic Character in Shakespeare (Valencia)

Shakespeare's power to give his actors characters who delighted the audience must largely be due to his being, like Molière, himself an actor in a stable company that enjoyed sixty years' pre-eminence in London. From 1594 to 1642, they remained a self-directed, self-controlled group. Richard Burbage (c. 1567–1619) did not dominate in the way that Edward Alleyn, the tragedian who created Marlowe's tragic roles, dominated through his wealthy father-in-law the troupes at the rival theatre of the 1590s, the Rose – and later at the Fortune. This partnership, which started with a wedding in October 1592, maintained an older tradition of spectacle – fireworks, cannon, gorgeous costumes, perhaps interludes of performing animals. A team of hired playwrights worked to order on Marlovian tragedy or farce. Burbage and Shakespeare offered the power of the word, of dramatic poetry, in which the protean Burbage made his name with the tragi-comic role of King Richard III, in the oldest play to stay on the boards continuously from 1592 until today.

This tragic hero emerges as both human and superhuman; his relation to the medieval devil is obvious. In the 1985 production of the Royal Shakespeare Company, Antony Sher makes Richard so demonic that he cannot change into the remorseful dreamer of Act V; Sher's Richard, an emanation of fiendish exuberance and boundless resource, cannot be brought back to humanity by the final recognition which unkings him: 'Richard loves Richard, that is, I am I'. Offering an astounding *tour de force* which is its own justification, it debars the growth of character which for the great eighteenth century actor, David Garrick, had given the supreme tragic moment, which foreshadows future developments.

Nevertheless, in December 1985, Antony Sher was voted best actor of the year in the Laurence Olivier awards for his performance as Richard III, and himself has written an account of his part.

Richard, who opens with a self-revealing soliloquy, is an actor who can assume any role he chooses to play, for the devil too was an expert in appearing as an angel of light – in *Dr Faustus* he is disguised as an old Franciscan friar. Evil of two generations of civil war, all concentrated in him, make him a portent, an 'embossed carbuncle' in the body politic, with an extremity of isolation from humankind that twists an opponent's words against him, an ironic repartee that parodies traditional speech, as in response to his mother's plea.

> Amen: and make me die a good old man.
> That is the butt end of a mother's blessing.
> I marvel that her grace did leave it out
>   (II.ii.109–11)

Richard begins where Macbeth at the end of his tragedy was to arrive. But the chorus of ghosts – their faces whitened with flour, their choric refrain 'Despair and die!' – brings him to rebirth as a man. It was the last act that made the part so famous. The cry 'A horse, a horse, my kingdom for a horse' sets fighting at a higher price than rule; it is a perfectly built line, the panting of the battle-weary, the defiance of the implacable. A character built up consistently is suddenly transformed, but with an instant effect of conviction. The part of a Shakespearean tragic hero may at first look traditional, but an individual emerges in both hero and villain. The tremendous effect of

> Yet Edmund was belov'd . . .
> I pant for life; some good I mean to do . . .
>   (*King Lear* V. iii. 240, 244)

or the total closure of

> Demand me nothing. What you know, you know:
> From this time forth I never will speak word.
>   (*Othello*, V. ii. 300–2)

transform the antagonists; merciless Edmund melts, loquacious Iago refuses any traffic with mankind.

The star actor, that 'delightful Proteus' who 'never put off his part, as much as in the tiring house', was supported by actors who over the years came to know each other intimately, intermarried, remembered each other in their last testaments. But they left no record; these belong to their rivals at the Rose, where Alleyn dominated physically; a cluster of dramatists worked to his orders. No care was taken of the texts; Marlowe's were very wretchedly corrupt when at last they appeared. An actor-playwright of that rival group printed *The Jew of Malta* as late as 1634 only because the new leading man wanted to play Alleyn's part.

The word had not the shaping or moulding power for Alleyn's company that it had for Burbage's. They sometimes copied their rivals – *Sir John Oldcastle* blatantly exploited the popularity of Shakespeare's *King Henry IV*. Little was printed; when Henslowe and Alleyn's later theatre, the Fortune, burnt down in 1622, their playbooks were destroyed, so from their records we have the names of many lost plays.

Shakespeare, who according to Ben Jonson 'flowed with such facility that sometimes it was necessary he be stopped', used no collaboration other than discussing the play with his fellow actors; he was the only member of the company who wrote, and they kept his scripts with care, for seven years after his death they could bring out the First Folio containing some very early drama. He himself was a supporting actor; by repute he played old men whether Adam in *As You Like It*, or the Ghost in *Hamlet*. His troupe were described as 'men of grave and sober behaviour'[1] and incontestably led the rest when in 1603 they became the King's Men.

A third group, the choristers of St Paul's Cathedral and of the Chapel Royal, who plays indoors, within the City, during the 1580s and from 1599 to 1608, was dominated by the dramatists, not by the actors or the financiers. John Lyly directed the choristers, his light elegant comedies furnishing Shakespeare with a model for the witty word combats of *The Two Gentlemen of Verona* and *Love's Labours Lost*, and for the symmetrical pairing of characters in deft satiric backchat. The plays in the children's repertoire were published, so that they strongly influenced other players, and set up a standard of plays as literature, not merely as theatrical scripts. A disproportionately large number of the texts have survived, whilst almost nothing remains of the spectacular tradition. The record we have is as distorted as an anamorph, or trick portrait.

In *Hamlet*, when the Prince objects on the one hand to those actors whose strutting and bellowing proclaim the work of 'nature's journeymen' and on the other to the 'little eyasses' or callow birds of prey who 'cry out on the top of question', he is taking a position midway between the two rivals, where Shakespeare and Burbage themselves were poised and balanced.

In addition, the wandering to which the actors visiting Elsinore are driven depicts that of the troupes who in the 1590s toured Northern Europe, as shown in the recent study by Jerzy Limon, *Gentlemen of a Company*.[2] They played in English and so tended to be led by clowns; farcical gymnastic feats alternated with music and dancing although they also played in *Titus Andronicus* and other early Shakespearean plays.

Titus Andronicus is a play where the hero becomes demonic and might well wear the mask of Revenge. Revenge tragedy purported to derive from the Roman tradition of Seneca (who wrote not for the theatre but for rhetorical declamation), imposing outward duty to kill in a world from which Justice has been banished. But suppressed rage and a sense of cosmic dislocation fires the great soliloquies; irony speaks both in and through the mask, showing both the mask and the face.

This double being is the obverse of the hero in the Japanese drama of masks, the Noh. As Zeami, founder of the tradition and himself an actor as well as dramatist explains, the First Actor must study his mask (probably an ancestral treasure) till he becomes the character of the mask, and yet by this act releases an inner force from his own being. In these plays the character first appears as human, in the second half being transformed into a divine or demonic being. In Shakespeare, one who appears at the first more than human is revealed in the second half to be a man — whether Richard the King, or Hamlet the Dane or Coriolanus, incarnation of the God Mars.

The Spanish Tragedy, prototype of Revenge plays, no doubt differed in Burbage's interpretation from Alleyn's, and by 1602 poignant additions to the hero's part show how much inward life had been imparted in a dozen years on the boards.

Romeo literally dons a mask for the Capulet's ball; as she confesses her love, Juliet says

> Thou know'st the mask of night is on my face,
> Else would a maiden blush bepaint my cheek . . .
> *(Romeo and Juliet*, II.i.127–8)

whilst later she puts on the mask of compliance and then the mask of death to escape her family. Modern productions often play up the family feud, which Shakespeare's audience would have taken for granted.

With *King Richard II*, however, Shakespeare reached the characteristic structure of his mature tragedies, interlocking the parts by a series of relationships, where the hero is exposed not only to suffering, but to judgement from within the play; this is a potentially comic or satiric aspect which is absorbed or contained in the final transformation.

Dispute continues about the balance of sympathy in this tragedy. W.B. Yeats opted passionately for Richard but in the latest New Cambridge edition, 1985, the editor, Andrew Gurr, suggests that what was seen originally as a balanced presentation of a central political issue has been transformed into a poetic tragedy by modern approaches. At the Royal Shakespeare Company in 1973 Ian Richardson and Richard Pascoe alternated between Richard and Bolingbroke at successive performances.

Gurr analyses the wealth of emblematic poetic and stage imagery. In the deposition scene where Richard is full of words and Bolingbroke, a 'silent king', issues orders, the new king corrects Richard's histrionic smashing of the mirror

> The shadow of your sorrow hath destroy'd
> The shadow of your face
>   (*Richard II*, IV.i.291–92)

looking back to the anguish of his own banishment from his country and his father, Gaunt, who had acted as the voice of judgement upon Richard, the unworthy ruler.

Richard is suddenly enlarged by his isolation; the divorce between himself and the crown, between himself and his wife has been the direct result of his impossible denial, his refusal of natural justice. English earth is the substance of Gaunt's dying speech. The unseen presence behind the actor is not a deity but a native land, an unweeded garden. Bolingbroke's lament is for his native land 'my mother and my nurse, that bears me yet', but in the deposition scene Carlisle warns him 'the blood of English shall manure the ground'. The Gardeners' scene is an emblematic presentation of this recurrent imagery.

By transformation the new Richard emerges as in prison, deprived of his kingdom, he strives to recreate it from within, to make a whole world out of his thoughts. Yet he knows that he is now outside the world of Time which

> Runs posting on in Bolingbroke's proud joy
> Whilst I stand fooling here, his Jack o' the clock.
>   (V.v.59–60)

The separation of 'the King's two bodies' – his regal and his personal identity – does not prevent Richard dying as king

> Exton, thy rash hand
> Hath with the king's blood stain'd the king's own land
>   (V.v.109–10)

whilst Henry finally laments that 'Blood should sprinkle me to make me grow' (this was done to vines, it was believed).

Richard's posthumous life in prison begins a new quest; it is the quest that is continued in *Hamlet*.

Some five or six years later, in 1600 or 1601, Richard Burbage created this greatest tragic role of the English stage. It was refashioned from an old play by the author of *The Spanish Tragedy*, Thomas Kyd, which Shakespeare, his fellow actors, and his audience must have known well. If he did not have collaborators, he continually recycled the material of his art; only by being traditional could he become so innovatory.

The play is always cut for the stage and exists in three separate versions. The part of Hamlet is a challenge for every reader as well as being the ultimate goal for every actor. Dr Johnson said the characteristic virtue of the work was its variety. 'You would pluck out the heart of my mystery' Hamlet tells his false friends; but no one has yet achieved it. The latest Hamlet I have seen was a young Chinese actor in Shanghai; he played it very quietly but in extreme shock. He was a young man who had met a ghost, the young man described by Ophelia to Polonius. This was in tune with the interpretation of Michio Masui, the professor at Hiroshima who told me he had a dream about Hamlet: 'Hamlet has met death – met death inwardly and it changed his life. He lives in a different way. . . .' This is the Hiroshima version. *Hamlet* marks the beginning of modern drama; in G.K. Hunter's words, 'it represents an enormous effort to move forward to the heroism of the individual without abandoning the older social and religious framework of external action',[3] yet it is built upon the dramatist's own achievement, at once a forward leap and a culmination.[4]

Hamlet the Prince assumes more than one mask. The antic disposition, used chiefly to Ophelia and Polonius, had become familiar in Revenge plays; the device of the 'play' and the Tragedy of Gonzago corresponds with the 'play' in *The Spanish Tragedy*, and the murder in a masque featured in *Antonio's Revenge* and *The Revenger's Tragedy* by Marston and Tourneur. Marston's bitter tragicomedy *The Malcontent* ended with an equivocal scene of dancing and daggers, an antic disposition with a difference. This play, written for the choristers, was adapted for Shakespeare's company.

Hamlet is his own clown; Yorick, the jester, appears only as a mocking skull. Osric, a character out of Marston's satiric comedy, is fashionable in his jargon. Polonius affects oratorical art, Hamlet himself rants in the grave, addresses Claudius with mock deference, writes to the King of England in flowery compliments. His variety of verse and prose, his sudden bouts of self-criticism when he finds himself unpacking his heart with words, the mystery he invokes when words fail, orchestrate the action; nowhere else is change of tempo so masterly, or jesting so intrinsic a part of heroic character.

In accordance with Shakespeare's usual plan, three large public scenes occur; the court scene at the beginning, the play scene and the final duet alternate with the four soliloquies which present Hamlet's inward self; as previously the trial scene, the deposition scene and the death scene made up the triad of *King Richard II*. The only other public scene in *Hamlet* is the funeral of Ophelia with its 'maimed rites'; the play scene is another maimed rite: more dramatically yet, the final duel embodies the broken and disturbed condition of the whole land, manifested in the first appearance of the Ghost.

Like the portents at the death of Julius Caesar, which are recalled just before its second appearance, it supernaturally registers a natural disturbance; its plea is for the kingdom of Denmark. The faithful soldiers and Horatio see it. Like the witches in *Macbeth*, it portends fear and horror foreknown, from which also it results. The ghost must overwhelm and command the scene; only in the closet scene it appears in a more private form to make a more personal appeal and is seen only by Hamlet, as the ghost of Banquo is seen only by Macbeth.

Unlike most Elizabethan ghosts it is at first silent, its 'shape' is to be 'questioned'. Like the ghosts in *King Richard III*, which appeared to prophesy, but also represented the spiritual forces that had accumulated, it is yet more than some bacteriological blight which destroys by an inward invasion. The ghost originates from the act of Claudius as directly as the ghost of Banquo issues from the act of Macbeth; Hamlet is 'on the wave length' or 'in the current' to encounter it. It is no private invasion of his psyche as some would believe. If Burbage challenges the spectators when Hamlet first denies to his mother that he is but seeming engaged in 'actions that a man might play', at his most violent, in the graveyard scene, Hamlet was probably muffled again in an inky cloak – which was the regular wear for the Prologue. Here in fact he begins the second half of the play; after his miraculous escape from death and his return to Denmark, he has resigned himself to Providence. The extraordinary calm and tranquillity in the last scene's opening leads to the decision and brevity of the last speeches. Hamlet is perhaps not surprised to find he is dying. His personal disposition – generous, impulsive, vulnerable – is recognisable in all Shakespeare's tragic heroes, not excluding Macbeth; his manic-depressive surges have attracted the medical profession continuously, whilst decisions what to leave out and what to stress make every performance into a new play. *Hamlet* is self-renewing; in its own day it offered a daring blend of ancient and modern, so that modern performances (starting with Barry Jackson's modern dress production of 1925) only adjust to what the Elizabethans must have seen in the blend of archaic history and modern courtly manners – an educative year in Wittenberg, a duel with rapiers. The fashions of Osric and Laertes were contemporary. Ophelia is buried in a Warwickshire graveyard after drowning in a willow-fringed Warwickshire brook. The castle of Elsinore, with its famous battery of guns guarding the entrance to the Baltic and its cellerage where three thousand men could lodge, had been visited by English actors. It was as modern as putting Hamlet into jeans or piping the Ghost's voice through the air conditioning system.

It was but a few years after its first showing that a critic recommended a play 'should please all, like Prince Hamlet',[5] there have been West Indian Hamlets and Siberian Hamlets. The network of characters works in any setting, though some characters are still liable to be cut (Fortinbras especially). A strong Claudius and Gertrude are essential, a weak Ophelia can be very damaging, Laertes and Horatio must be capable of fire, and the Ghost of dominance; Hamlet's wit can turn some stretches into comedy.

The paradox is that a character is most firmly built upon mutability upon the protean powers of both Shakespeare and Burbage; the whole group were used to playing for an after-dinner audience in a palace, or perhaps giving a scene or two for some distinguished patron; they performed also in the universities of Oxford and Cambridge. The plays which set out to imitate *Hamlet* selected various aspects; satire predominated in Marston and Tourneur, pathos in Fletcher's *Philaster*, a tragicomedy; in Webster's *The White Devil* ruthless and embittered jests contrasted with the lament of a distracted mother, in Ophelia's style, over the corpse of her slain son.

Later playwrights copied other parts: Massinger seemed fascinated by Othello, Chapman in *The Revenge of Bussy d'Ambois* had his hero commit suicide on the grounds rejected by Hamlet in 'To be or not to be'. No one equalled Shakespeare in building a part that related to an ensemble; they were interested only in his heroes, with the exception of Ford in *Perkin Warbeck*. Complexities of the great tragedies forbid an extended survey so I shall end with the latest, *Coriolanus*, last edited by Philip Brockbank for the New Arden in 1976, where he dates it early in 1608. It had been frequently revived and adapted; Quin in the eighteenth century, Macready in the nineteenth were equalled in 1938 by the young Olivier, playing with Sybil Thorndike as Volumnia. He has played it since many times. In France this play provoked political riots in the 1930s; the Berliner Ensemble adapted it from Brecht in 1964, showing the tribunes at the end deciding not to commemorate Coriolanus but to build a new viaduct. It is a play which challenges variety of readings, but revives the conflict between man and office from *King Richard II*.

A hero of laconic brevity is given only fifteen lines to proclaim, not debate, his change of allegiance. His enemy imparts a series of conjectures

> Whether 'twas pride
> Which out of daily fortune ever taints
> The happy man; whether defect of judgement,
> To fail in the disposing of those chances

> Which he was lord of; or whether nature
> Not to be other than one thing, not moving
> From the casque to the cushion . . .
>
> (IV.vii.37–43)

After leaving with the promise his family shall hear nothing 'but what is like me formerly' he reappears in the black cloak of the Prologue at the threshold of the enemy – for like Hamlet in the graveyard, he is starting a new Revenge play – to be foregone in the end, and shot through with ironic comedy. Shaw indeed termed it Shakespeare's best comedy.

There is a sense in which Coriolanus stands for the virtue of the tribal leader; but Rome is a City, no longer tribal. The iron god-like mask of Mars is not so spontaneous as it may seem:[6]

> Would you have me
> False to my nature? Rather say I play
> The man I am
>
> (III.ii.14–16)

provokes from his mother:

> You might have been enough the man you are
> By striving to be less so.
>
> (III.ii.19–20)

Being fashioned only for one kind of life and looking with disdain on any other, the God-Mask of Mars, as in T.S. Eliot's 'Coriolan' turns for him into the prisoner's iron mask. When he exclaims

> You have put me now to such a part as never
> I shall discharge to the life
>
> (III.ii.105–6)

his friends assure him. 'We'll prompt you'; he assumes the false mask only to tear it off.

In a prologue to the BBC's television version, General Sir John Hackett considered him a very dangerous member of an army staff, devoid of the prime need of insight into himself and his enemy. Only the silent Virgilia has this quality; but in a Rome of power politics, she is powerless.

Coriolanus's pride and humility alike alternate to his disadvantage. In Part II his new role becomes more and more of an effort; it hurts him to repel Menenius; in the supplication scene he capitulates with the first words to his wife:

> Like a dull actor now
> I have forgot my part and I am out
> Even to a full disgrace.
>
> (V.iii.40–2)

At the climax there is an end of Volumnia's eloquence; the family kneel silently. In that silence, taking her hand, Coriolanus sees the great dome of the heavens open, where the gods sit laughing at this 'unnatural scene', as the pretender to deity turns human again.

For this is a truly Palladian temple of a play to set against the Gothic of *King Richard II*.

If the boy Marcius is allowed a comic line in final parody of his father, if even in the death scene, Coriolanus's response to Aufidius's 'Boy!' is that of a bull in a bullring, yet his own final image of himself as 'an eagle in a dovecote' is one of divine rule. Jupiter's eagle brings him apotheosis, through the agony of death unarmed, among a mob, like Hector among the Myrmidons. From the fable of the belly onward, this is an intensely physical play; the stinking breath of the multitude, whichever way they may be shouting, the wounds that Coriolanus must put up to auction produce the gymnastic feats of Laurence Olivier, who delights in swinging on a rope or hanging by one foot upside down. In the 1986 production, which brings some of the audience onstage, the vigorous sword swinging of Ian Mc Kellen has occasionally hazarded their lives. Yet in the television production, the fights became an inner dream (compare Aufidius IV.v.122–7). Curses are not shouted but whispered; all happened within.

This is not the Palladian design. Shakespeare had acted in Jonson's *Sejanus*, a tragic satire on Rome's power politics, and in the magnificent classical masques which Jonson and Inigo Jones were now producing at court. The King's Men, after many years' waiting, were triumphantly taking over their new theatre at Blackfriars, within the gates of a city hitherto barred to them. Perhaps the Jacobean Banqueting Hall, which did not appear till after Shakespeare's death, gave a fitting royal setting to a play where the hero emerges from the sharp tests of deflating comedy and satire, closest to the plebeians in his capacity for being manipulated.

Under King James, whose motto was *Beati Pacifici* warriors were out of fashion; but Roman grandeur was much in vogue. King James would not have been totally averse from a little satire at the expense of his loyal City of London, which was already proving less accommodating than he would have wished.

Notes

1   James Wright, *Historia Histrionica* (1699) B8r.
2   Cambridge, Cambridge University Press, 1985.
3   G.K. Hunter, 'The Heroism of Hamlet' in B. Harris and J.R. Browne (eds), *Hamlet* (London, Edward Arnold, 1963), p. 108.

4 Sir William Empson in 'Hamlet when new' (D.P. Pine, ed., *Essays on Shakespeare*, Cambridge, Cambridge University Press, 1986) dealt brilliantly with this.
5 Antony Scoloker, *Daiphantus*, 1604, A2v.
6 See Philip Edwards 'Person and office in Shakespeare's plays' in Kenneth Muir (ed.), *Interpretations of Shakespeare* (Oxford, Oxford University Press, 1985) pp. 109–10.

IV.

Social Nuances in Shakespeare's Early Comedies (Oslo)

At the closure of a comedy, amid epithalamion, final dance and flattering epilogue, delicate social nuances of a single word, if it invoke habits unfamiliar, may breed disquiet. Modern dissatisfaction occurs notoriously at the end of Shakespeare's first love comedy, *The Two Gentlemen of Verona*, as Valentine forgives his false friend, whom he has just prevented from raping the heroine – although since he is lurking nearby, she was in no danger, and has moreover proclaimed her fidelity to her banished love: 'O heaven, be judge how I love Valentine!' Yet when Proteus begs forgiveness, Valentine not only declares himself 'fully paid' but

> that my love may appear plain and free,
> All that was mine in Silvia I give thee.
>
> (V.iv.82–3)

(See below p. 48) If Valentine is holding Silvia by the hand, whilst Proteus kneels, the penitent is being readmitted to the honour Valentine had formerly begged for him, of being the lady's 'servant', from which legitimate and public rank he himself has risen. Though locked in a tower at night by her ducal father, the heiress of Milan would be attended by attached gentlemen servants – secretaries, hunters, gentlemen ushers. Queen Elizabeth had her gentlemen pensioners, her squires of the body, gentlemen of the privy chamber. In assuming the right to grant an honour, but no abdication, Valentine asserts the possession he was soon to maintain against Thurio in the presence of the Duke himself.

When Valentine invites Silvia to extend her hand in forgiveness to the kneeling Proteus, the gesture reminds disguised Julia of Silvia's returning her own ring, for rejection; such reconciliation renewing a threat for her, she faints. After which, by returning to Proteus the love token he had originally given her, she reveals herself as his forsaken mistress, which as if by magic, reconverts him; no Puck has sprinkled a love juice, but with the ring he re-enters his new servant's older service. Final recognition and reversal is effected by the ring, which was to feature more powerfully in *The Merchant of Venice.*

To give away a love token is an affront of which the author of the *Sonnets* was himself guilty; his tablets – sensitively chosen for a writer, and perhaps an exchange since he had given a table book in Sonnet 77 – awaken in the apology, Sonnet 122, conceits that were to echo in *Hamlet.*

> Thy gift, thy tablets are within my brain
> Full character'd with lasting memory . . .
> Therefore to give them from me was I bold
> To trust those tables that receive thee more:
> To keep an adjunct to remember thee
> Were to impute forgetfulness in me.
>
> (1–2, 11–14)

That rhetorical *tour de force* and most elaborate set of wit well played, *Love's Labours Lost*, ends with a musical conceit that has been overlooked, in the final song of Hiems and Ver.

The lovers are bound to a year of probation which Berowne declares too long for a play; the present season is fixed by the deer hunt, a signal that any Elizabethan would pick up as late summer or early autumn. Spring will not be merry, and the cheerful note of the cuckoo takes on a note of menace. In winter, a year will have passed, and the 'staring owl', not always taken as a cheerful songster, will sing

> Tu whit,
> Tu who! a merry note
> Whilst greasy Joan doth keel the pot.

I have pointed out elsewhere that 'To it!' is the huntsman's cry of encouragement to his hounds, as they close up on the quarry.[1] In *Tom Jones*, the hunting Squire Western, as Tom ventures finally to embrace and kiss Sophia, bursts in with 'To it, little honeys, to it, O that's it!'. The Elizabethan song 'Quoth John to Joan' uses the vibrato of the owl for the last phrase of the refrain.

> O say, my Joan, will not that do?
> I cannot come every day to woo! – oo-oo!

'To woo' is Longaville's merry note as he cries 'Shall we resolve to woo these girls of France? (IV.iii.369) at the end of the discovery scene.[2] The song envisages a wider set of wooers than the court, with Tom and Dick, Marion and Joan, who is 'greasy' – that is, fat of body, like the greasy amorous cook in *The Comedy of Errors*; to keel the pot is a direct sexual image and presumably the song was enlived by gestures, ending in one that includes the audience as well – 'You that way, we this way.' If for the royal party 'Jack hath not Jill' (V.ii.263), perhaps in a twelvemonth, he will; and the audience has no need to wait longer than it takes to get home. Confined within the bounds of the royal park and the royal households, this 'great feast of languages' relies throughout on social nuances, or their mistakings. In a succession of episodes, the interweaving of social judgements and the unwinding of the plot progresses through the Nine Worthies' play and quarrel, the tragic entry of the messenger of death, the judgement of the lovers' suit and the bonding of all by the song. In *A Midsummer Night's Dream*, promise that 'Jack shall have Jill' comes not indeed at the end, but in the third act (III.ii.461–3); action moves through a hunting scene back to the palace, the mechanics' play, Theseus' orders for bed followed by the return of the magic band and a fairy dance, with Puck's plea to the real audience. The same types of ingredient are mixed a little differently.

The next comedy, *The Merchant of Venice*, also appears to end the main action with Act IV; and here sometimes the play ended, in performances of the nineteenth century. Shylock dominated absolutely. But feminist interest in Portia has brought back not only the action she initiates, the comedy of the rings (which was in the source), but a new series of questions about the significance of her riddling game. In *The Two Gentlemen of Verona* Julia's ring is already associated with a woman playing a man, and a man breaking an oath:

> Behold her that gave aim to all thy oaths,
> And entertain'd 'em deeply in her heart . . .
> Be thou asham'd that I have took upon me
> Such an immodest raiment, if shame live
> In a disguise of love!
> It is the lesser blot, modesty finds,
> Women to change their shapes than men their minds
>
> (V.iv.101–9)

Riddles, trials, wagers and testing points match and reflect each other in different tones and colourings; the play was felt as early as Theobald's commentary to touch upon the tragical, but from the time when Goethe exclaimed 'The poor man is wronged' almost assumed its alternative Elizabethan title, *The Jew of Venice*.

Primarily the comedy of the rings is the revenge by Portia and her confidante, Nerissa, for their bridegrooms' declaration at the trial in Venice that they would sacrifice their brides to deliver Antonio from Shylock. Bassanio first offers his own life; indeed 'all the world' as well. In the last act, Portia plays the role she had envisaged to Nerissa in assuming her disguise, a role which had no place in the Venetian courthouse, but which comes to her with reassuming woman's dress:

> I'll prove the prettier fellow of the two . . .
>   and tell quaint lies
> How honourable ladies sought my love . . .
>   (III.iv.64, 69–70)

In the trial scene Shylock had joined the men's vow, in remembrance of his defecting daughter:

> These be the Christian husbands. I have a daughter –
> Would any of the stock of Barabas
> Had been her husband rather than a Christian.
>   (IV.i.295–7)

Jews marrying Christians were declared 'dead' in acts of ritual mourning, and much earlier he had 'buried' her inside a casket, with his wife's love token which she had carried off.

> I would my daughter were dead at my foot and the jewels in her ear would she were hearsed at my foot and the ducats in her coffin.
>   (III.i.87–9)

Jessica may have regarded what she took as the equivalent of a dowry – which plays an important part in Jewish marriage rites.

The casket she steals and the casket in which Shylock wishes her lying link Jessica, no less than her page's disguise, as Portia's shadow, and it is part of the harmony of Act V that it begins on a rarefied level, the highest Platonic level since Portia and Bassanio felt that moment of transfiguration that led to her gift of the ring. Such moments can be neither sustained nor forgotten.

A man gives a woman the wedding ring when she takes his name; this relic of subjection, the riveting or branding of his chattel was enlarged by Posthumus into the 'manacle of love' for one already wedded. The woman's gift of a ring rather symbolises the ring of investiture, given to an inferior by a superior. The coronation ring, the episcopal ring or the ancestral signet (such as Bertram gives away in Florence for the royal pledge of the King of France to Helena): Portia, Imogen, and the Duchess of Malfi give such a ring – the Duchess, her wedding ring, given to Antonio ('to help your eyesight'): Julia, Olivia give rings, Rosalind a chain; jewels and gloves were among the 'fairings' sent by the wooers in *Love's Labours Lost*. Rings were often credited with magic powers, because of the 'virtues' in the jewels; the crown as supreme token of authority became one of the chief objects of dramatic confrontation, but Shakespeare was also later to use Hamlet's love tokens, the pledges of Troilus and Cressida, Othello's handkerchief and the bounty by which Timon ruins himself; Lear perhaps sees the division of the crown in such a light.

Leo Salingar has asked 'Is *The Merchant of Venice* a problem play?'[3] suggesting that it displays the 'mingled yarn' of life, not in the manner of Italian tragicomedy as later introduced by Fletcher, but by working on a multiplicity of levels, a variety of tones, with something for each member of the audience, so that the scenes may change from high romance to bawdy jokes, and the leading figures are open to a variety of interpretations.

The debate whether Shylock is monster or victim is about two hundred years old; but Shylock is banished at the end of Act IV, and the equivocal relations of Bassanio, Antonio and Portia present new problems for a modern reader, which may be only intensified by the final episode of the rings. Linked with the trial scene, it is in effect a new trial, with Portia this time not as judge and defence counsel but as judge and prosecutor.

Harold Goddard went so far as to term Shylock the leaden casket containing gold – a genuine wish to join the merchants of Venice by forgoing interest – whilst Portia's ruthless conduct of the end of her case is compounded by her torturing her husband and his friend by withholding the second and crucial charge (conspiracy by an alien) and her mockery of 'the most heartfelt and noble lines her lover ever uttered'.[4]

The development of homosexual elements in the relation of the two men is a recent reading that gives Portia a stronger case for resentment. Lawyers have examined her handling of the case, and feminists her handling of her charge about the rings. Lord Normand, a high court Judge, observed that a wise judge would not tell the creditor she was trying to persuade that he was certain to win if he persevered; and a fair judge would not do so if she knew that the case could in fact be overturned. But other legal experts say that Portia has to establish Shylock's enforcement of the bond in open court before she can produce her second defence; adding however that she might have pleaded fraudulent misrepresentation, since before witnesses the bond had been tendered as having no legal significance 'and Bassanio and Gratiano would have done their friend a greater service by remembering it than by reiterating their undying friendship for Antonio and annoying Shylock still further'.[5] In England, a woman presided 'over all causes, as well civil as ecclesiastical supreme' and Spenser depicted her as Mercilla. Anne Barton puts a moderately feminist case, feeling 'the situation must be clarified,' and concluding 'there is room for friendship in the house of love, but love holds the upper and controlling hand'.[6] A more reductive but psychiatric conflict is presented in an article 'The nature of Portia's

Victory' by Keith Geary, which turns the ending into the defeat of
Antonio's emotional blackmail of Bassanio, and Portia into an
earlier version of Maggie Verver, the innocently undefeatable mil-
lionairess of Henry James's *The Golden Bowl* – in this story 'the
most adept business man of them all' – probably fudging Antonio's
recovered fortune.[7]

The professional view, whether legal or psychological, and the
feminist approach are but variants on the use of standards applicable
to those in real life and living at the present time. The two lesser
heroines shadow or contrast with Portia, and she herself radiates or
diminishes her intensity. After Bassanio's departure she is praised by
Lorenzo for her understanding of 'true amity', and he anticipates the
figure used in the 'quarrel' of Portia and Bassanio, in his praise of
Antonio:

> If you knew to whom you shew the honour
> How true a gentleman you send relief . . .
> (III.iv.5–6)

which she counters by saying that since they love each other, Antonio
and Bassanio share a soul and she is but purchasing 'the semblance of
my soul/From out the state of hellish cruelty' (III.iv.20–21). This is to
recall her own moment of ecstatic union:

> Myself and what is mine to you and yours
> Is now converted . . .
>   I give them with this ring.
>   (III.ii.166–7, 171)

and this is the note on which Lorenzo and Jessica open the final
scene. They move from Platonic heights to lovers' banter, in which
anticipating the quarrel, Jessica accuses her lover of infidelity, and he
responds.

> In such a night
> Did pretty Jessica, like a little shrew
> Slander her love and he forgave it her
> (V.i.20–22)

Portia's arrival to the music of her domain makes her think that
the season itself lends 'right praise and true perfection'; and at the
approach of Bassanio, she feels night turn to day which he repeats in
a courtly hyperbole that is later to be used by Prince Ferdinand to
Miranda (*The Tempest*, III.i.33–34). Portia's reply is a telling jest on
'lightness' and she jests also with him about Antonio, and being
'bound' to one another; Antonio's 'No more than I am well acquitted
of' brings forward the memory of the court scene as a subject now for
jests. When accused of unfaithfulness as well as perjury, Bassanio

freezes from 'Sweet Portia' to a respectful but outraged 'Madam' and 'Fair lady'. Portia had answered his highly rhetorical plea

> If you did know to whom I gave the ring,
> (V.i.193)

– which of course, she does – with an exactly matched set of lines in accusation, reversing his words in a manner much approved by pleaders. When Antonio – who had persuaded Bassanio to give the ring – pledges his soul for Bassanio's good faith, Portia plays her final jest of having already slept with Dr. Balthazar.

Portia is now entering not only the closed masculine world of the law, and of Venetian gentlemen, but that of young 'wags' in jests which, especially in London at the Inns of Court, could be 'stagey', as Ben Jonson later exemplified where his stagekeeper recommends them for comedy:

> Would not a fine pump ha' done well for a property now? and a punk set upon her head, with her stern upward, and ha' been soused by my witty young masters o' the Inns of Court?
> (*Bartholomew Fair*, Induction)

Serious feminism will not serve here, any more than serious law. If Portia-Nerissa-Jessica and Lorenzo-Bassanio-Gratiano form composites, it is Jessica who complements Portia by sounding the cruder notes in the vulnerability of women and their revenges; Nerissa is simply a duplication, whose presence however reduces the possibility of taking this action seriously. The women acting in chorus anticipate that spirited duet in which, in *The Importance of Being Earnest*, Gwendolen and Cicely unite to proclaim their demands for a properly christened fiancé, Gwendolen beating time. The men's reactions are left to the actors; Antonio's 'I am dumb', Bassanio's 'Were you the doctor and I knew you not?' imply vistas opening; Portia has stepped down from her pedestal for him; he will have to incorporate the doctor. Portia, gracefully consigning herself to the position of a defendant, concedes that Bassanio also is entitled to a full explanation:

> Let us go in,
> And charge us there upon interr'gatories
> And we will answer all things faithfully.
> (V.i.297–99)

This invocation of the legal procedure by which those charged with contempt of court must answer written questions upon oath, answers Bassanio's acceptance of the masculine aspect that Portia's wit has retained:

> Sweet Doctor, you shall be my bedfellow,
> When I am absent, then lie with my wife.
>
> (V.i.284–5)

Gratiano joins in, when he announces his first interrogatory for Nerissa, implying bed first and talking afterwards. His last word, and the last word of the play is his direct sexual pun upon the meaning of the ring, the direct contrast with the Platonic opening of this final scene:

> Well while I live, I'll fear no other thing
> So sore, as keeping safe Nerissa's ring.
>
> (V.i.306–7.)

The notable feminist, Germaine Greer, in her recent book on Shakespeare[8] ends her chapter on Shakespeare's poetics with a quotation from the philosopher Wittgenstein:

> Shakespeare displays the dance of human passions, one might say. Hence he has to be objective; otherwise he would not so much display the dance of human passions as talk about it. But he displays it to us in a dance, not naturalistically.

In her chapter on sociology, Germaine Greer observes 'In the theatre, the audience is the medium'.[9] Lacking a formal epilogue, the end of *The Merchant of Venice* is audience-directed, the characters of the play being subordinate to the moods they create. In 1582 the comic ending had been described by the unfriendly Stephen Gosson in *Plays Confuted in Five Actions*:

> The beholders rose up, every man stood on tiptoe . . . when they sware, the company sware, when they departed to bed, the company was set on fire, they that were married posted home to their wives, they that were single, vowed very solemnly to be wedded.
>
> (Sig. G. 52)

'You that way, we this way'.

Notes

1 *Shakespeare Quarterly*, vol. 33, No. 1, 1982, pp. 94–5.
2 Confirmation of this reading of the song in *Love's Labours Lost* has come to hand in John Lyly's *Endimion* (3.3. 160ff)

> There appeared in my sleep a goodly owl, who, sitting upon my shoulder, cried 'Twit, twit! . . . I marvelled what the owl said, till at the

last I perceived 'Twit, twit', 'To it, to it' only by contraction admonished by this vision to make account of my sweet Venus.
Endimion was first published in 1591.

3   In *Dramatic Form in Shakespeare and the Jacobeans* (Cambridge,
    Cambridge University Press, 1986).
4   In *The Meaning of Shakespeare* (Chicago, University of Chicago Press,
    1951) p. 151.
5   George W. Keaton, *Shakespeare's Legal and Political Background*
    (London, Pitman, 1967) p. 133.
6   In *The Riverside Shakespeare* (Boston, Houghton Mifflin, 1974) p. 253.
7   *Shakespeare Survey*, vol. 38, 1984, pp. 55–84.
8   *Shakespeare* (Oxford, Oxford University Press, 1986) pp. 67–8.
9   *Ibid.* pp. 125–6.

V.

Love and Courtesy in *The Two Gentlemen of Verona* (Verona)

It is a great honour to be invited in this ancient city to celebrate a poet who wrote of this region with varying degrees of knowledge but always with reverence, as of a visionary country, a country of the heart. On the stage of his day, Italy was depicted either as very beautiful or very, very wicked. There was nothing in between a country full of lovers and a country full of murderous ducal feuds. No ordinary lives at all; the moonlight of the summer garden was heavenly or else the 'smiler with the knife beneath the cloak', Iago or Iachimo, trapped the unpractised alien. From the beginning to end of his career Shakespeare turned to Italy, and his last play celebrated a unification which had happened between parts of the British Isles; he shows the heiress of Milan betrothed to the heir of Naples.

Today I wish to look at his comedy of courtly love, named from this city – *The Two Gentlemen of Verona*, for him *par excellence* the City of Lovers. I would place it in 1593, the year when plague closed London theatres and the young writer (he was 29) retired to the country to write *Venus and Adonis*. It has not received as much attention as later comedies, but it is a beautiful and delicate piece of *sprezzatura*, that links it not with the later comedies of love, several of which are also set in Italy, such as *Much Ado about Nothing*, but rather with last romances, *The Tempest* particularly in which Shakespeare turned back to memories of earlier traditions. But Shakespeare's work, though so full of variety, is also deeply unified. The element of fantasy in his art struck his contemporaries.

The early morning freshness of *The Two Gentlemen of Verona* was very well caught visually in the BBC's television production. Many plays were given an Italian flavour – *Antony and Cleopatra*, in Renaissance style, was heavily flavoured with the opulence of Titian. *The Two Gentlemen of Verona* was based on Fra Angelico and the early Botticelli of *Primavera*. Lightness, innocence, delicacy and grace were embodied in the heroine, with her transparent draperies, her garden setting; her wooers also reminded me of Botticelli's young men.

The Two Gentlemen of Verona is built on a tale of love and friendship, not for the sake of developing characters, but for exploring moods embodied in manners; for displaying sentiments, not conflicts – sentiments in the psychological sense of habitual sets of feelings emerging from implanted disposition, not innate. This is the Italy of Petrarch and Castiglione, perhaps of Ariosto.

No supernatural beings hover in the summer air, but something like the music of Ariel is heard in the aubade procured by the two unworthiest of her suitors to be sung at Silvia's window – in Schubert's setting, the best known words of this play:

> Who is Silvia? what is she
> That all our swains commend her?
> Holy, fair and wise is she:
> The heaven such grace did lend her
> That she might admired be.

> (IV.ii.38–42)

'Admired' – a wonder, like the 'most admired' Miranda; not a mortal but to her lover 'the goddess on whom these airs attend'. Silvia indeed radiates the grace of heaven; she is 'excelling', sent from on high. Her father's courtiers are her servants in the sense of professing to love her, without daring to aspire to her hand, rendering the service of '*fin amours*' like the trouvères.

England indeed knew such a divinity; although no longer either young or fair, Elizabeth now enjoyed the height of her literary cult among poets, all vying to assert her eternal beauty in terms often borrowed from the cult of the Virgin Mary. In Spenser, presented as Belphoebe

> Her face so fair as flesh it seemed not,
> But heavenly portrait of bright angel's hue . . .

to Ben Jonson she is a heavenly being from an older religion, Cynthia, still excelling.

> Queen and huntress chaste and fair,
>   Now the sun is laid to sleep,
> Seated in thy silver chair,
>   State in wonted manner keep.
>   Hesperus entreats thy light,
>   Goddess excellently bright.

John Lyly wrote plays in her praise, as he also wrote wittily to provide models of conversation for the Court. His plays were given

by the choristers of her chapel and these have the most powerful and
refining influence on Shakespeare's court comedies of love, although
he outgrew Lyly. Here is the praise of Cynthia by Endimion in a play
upon which Shakespeare closely depended:

> Such a difference hath the gods set between our states that all must be
> duty, loyalty, reverence; nothing (without it please your highness) be
> termed love. My spotted thoughts, my languishing body, my discontented
> life, let them obtain by princely favour that which to challenge they must
> not presume, only wishing of impossibilities; with imagination of which, I
> will spend my spirits, and softly to myself, that no creature may hear, call
> it love. And if any urge to utter what I whisper, then I will term it honour.

Shakespeare's first sixteen sonnets exhort marriage on the model of
the early pleas to the Queen; but in this comedy wooing instruction,
whether the First Gentleman's to the Duke or the Second's to his
rival, are farcical and lead to entrapment.

The first of the two Gentlemen to be sent from Verona to Milan is
a professed mocker of his lovelorn friend but his role as true lover is
proclaimed in his name, Valentine, named for the patron saint of
lovers, on whose feast not only men but birds chose their mates. He
falls instantly into worship of the heiress of Milan, the divine Silvia,
but does not aspire to woo her; she instead asks him to write a love
letter for her to one she loves, which she then tells him to keep. His
witty page has to enlighten him that this modest device is to make
him aware of her favour. For the little love god blinds his votaries;
the engagingly silly infatuation of first love was to receive affectionate banter and very clear demonstration in Shakespeare's later
comedy, *A Midsummer Night's Dream*, where the Duke describes
the lover's frenzy that can

> see Helen's beauty in a brow of Egypt.

The Duke of Milan, with his own blindness, is encouraging the rich
but stupid Thurio to court his daughter, and Valentine engages in a
sharp duel of wits with him. But when the second Gentleman arrives
and is generously introduced by Valentine with the request that he be
enrolled Silvia's courtly servant, Proteus, though now betrothed by a
ring to Julia, keeps neither friendship nor vows, although he has not
been given any magic love juice by a fairy; but he has already termed
himself metamorphosed by love, and now proves his name from the
great shape-changer Proteus to be fitting. He debates quite sharply
within himself: for he has been told by Valentine that his own love
for Silvia is of the heart.

> To leave my Julia, shall I be forsworn:
> To love fair Silvia, shall I be forsworn:
> To wrong my friend I shall be much forsworn.
> And e'en that power which gave me first my oath
> Provokes me to this threefold perjury:
> Love bade me swear and love bids me forswear.
> O sweet-suggesting love, if thou hast sinn'd,
> Teach me, thy tempted subject, to excuse it.
>
> (II.vi.1–8)

Wronging his friend is the worst sin. But prompted by love, he puts the counterplea, as in a later play, 'some salve for perjury' had to be found at another court.

> At first I did adore a twinkling star,
> But now I worship a celestial sun.
>
> (9–10)

With the same wit that earlier he had defended himself against Valentine's mocks he crowns his sophistry:

> Julia I lose and Valentine I lose.
> If I keep them I needs must lose myself:
> If I lose them, thus find I by their loss:
> For Valentine, myself; for Julia, Silvia.
>
> (19–22)

This is but wordplay; in the last scene, when Valentine discovers the depths to which Proteus has been brought, *he* feels a loss which is not that of self-sufficiency but of the vulnerable self that is invested in honourable trust. Valentine, like a later hero, is 'most generous and free from all contriving'; in fact his contriving to elope with Silvia had been deftly uncovered by the Duke, prompted by Proteus. Finally, he witnesses Proteus' threat of force towards his lady

> Treacherous man,
> Thou hast beguil'd my hopes; naught but mine eye
> Could have persuaded me. Now I dare not say
> I have one friend alive; thou wouldst disprove me.
> Who should be trusted now, when one's right hand
> Is perjured to the bosom? . . .
> The private wound is deepest. O most accurst!
> 'Mongst all foes that a friend should be the worst!
>
> (V.iv.63–72)

Confronted with depth of grief, Proteus is immediately struck into deep remorse; and then comes the turn of events which is universally misunderstood, universally considered to destroy the play. I think the lines are misconstrued and they do not destroy it at all, but depend on the contrast between private and courtly status.

What has happened is that after betraying the lovers to the Duke, Proteus follows Silvia in her flight to the banished Valentine. Meeting her in a wood, where Valentine had earlier been turned into the captain of a band of outlaws, he begins to woo her, and on repulse, attempts to rape her. Valentine who has overheard it all, has heard his lady declare her love of himself:

> O heaven be judge how I love Valentine
> Whose life's as tender to me as my soul
> (V.iv.36–7)

and the words with which he delivers her are those of courtly decorum, very restrained (but presumably he has drawn his sword):

> Ruffian, let go that rude, uncivil touch,
> Thou friend of an ill fashion.
> (60–1)

After Proteus' repentance, his 'forgive me', he proceeds:

> Then I am paid;
> And once again I do receive thee honest.
> Who by repentance is not satisfied
> Is not of heaven nor earth, for these are pleased.
> By penitence th'Eternal's wrath's appeased.
> And that my love may appear plain and free,
> All that was mine in Silvia I give thee.
> (77–83)

The outcry is all but universal. 'By this time, there are *no* gentlemen in Verona!' exclaimed Sir Arthur Quiller-Couch. But the verb is all important: 'was' is not 'is', as another wise character was to remark. (See above p. 35.) Proteus, who is on his knees before Valentine, may be invited, kneeling, to kiss the lady's other hand. What is offered to Proteus is public reinstatement to the position they had formerly shared and Valentine had procured; what had been theirs was the position of courtly servant to the lady but Valentine is now speaking as Silvia's betrothed lover (II.iv.176) and protector – a generous but not preposterous act. Valentine in the wood assumes an authority which enables him, when the Duke arrives as captive to the outlaws, to defy Thurio with a physical directness which comes from the new relation that his rescue and Silvia's declaration of love had conferred:

> I dare thee but to breathe upon my love!
> (V.iv.132)

He ends with great assurance, though in the Duke's presence, by inviting Proteus and his restored Julia to be married on the day he marries Silvia. Proteus never addresses Silvia. And Silvia says nothing at all. Outside the charmed circle of the court, she does not now speak to Proteus, or to her father. In the opening scenes Julia had nothing to say by way of farewell to Proteus. And now, at this point, present in disguise as Proteus' page, she swoons. It may be thought that this confirms the modern idea that Valentine is relinquishing Silvia to Proteus, but is it not the hand-in-hand postures of the lovers that recalls to her betrothal-ring (and Proteus' ring) both now in her keeping?

Valentine had first, after entreating Proteus' admission as 'fellow servant to your ladyship', exalted her to Proteus 'a heavenly saint' to which Proteus replies 'No, but she is an earthly paragon'; and in his new feelings, the grosser level is stressed "Tis but her picture I have yet beheld' (II.iv.207). His stupid servant Launce presents the divine Silvia instead of Proteus' toy dog with a rough cur of his own, who befouls her farthingale; and the animal level of Proteus comes out in the wood. Valentine is re-educating him, using that line of the Paternoster that echoes down to the epilogue of *The Tempest*: Forgive us our sins as we forgive those who sin against us.

Julia's first acts are Protean; she tears up the letter that her lover sends her, then picks up the torn pieces and puts them together. Her maid is well versed in the feminine perversity that 'says nay and takes it': her resolution to follow her lover in disguise is a familiar romance complication. He employs her as a page. It is not necessary to stress on the stage the very intimate attendance this implies, helping her master to dress and undress. In *Love's Labour's Lost* Don Armado's page knows him in this way. This it is which makes her apologise not to, but on behalf of Proteus when she recovers from her swoon:

> O Proteus, let this habit make thee blush!
> Be thou asham'd that I have took upon me
> Such an immodest raiment, if shame live
> In a disguise of love.
> It is the lesser blot, modesty finds,
> Women to change their shapes, than men their minds.
>   (V.iv.105–10)

The shock for Proteus, as in *Twelfth Night* for Orsino, is to discover that it is a woman who enjoyed such intimacy 'so far beneath your soft and tender breeding'.

Julia and Proteus are the more interesting couple to modern readers since they seem, because more changeable and more physically expressive, to be individuals. The difference between the two levels may be illustrated from the life and poetry of Sir Walter Ralegh, who at this time (1592) had incurred the Queen's displeasure and imprisonment for first seducing and afterwards secretly marrying one of her maids of honour. (Shakespeare's patron was to do the same.) He wrote an ingenious poem in which he adopted one

of the regular defences of a courtly lover (one which appears in the
discussion of love between Julia and her maid, (I.ii.29–30) as well as
in the opening discussions in Castiglione *Il Cortegiano*, that the
truest lover does not declare his love). In the lyric 'Wrong not, dear
Empress of my heart' Ralegh writes

> For knowing that I sue to serve
> A saint of such perfection
> As all desire, but none deserve
> A place in her affection . . .

He anticipates that kind of humility which adopts a disguise of
poverty, which Castiglione thinks may enhance the nobility of a
knight, and which in Silvia's aubade describes her wooers as 'swains'
and their offering a pastoral 'garland'.

The sentiments, tone and mood of Castiglione are to my mind
more relevant and more illuminating than the narrative sources
which are so carefully collected in such works as Geoffrey Bullough's
eight learned volumes. The narrative lines are all of romance commonplaces, even the story of Julia's disguise which is the closest and
comes from the Spanish *Diana Enamorada* of Jorge de Montemayor,
a work beloved of Sir Philip Sidney's Mistress, the heroine of his
beautiful sonnet sequence *Astrophil and Stella*, first printed in 1591,
the most powerful set of love sonnets before Shakespeare's own. But
I think the mood, sentiments and tone are more important than the
narrative line, and these come from Castiglione through Sidney –
who stole away to the wars, where he met his untimely death in
October 1586, with a copy of Castiglione. The chivalrous treatment
of wars as jousting, forbade him to put on his thigh pieces because a
friend had ridden out without them. He received his death wound
and England mourned one who was a model of chivalry.

Il Cortegiano had first appeared in print in 1527, two years before
Castiglione's death at the court of Spain where the Emperor Charles
V exclaimed 'I tell you that one of the best *caballeros* of the world is
dead'. Sir Thomas Hoby's translation, *The Courtyer* was published
in 1561.

In this book the courtly games played at Urbino in the presence of
the Duchess are moderated by her deputy, the Lady Emilia Pia. The
Duchess herself is Surrogate for her lord, the highly judicious and
watchful though crippled Duke. In the preliminary choice of the
game, questions of love like those of ancient Provençal Courts of
Love, are proposed and laid aside; such as which are the greater, the
joys of love or its sorrows? Which lover shall a lady take, one who
confesses his love or one who does not dare to do so? A question as
we have seen posed between Julia and her maid in *The Two*

Gentlemen of Verona (I.ii.29–30) and the basis of Ralegh's plea to his Queen. However, the game chosen at Urbino, the definition of the perfect Courtier, is not of this kind; it leads to deeper self-examination. Every barbed and searching point is made with 'laughter'. The most realistic and even shameless opportunism is concealed under exquisite refinement; and the facts of history are dexterously rearranged for the most favourable construction. When the Duchess asks Ottaviano what he would do if he won the Prince's favour so completely that he could tell him anything, he laughs and replies that if he were able to tell the Prince what he thinks 'I fear I should soon lose that favour' (IV.26). The final hymn to Platonic love from Pietro Bembo stuns the company into silence, because it goes beyond the game into the realm of Petrarch's Laura and Dante's Beatrice, and the Lady Emilia Pia, taking Bembo gently by the sleeve, says 'Takes care, Messer Pietro' (IV.71).

The limitations of the charmed circle are well understood; *grace* and *sprezzatura* – those key words of the definition – were absorbed by Sidney; Beauty can be attained only by ease and cannot be reached by directly taking pains; it emanates from the graceful negligence that conceals art after long practice, the irony and self-depreciation that Sidney practised with such wit. He ridiculed false Petrarchism: so later did Shakespeare: 'My mistress' eyes are nothing like the sun' (*Sonnet* 130).

The Two Gentlemen of Verona is founded upon the courtly assumptions of the 'game', which includes a good deal of parody. Valentine and Proteus open with a sharp bout of wit about the folly of love; later Valentine and Thurio attack each other with unbaited rapiers of wit and are separated by Silvia. Of course the assumptions are tested and parodied, this gives a frame to the romance. The true lover is given the malicious and witty page Speed; the dissembling Proteus is given the clown Launce, a character of immense vigour whose parting from his family to accompany Proteus is a parody of the previous scene, the parting of Proteus and Julia. Launce's dog is theatrically a winner, and often steals the show as outrageously as ever he stole a pudding. Animals are utterly natural and do not play a game with the audience as the actors do. Launce's catalogue of his mistress's charms parodies those of the divine Silvia. She is black as ink, but 'she hath more hair than wit, more faults than hairs, and more wealth than faults' (III.i.343–4). He is the Sancho Panza to Valentine's Quixote; while Speed explains to Valentine the riddle of Silvia's letter and advises joining the outlaws 'Master, be one of them; it's an honourable kind of thievery' (IV.i.39). Launce, having lost the toy dog Proteus was sending to Sylvia, gives her Crab; and just such an ill-mannered animal does Proteus himself become. For

throughout the play we are conscious of that freedom of man to
ascend and become a god or descend to a beast which was the theme
of Pico della Mirandola's oration on the Dignity of Man.

Of course the story is comic, in the way that in Ariosto the knights
are comic, when two mounting one horse in pursuit of their lady,
urge the horse by the pricking of four spurs instead of two, to an
unwonted pace. But in the last Act the clown and the page both
disappear, for the final scene must maintain the courtly game against
the counterpoint of the outlaws and the wood, and the important
servant is the page, Julia in disguise – other servants must fade. This
use of the wild wood was to be much further worked into the action
in *A Midsummer Night's Dream*.

The comedies of Lyly included pages, and sometimes clowns; early
wit combats do not give much more skill to courtiers than to their
pages.

Silvia:	Servant, you are sad.
Val.:	Indeed, madam, I seem so.
Thurio:	Seem you that you are not?
Val.:	Haply I do.
Thurio:	So do counterfeits.
Val.:	So do you.
Thurio:	What seem I that I am not?
Val.:	Wise.

(II.iv.8–15)

The deeper feelings are given in soliloquy and when called for in the
dialogue, they simply are not there. Courtship is always in another's
presence; so much is obliquely done by letters, tokens, gifts. Unlike
other great ladies, Silvia has not even a waiting gentlewoman for
confidante; moving only among courtiers or priests. The most
poignant and self-revelatory of her scenes is when Julia, disguised as
a page, brings Silvia as a love token the very ring she had given
Proteus. Silvia knows its history and returns it; Julia, speaking out of
part, gives her thanks.

Silvia:	She is beholding to thee, gentle youth.
	Alas, poor lady, desolate and left!
	I weep myself to think upon thy words.
	Here, youth; there is my purse; I give this thee
	For thy sweet mistress' sake, because thou lov'st her

(IV.iv.170–4)

'Pity runneth soon in gentle heart', as Chaucer said more than once.
If this were an allegory, Silvia would stand for the Divine Imagination and she appeals to the highest level of the *audience's* response. In

this, she anticipates again the divine Miranda of Shakespeare's last play, *The Tempest*, who wept to see the shipwreck, suffered with those she saw suffer; 'O, the cry did knock against my very heart'. To which her father replies:

> tell your piteous heart
> There's no harm done.
> (I.ii.15–16)

Silvia and Julia's mutual sympathy delicately balances the friendship of the two gentlemen. Julia has been sent to get Silvia's picture, but this decorous mode of worship is not what Proteus has in mind; for he said before 'Tis but her picture I have yet beheld' (II.iv.207) – he hopes to look on her 'perfections' later. Valentine uses this word in his poignant soliloquy upon his own banishment, engineered by Proteus.

> What light is light if Silvia be not seen?
> What joy is joy, if Silvia be not by?
> Unless it be to think that she is by
> And feed upon the shadow of perfection?
> Except I be by Silvia in the night,
> There is no music in the nightingale;
> Unless I look on Silvia in the day,
> There is no day for me to look upon.
> She is my essence, and I leave to be,
> If I be not by her fair influence
> Foster'd, illumin'd, cherish'd, kept alive.
> (III.i.174–84)

This is almost in that realm of high constancy which Pietro Bembo celebrated; the most beautiful lines given to Proteus celebrate, again, the world as mirrored in the beloved.

> O how this spring of love resembleth
> The uncertain glory of an April day,
> Which now shows all the beauty of the sun,
> And by and by a cloud takes all away
> (I.iii.84–87)

The Two Gentlemen of Verona belongs (one might say) to the State of Innocence. The delicate acquarelle tints cannot be fully appreciated if Launce and his dog are taken for the more real, the more developed characters, although in the present culture they appear more 'rounded'. Nothing could well be further removed from the Court of Urbino than the sentimental animal lovers of today, but they would welcome the self-sacrifice of Launce. The first great clown, Richard Tarlton, had a man-and-dog act; he fought a combat with Queen Elizabeth's lap dog. Launce's dog represents all that is excluded from Royal Courts; as the horse and jennet, the little hunted hare in *Venus and Adonis* represent in animal shapes the love-making of Venus, the hunt that destroys Adonis; the monstrous animal form of the boar appears only in vision. Here is Crab:

> He thrusts me himself into the company of three or four gentlemen-like dogs under the Duke's table; but he had not been there, bless the mark, a pissing while but all the chamber smelt him. 'Out with the dog!' says one; 'What cur is that?' saith another; 'Whip him out' says a third: 'Hang him up' says the Duke. I having been acquainted with the smell before, knew it was Crab, and goes me to the fellow that whips the dogs. 'Friend,' quoth I 'you mean to whip the dog?' 'Ay, marry do I' quoth he. 'You do the more wrong' quoth I; ''Twas I did the thing you wot of.' He makes me no more ado but whips me out of the chamber. How many masters would do this for his servant?
>
> (IV.iv.15–28)

This breaks right out of the frame and addresses the audience directly, like an epilogue, and marks the grand exit of Launce (and Crab) immediately preceding the scene between Silvia and Julia, the high note in selflessness and sympathy. I do not think the collocation is an accident. But one of the most experienced editors, Clifford Leech, thinks that the play was rewritten and that Launce belongs to a later stage than the rest of the play.

The text that has come down to us is a bad one – it seems to have been torn in pieces like Proteus' love letter and put together by the playhouse scribe, Ralph Crane, from Shakespeare's rough papers. Yet his old friends, who collected his plays seven years after his death, put it second in the volume, immediately after *The Tempest*, his last play, given at Court as a wedding play. A lifetime of experience lay between these two. I shall end by trying to suggest something about its place of Courtesy in the context of its time.

I have already mentioned that I would place it in 1593, the time of plague, when London theatres were closed and the actors disappeared; many companies broke up. The best refuge was in some noble household in the country. At this time Shakespeare published his first poem with a dedication to the Earl of Southampton, whom most people identify with the fair youth of the Sonnets that circulated privately and which are most probably belonging to the years 1594–6.

As the courtly figures of the opening to the *Decameron* retreated into an enclosed garden in the time of plague, Shakespeare took to the rich woodland scene of *Venus and Adonis*; its country sports, the deep woodlands of Hampshire and a frank eroticism which is fleshly enough. Venus sweats, pants almost overpowers the boy. Love is 'deaf and cruel when he means to prey' as the poet who was probably Shakespeare's rival, Christopher Marlowe had commented in his own erotic masterpiece of *Hero and Leander*, the very poem Proteus is reading at the opening of *The Two Gentlemen of Verona* (I.i. 21–2).

In this Court, however, we are in the realm not of Venus but of Cupid, the innocent world – well, very nearly innocent – of Lyly's courtly elegance. Our poet's epigraph to *Venus and Adonis* would better fit the comedy:

> *Vilia miretur vulgus: mihi flavus Apollo*
> *Pocula Castalia plena ministret acqua.*

which Marlowe translated

> Let base-conceited wits admire vile things,
> Fair Phoebus lead me to the Muses' springs
> (*Elegy* XV.35–36)

To live within a noble household would give a unique opportunity for a sensitive receptive poet to absorb the finer nuances of courtly life, as they could never be learnt from outside. The young Earl was nineteen years of age, handsome and self-willed, decidedly a Proteus in matters of love and frustrated of his wish to visit Italy by the Queen's refusal to allow it. Perhaps she feared the influence of the Roman church, for the family were Catholics, and so the young man had been first brought up. Among his retinue was John Florio, the most famous Italian teacher in England. Shakespeare showed himself acquainted with Florio's works before he published the translation of Montaigne which so pervasively influenced the writing of *Hamlet*.

Here, then, if he were in the Earl's country house, Shakespeare would be under new and excellent literary influences. He would find a library. But he would also find a household and a patron to whom he might modestly hope to show the ideal courtly life. The growth of Shakespeare's art was phenomenal, under any consideration; he was famous as a writer already, with the plays on King Henry VI. But *The Two Gentlemen of Verona*, I think, was written for boy players, with one part for a professional actor, that of Launce; a regular clown's role, as Tarlton and Kempe had created it on the public stage. In a noble household the children of the private chapel, or of a local school, or the household pages might be recruited; in this same plague time Thomas Nashe wrote such a play for the Archbishop of Canterbury's country house, with a part for one mature actor as jester.

The air of modest but lofty exclusiveness implies an audience who savoured the cult of fine manners. Boys can be sharply satiric, mimicking absurdity and affectation, and they can sing with piercing purity of tone impossible to the adult voice. Their range however is limited. There are no duels and no ensemble scenes; as Stanley Wells noted, the dialogue consists of duets, solos, soliloquies; even if more than two people are together on stage they do not engage as a group.[1] This is surely not incapacity in the writer but in the actors; they are amateurs, and cannot manage anything complicated — technically complicated. Apart from its perfect song, the play has achieved no great fame. The vision of an enchanted enclosure, a world whose reticences and limitations define its beauty, the fragility of first love, a violet in the youth of primy nature, the perfume and suppliance of a minute are found in the first tentative Sonnets of Shakespeare's sequence (1–17)

> Music to hear, why hear'st thou music sadly?
> Sweets with sweets war not, joy delights in joy
> (8.1–2)

or

> Thou art thy mother's glass and she in thee
> Calls back the lovely April of her prime
> (3.9–10)

or

> Shall I compare thee to a summer's day?
> Thou art more lovely and more temperate
> (18.1–2)

Valentine's admission of idolatry (II.iv.142) is rebutted later with words that chime with the praises of Silvia, who is kind as she is fair:

> Let not my love be call'd idolatry . . .
> Fair, kind and true is all my argument
> (105.1.9)

That very perceptive critic, Inga-Stina Ewbank, comparing this play with the Sonnets, thinks its dependence on verbal techniques fails to reach the fully dramatic terms, the truth to complex human relationships that is achieved in the Sonnets — for perhaps the contribution of the Veneto to Shakespeare's work, represented by the advent of the Dark Lady, had not yet appeared.[2] Was she Emilia Bassano? I am not so sure as A.L. Rowse.

Roger Prior has made out a strong case for identifying the whole group of the Bassano family with this region; they were Jewish musicians who came to the royal court in the reign of Henry VIII, where they formed a compact little enclave. By tracing their wills, he has unravelled their history.[3] If Emilia Bassano, the mistress of the

Lord Chamberlain, whom Shakespeare would have encountered in that household when he joined the Lord Chamberlain's company in 1594, is indeed the dark lady, as Rowse and others have considered her, the deeper knowledge of *The Merchant of Venice*, the distancing of the magic garden of Belmont, would be explained. The tragic notes of *Romeo and Juliet* followed *The Two Gentlemen of Verona* very quickly, indeed Shakespeare may already have read the English poem from which he took this story; but its form and the depth of its passion belong to the public theatres, to which he returned. *The Two Gentlemen of Verona*, with the bloom of dawning that is not quite full day, has its own particular magic – a magic which Wordsworth echoes in his line on first love:

> Earth moved in one great presence of the spring.

In the future lie the passions of Venice, but in the garden of Belmont the arrival of Bassanio's messenger brings hope of what is to come:

> Yet I have not seen
> So likely an Ambassador of love,
> A day in April never came so sweet
> To show how costly summer was at hand,
> Than his forespurrer comes before his lord.
> (*Merchant of Venice* II.ix.91–5)

Such a forespurrer is this comedy, which I do not think was ever clapper clawed with the palms of the vulgar.[4]

Notes

1 *Shakespeare Jahrbuch* XCIX, 1963.
2 *Shakespearean Comedy* (London, Stratford upon Avon Studies, 14, 1972).
3 His article appeared in *The Literary Supplement of The Jewish Chronicle* for June 1979; see also 'Jewish musicians at the Tudor Court' *The Musical Quarterly* Spring 1983, 258–65.
4 In a later study I suggested that the modern reading might have been that of the popular stages, where ordeals in the last minutes were the custom. ('Castiglione, Lyly and Shakespeare's *Two Gentlemen of Verona*', listed p. 211).

VI.

Romeo and Juliet in Performance
(Valencia)

That *Romeo and Juliet* is a lyric tragedy has become a critical commonplace. That it is essentially a play for performance has been attested from the beginning. In 1598 young John Marston, a student of the Middle Temple devoted to plays, wrote:

> Luscus what's played today? faith now I know,
> I set thy lips abroach, from whence doth flow
> Naught but pure *Juliet* and *Romeo*
> (*The Scourge of Villainy*)

Other playwrights were echoing its most popular lines; the first adaptation was by the actors themselves, for the first edition of the play to appear, *The most excellent conceited tragedy of Romeo and Juliet*, 1597 was a pirate edition, or Bad Quarto, evidently derived from the memories of some leading actors and the copied part of the Nurse, who would be played by a man. An authorised edition followed in 1599, and this forms the basis of the modern text we have; it obviously comes from a stage script because the name of Will Kemp, the leading comedian of Shakespeare's company, appears for Peter, the Nurse's servant.

Shakespeare became famous as a love poet after the publication of *Venus and Adonis* in 1593, so presumably the players wanted something from him that would appeal to the same audience. It was the young students in the London audience who found this tragedy of love irresistible. The orchard scene in the folio at the Bodleian Library is heavily thumbed; for the vividness and directness of the love dialogue was something quite new. However powerful the description of lovemaking in *Venus and Adonis*, it is not reciprocal; here the love duets, the teasing jests that spring from a kind of mutual security and trust come in the first meeting when the two jest about the Petrarchan image of Love's Pilgrim, ending with Juliet's 'You kiss by the book' – that is, you are wooing according to the proper authorities; or the exchanges in the orchard scene, when Juliet compares Romeo's departure to that of a bird kept on a string by a young girl. Philip Sidney had written a sonnet about Stella's pet sparrow (also called Philip), of whom he had become jealous, because the little creature could touch Stella's lips. 'Leave that, Sir Phip, lest off your neck be wrung!' Juliet's conceit leads Romeo to say 'I would I were thy bird!' and she replies

> Sweet, so would I,
> Yet I should kill thee with much cherishing.
> (II.ii.182–3)

The line is part of the unstressed ominous imagery. Just before, she had tried to lure him back with a falconer's soft call

> Hist, Romeo, hist! O for a falconer's voice
> To lure this tassel-gentle back again!
> (II.ii.158–9)

The use of bird imagery for lovers gave a kind of warmth unmixed with sensuality to love allegory like Chaucer's *Parliament of Fowls*, a poem of wooing for St Valentine's Day in which a royal falcon wooed his mate. And Romeo turning back at her call of his name says 'My niesse!' The niesse is the same as the little eyas of the play scene in *Hamlet* – a young unfledged nestling high up in the nest of the hawk.[1] Juliet up on her balcony is the young unfledged bird – and it is she, after all, not Romeo, who is tied and constricted by her parents. All this imagery of flight and recalling is beautifully theatrical, and the balcony scene is the most brilliant exploitation of stage possibilities for the emotional relation of movement to poetry, the enactment. The bad quarto does not get this conceit and makes Romeo reply 'Madame' – it was Dover Wilson who interpreted Q2; neece: Folio 1 was 'My deere' and Folio 2, 'My sweet'. The good quarto reads 'My neece', which of course sounds impossible, but the difficult reading is always to be preferred. If this close, playful game of endearment was perhaps too subtle for the actors – yet it is related to the rougher wit-games of Romeo and Mercutio. Their tenderness is lacking in *Love's Labours Lost,* the nearest comic equivalent – except at the end.

Such intimacy and delicacy combined distinguishes Shakespeare from Marlowe, whose *Hero and Leander*, with its star-crossed lovers, also kept asunder by the Hellespont and by her vows as Venus' nun, had in 1593 enchanted young readers. *Romeo and Juliet* appeared probably the next year, 1594. I think myself it may have been given before the Lord Chamberlain's group separated off at the Theatre Shoreditch from the Alleyn-Henslowe troupe; the theatres had been closed because of the plague for nearly two years, so perhaps Alleyn played Romeo too, as well as Burbage. Marston asks his stage-struck Luscus:

> Say, who acts best? Drusus or Roscio

and this was one of Burbage's most celebrated parts. The speech about Queen Mab in the Bad Quarto describes an agate ring as 'on the forefinger of a burgomaster' instead of 'an alderman'. This might be the word used by an actor who had contact with overseas players – and we know *Romeo and Juliet* was popular with the overseas players who went out from Alleyn's group to play in Denmark and the Low Countries and Germany. Shakespeare's father had been an alderman and would have worn the alderman's seal ring in his days of prosperity, which was used for attesting bonds, or giving guarantees. The rather touching recall of this lost dignity in connection with Queen Mab is in keeping with the fancy, composed of tenderness and mockery, which Mercutio, though in a very different key from Romeo, displays in this famous bravura speech.

Tragedies of separated lovers had been seen before, the most famous being *Tancred and Gismund*, a ferocious tale, written by a group of gentlemen from the Inner Temple, one of the Inns of Court, first performed in 1566 and revised and published by Robert Wilmot, one of the original authors, in 1591. He dedicated it to two ladies of the court, to his friends at the Inns of Court. The tragedy is seen as the revenge of Cupid upon King Tancred, aided with a Fury. The lovers, Gismund and the Count Giscard, a courtier, are never shown on stage together, the play showing single passions of her father, Tancred, herself – to whom her father sends the Count's heart in a cup – and the Count, a relatively minor figure, whose death is merely reported. Gismund poisons herself, and her father, having ordered that she and the Earl are to be buried in one tomb, puts out his own eyes and kills himself, wishing to be buried with them. Gismund's dying speech may have been in Shakespeare's mind for Juliet's end, and earlier at her drinking of the cup; Gismund says

> Lo, here, this hearty draught
> Dreadless of death, mine earl, I drink to thee
> So now, work on, now doth my soul begin
> To hate this light, wherein there is no love.
>
> (lines 1717–21)

The extraordinary series of dramatic laments are broken only by rebukes of the King to his daughter. That this play was published only three years before *Romeo and Juliet*, in response to requests as it would appear, gives a measure of the theatrical shock and excitement that the fellowship of players generated.

The young gentlemen of the Inns of Court had been content each to get up in turn and put out his oration in a Senecan play, with chorus as well as gods and furies. Some have taken it that the King Tancred's implacable opposition to his daughter's wedding was aimed at the Queen's well known ferocity towards marriages at Court, particularly that of her cousin Lady Katherine Grey, next in succession if the Scottish claim were disallowed.

The Bad Quarto's stage directions, clearly derived from perform-ance, include, for the scene at the Friar's cell 'Enter Juliet rather fast and embraceth Romeo' (II.vi.15) 'Enter Nurse wringing her hands with the ladder of cords in her lap' (III.ii.5) – where incidentally, Juliet's epithalamium has been cut to the first four lines. The Nurse also prevents Romeo from stabbing himself after banishment, and in her final exit, Juliet is told 'She lookes after Nurse' before 'Ancient damnation'. Evidently the Nurse was a collaborator in this piracy.

Presumably the leading actor's prentice played Juliet, which means that they would be on familiar terms – Alleyn's prentice, John Pyk, from the Henslowe papers jested with the family. The prentice lived with his master and became one of the household; Mrs Burbage was kind to her husband's boys. Juliet's part was unusually impor-tant and on the modern stage she can dominate. It is possible that on the Elizabethan stage, some of her big solo acts were shortened, as the poison drinking in the bad quarto, and even her final relatively brief lines.

The rush to finish a play always tends to cram the final scene, which in any event rely on spectacle and tableaux for a grand finale. It was probably followed by a jig for Will Kemp, who has only a very small part in the tragedy and would need to be compensated.

As Bad Quartos go, the actors' version of *Romeo and Juliet* is not impossibly bad. It isn't in the same field as the Bad Quarto of *Hamlet*. There are a few lines made up by the actors:

> O serpents hate, hid with a flowering face
> O painted sepulcre, including filth

is Juliet's exclamation when she hears Romeo has killed Tybalt. On the other hand, the actors' version preserves 'Romeo I come; this do I drink to thee!' after which 'she falls upon her bed within the curtains'. Modern editions (the two best are Brian Gibbons's Arden, 1980 and Blakemore Evans's New Cambridge, 1984) make good use of this Bad Quarto.

Pepys saw the play soon after the reopening of the theatres, which had been closed for eighteen years during the Civil War. On March 1st 1662, he recorded in his Diary:

> thence to the opera and there saw *Romeo and Juliet*, the first time it was ever acted. But the play is of itself the worst that ever I heard in my life, and

the worst acted that ever I saw these people do; and I am resolved to go no
more to see the first time of acting, for they were all of them out, more or
less.

They had not learnt their lines.

The Restoration saw most of the plays of Shakespeare 'improved'
to meet the taste of a very different stage. These performances must
not be judged from our point of view, as travesties of Shakespeare,
but as evidence of what the age that enjoyed them was like. They are
part of dramatic history and the history of culture; and the measuring rod of Shakespeare gives proof of how far the basic appeal could
remain and where that basic appeal was. The parts which remain
relatively constant are the orchard scene, the parting, Juliet's drinking of the potion and the first part of the tomb scene. What was
constantly reshaped, and is most frequently reshaped today, is the
family feud, the tragic events surrounding the lovers. The two minor
parts that survive most clearly are Mercutio and the Nurse, high
comedy both, strongly characterised, and essential to the story –
though Mercutio is Shakespeare's invention. By the standards of
the later seventeenth century, Shakespeare was lacking in politeness, nobility, refinement of language. He was the poet of nature,
warbling his native woodnotes wild, as Milton put it. Of *Troilus and
Cressida* (1679), in Dryden's version, Duke, a friend of Dryden and
Otway, wrote 'You found it dross and you have left it gold'. This
was by adapting it to a French model, making Cressida faithful
but misunderstood, and putting all blame on her father Calchas.
The 'improved' version of *Romeo and Juliet*, the work of Thomas
Otway, a young playwright of 27, appeared also in 1679 as *The
History and Fall of Caius Marius*, based on the wars of the Roman
consuls, Marius and Sulla. The leading part, taken by the great actor
Thomas Betterton, was that of Marius but he was given a son,
Marius Junior, the Romeo of this classic play. The Juliet part,
Lavinia, a daughter of Metellus, one of the old nobility and allied to
Sulla, was taken by Mrs Barry, an actress of whom Otway was
hopelessly enamoured and for whom he wrote all his leading femi-
nine parts. She was the mistress of the Earl of Rochester. The story of
Marius junior and Lavinia gives the intimate private tragedy en-
closed within a tragedy of state; and in fact in a recent article
Matthew Wikander gives the political aspect of this play, to which I
shall return.[2] It concerns what English historians term the Exclusion
Crisis, the attempt to bar the King's brother and heir presumptive,
the Catholic James Duke of York, from the succession to the throne.
The Duke resigned as Lord Admiral on 29 January 1679, went into
voluntary exile in the Spanish Netherlands, returning in September
to Scotland. Otway wrote about this in his ode *The Poets' Complaint*

of his Muse. His last unfinished verses welcomed the succession of James. (It was still necessary for the present Duke of York when he took his seat in the House of Lords in February 1986 to sign a declaration that he acknowledged his mother, the Queen, as supreme and not the Pope!)

The love story provides a severe test of filial obedience as well as love. The tragedy opens with the Roman mob deserting Marius for Sulla at the behest of Lavinia's father and his friends. Marius and his two sons enter: Marius explains that he had offered marriage between his eldest and Lavinia — Metellus had been his original patron, for Marius is not of equal rank, though now of greater power.

> Why sigh'st thou, boy? still at th'unlucky name
> Of that Lavinia, I have observ'd thee thus
> With thy looks fix'd, as if thy Fate had seiz'd thee.

Marius Junior cannot assent to the vengeance sworn by his father

> Lavinia! O! there's music in the name
> That softening me to infant tenderness
> Makes my heart spring like the first leaps of life!

To which his parent retorts.

> Hell! Love her? Damn her. There's Metellus in her,
> In every line of her bewitching face . . .
> I'd rather see thee in a Brothel trapt
> And basely wedded to a Ruffian's Whore.

But the son persists that she is 'harmless as the turtle of the woods' and that Marius had encouraged his son to love her. Marius junior's confession of love gives Otway's languishment. The love is not exchanged directly; he confesses that he thinks Lavinia returns his feelings 'if eyes may speak the language of the heart'.

It is the heart that is struck, as he describes his own state.

> I lookt and gaz'd and never missed my heart,
> It fled so pleasingly away. But now
> My soul is all Lavinia's, now she's fixt
> Firm in my heart by secret vows made there,
> Th'indelible record of faithful love.
> You'd have me hate her. Can my Nature change?
> Create me o'er again — and I may be
> That haughty Master of myself you'd have me:
> But as I am, the slave of strong desires,
> That keep me struggling under; though I see
> The hopeless state of my unhappy love:
> With torment like a stubborn slave that lies
> Chain'd to the floor, stretch'd helpless on his back,
> I look to liberty, and break my heart.

This is poor Otway's own case, and the image of the slave, a contemporary one, suited to himself. The act ends with the arrival of Sulpitius (the Mercutio of the play) who recites the Queen Mab speech, and they plan to raise the citizens again at Sulla. Act II opens with Lavinia and the Nurse, and Metellus – her mother does not appear – telling her that he designs her for Sulla. She refuses, of course, and lets drop the name of Marius, whereupon her father threatens her with being turned out; the pathetic heroine then has a whole outburst about begging her bread, facing the 'proud and hard revilings of a slave' when she asks 'a little pity for my pinching wants', enduring the 'cold wet windy night' with 'a porch my bed, a threshold for my pillow'. She is told to forget her lover, cursed if she thinks of marriage; the scene concludes with the Nurse praising 'a young man' in lavish prose. And so to the orchard scene, where Lavinia appears after a bout between Sulpitius Granius and the lurking Marius.

> He laughs at wounds that never felt their smart.
> What light is that which breaks thro' yonder shade?
> O! tis my love.
> She seems to hang upon the cheek of night
> Fairer than snow upon a raven's back, (a line from the epithalamium)
> Or a rich jewel in an *Ethiop's* ear.
> Were she in yonder sphere, she'd shine so bright,
> That Birds would sing, and think the day were breaking.

Compared with Shakespeare this is most unfortunate. 'He jests at scars that never felt a wound' contrasts the ignorance about hidden hurt that shapes Mercutio's 'conjuring' with the sheer callousness of laughing at wounds, active pain. Marius has indeed shewn his hurt before Sulpitius. In the next line, the pacing is less varied than 'But soft, what light through yonder window breaks' with its extension

> It is the East and Juliet is the sun

– the imagery of light in darkness that persists up to the tomb scene.

A line from the opening meeting of the two, which is cancelled is inserted here, but eighteen lines are cut, and the couplet is dismembered that makes Juliet's eyes, translated to the heavens

> though the aery regions stream so bright
> That birds would sing and think it were not night.

But the lines most difficult to take seriously are the opening speech of Lavinia

> O Marius, Marius! wherefore art thou Marius?
> Deny thy Family, renounce thy name:
> Or if thou wilt not, be but sworn my love,
> And I'll no longer call Metellus Parent.

The jogging movement of this renunciation, suggests a restive horse throwing off an unwanted rider. 'I'll no longer be a Capulet' is an individual disclaimer, making firmly the greater independence of both lovers. In Otway they provide only the love interest of a political tragedy and might be termed its subplot. But when Lavinia continues

> Tis but thy name that is my enemy.
> Thou wouldst be still thyself, though not a *Marius*,
> Belov'd of me and charming as thou art.
> What's in a name? that which we call a Rose
> By any other name would smell as sweet. . . .

the idiom has altered the quality of the feeling: 'charming as thou art' has already something of the weak modern sense of 'charming' meaning 'very attractive', rather than 'magically compelling'. It was a very fashionable word. The scene ends with Marius going to rejoin his party. A confrontation and an attack by Marius' party upon Metellus brings temporary victory, but Sylla is at the gates, and Marius Junior sends a challenge into his camp. The Nurse comes to make an assignation, for the lovers have been married by a priest of Hymen off stage; after a new quarrel between the two Mariuses they rejoin the fight. This time Sylla conquers though not before the Nurse has had her comic scene of refusing to divulge her news, and Lavinia has opened this comedy with a shortened form of the epithalamium. Another fight between the opposing groups leaves Marius a prisoner with his family and all are banished; they swear a horrid revenge, but Marius junior goes to his tryst. Act IV opens with the aubade – 'Wilt thou be gone! it is not yet near Day'.

A message to her father from Sylla, temporarily at Capua, and a few lies from the Nurse 'to keep this family at peace' precede Lavinia's entering in disguise to flee. A comic scene with Marius' country servants follows; enter the destitute Marius, his sons, who go to beg food for him. Lavinia enters, feeds him with peaches and pomegranates 'both ripe and refreshing'. The lovers are reunited. Enter to soft music a Prophetess who proclaims that he is victorious after all. As some servants of a local lord are preparing to kill him, he is saluted by his own faction, but Lavinia has been seized and borne back to Rome. There she persuades the priest of Hymen to give her the sleeping draught, which she forthwith drinks off. It ends

> What? Sylla? get thee gone, thou meagre lover:
> My sense abhors thee. Don't disturb my draught:
> Tis to my lord. O Marius, Marius, Marius! *Exit*

Marius enters Rome, having received some humble Ambassadors, but he is determined on slaughter. He has some terrific speeches. The discovery of the supposedly dead Lavinia is followed by threatened slaughter of old men and infants in the forum (the infant is usually spared). According to Wikander, Marius senior is based on Lord Shaftesbury, villain of Dryden's *Absalom and Achitophel*, and the slaughtered infant appears in other Shakespearean adaptations of this period as emblem of civil war.[2]

Finally, Marius junior enters in a churchyard, is told the news of Lavinia's death, finds the Apothecary; 'scene draws and shows the Temple and monument' which Marius prepares to enter just as the priest arrives with a wrenching iron and in disguise. Marius kills him, 'pulls down the side of the tomb', and drinks the poison. Lavinia wakes before he expires; both are a little wandering in the wits, and he ends

> I'm all a God; such heav'nly joys transport me
> That mortal sense grows sick, and faints with tasting.

Marius drives in the captured Metellus, who falls and dies 'O, I am slain' and Lavinia, after some speeches of reproach, kills herself with his sword. He hears of a new attack from Sulla; is led off after one speech of repentance; and Sulpitius is led on to die with the last words of Mercutio 'I am peppered, I warrant for this world'. The epilogue, spoken by Mrs Barry is in the usual Restoration vein

> A mischief on't! though I'm again alive,
> May I believe thus play of ours shall thrive?
> This drumming, trumpeting and fighting play:
> Why, what a devil will the people say?

Both parties show the greatest contempt for the mob; Marius and Sulpitius openly denounce them. There are touches that recall *Coriolanus* in this political part of the play. Fear of civil war kept all parties restrained; the king profited by this fear.

Otway had just been serving in Flanders himself; he enlisted late in 1678 but after six months a peace was concluded and he was disbanded with his pay in arrears. The scenes of destitution in the tragedy represent his own pitiful state. He remained as always of the High Tory (the extreme right) party and was a firm supporter of the Duke of York, who was imperilled by an illness of the King, referred to in the prologue of the play where Otway humbly acknowledged the superiority of Shakespeare to himself, reversing his friends comparison of dross and gold.

> Though much the most unworthy of the throng,
> Our this day's poet fears he's done him wrong.
> Like greedy beggars that steal sheaves away
> You'll find h'has rifled him of half a play
> Amidst his baser dross you'll see it shine,
> Most beautiful, amazing and divine.

It is spoken by Thomas Betterton, who played Marius Senior; the epilogue, which refers to Otway's forlorn state as a disbanded soldier, was given to his adored Mrs Barry, who played Lavinia and the published work dedicated to the Viscount Falkland, whom he claimed as a former schoolfellow at Winchester. The story is in form not unlike that of his masterpiece, *Venice Preserv'd*, where the private love story and the political chaos of public uncertainty are set against each other. It was the helplessness of the lovers, their passive suffering which he rendered with sentiment. The revival of Juliet before the death of Romeo allows for extra pathos; this was the most permanent feature of his adaptation which held the stage till the mid-eighteenth century, over sixty years. Cibber and Garrick in 1744 and 1748 then produced more Shakespearean versions, but they kept that final love duet.[3]

The despair behind *Caius Marius* is poor Otway's own – military, amorous and financial; Shakespeare for him acted as a catalyst; it was the penetrative power of the original that shaped the adaptation. And this had continued to be its effect. The actors ensured its success; Mrs Barry says

> And now for you who here come wrapt in cloaks
> Only for love of Underhill and Nurse Noakes.

Underhill played Sulpitius (Mercutio) and Norris was ever after known as Nurse Noakes. Both comic parts were extended; the Nurse had an extra bawdy speech about Lavinia's behaviour in bed as an infant, and Mercutio survived to the last line.

David Garrick, arguably the greatest actor of the English stage, made his perversion of *Romeo and Juliet* in 1748 when he was directing at Drury Lane. He would be married in 1749 to Mlle Violetti, a French dancer, being himself of Huguenot descent, a year after his Romeo; in 1744 he had seen Theophilus Cibber playing Otway's version somewhat adapted at the Haymarket. His own adaptation retained the Otway-Cibber ending of Juliet's revival before Romeo's death, and on a second round of adaptation in 1750 he followed them in abolishing all reference to Rosaline (she was thought to detract from Romeo's nobility). He proceeded cautiously, stating that his aim was to 'clear the original, as much as possible, from the jingle and quibble, which were always thought of as great Objections to reviving it'. It will be remembered that Garrick's friend Dr Johnson said a quibble was Shakespeare's fatal Cleopatra, for which he lost the world and was content to lose it. He excuses himself for not having removed the references to Rosaline, as Otway and Cibber had done; but by 1750 she had vanished from his version. His first Romeo was Spranger Barry, and his first Juliet Mrs Cibber. But these two left him for Covent Garden in 1750 and he decided to play

Romeo himself, with a young woman, George Anne Bellamy as
Juliet. The tragedy opened at both theatres on 28 September 1750
and ran for twelve performance at both houses. This 'battle of the
Romeos' provoked a comment in the *Daily Advertiser* for 11
October:

> Well, what tonight? says angry Ned
>   As up from bed he rouses.
> Romeo again! and shakes his head,
>   Ah! pox on both your houses.

Garrick himself played Romeo for another ten years or so, giving it
up at 53. Shakespeare was cut heavily, from one third to one half in
each act. Barry also continued – for much longer – in the role, in this
version.

   Two very spectacular scenes were added; the masquerade ball,
and a funeral procession to Juliet's tomb, with tolling bells, a choir,
torchbearers, choristers and clergy in vestments, a dirge written for
Garrick to the music of William Boyce.

   Garrick-Otway's version of the final scene held the stage for two
hundred years. Produced in 1679, it was acted by Wyndham in 1875
and not discarded till Henry Irving's production in 1882. Romeo has
just drunk the poison when Juliet awakes with the exclamation
'Where am I? defend me, powers'; and a hundred lines follow in
which Romeo in ecstasy forgets that he has drunk poison, Juliet, half
awake, protests that she will not marry Paris, 'Romeo is my husband'; she tries to kiss him, but Romeo turns faint, explains to Juliet:

> My powers are blasted,
> 'Twixt death and love I'm torn, I am distracted!
> But death's strongest – and must I leave thee, Juliet?
> O cruel cursed fate! in sight of heaven –

Juliet:	Thou ravest; lean on my breast.
Romeo:	Fathers have flinty hearts, no tears can melt 'em.
	Nature pleads in vain. Children must be wretched.
Juliet:	O! my breaking heart!
Romeo:	She is my wife; our hearts are twined together.
	Capulet, forbear! Paris, loose your hold!
	Pull not our heart strings thus; they crack, they break!
	O Juliet, Juliet! (Dies)

(V.iv.121–35)

Friar Lawrence enters to find her fainting on his body.

> O fatal error! Rise, thou fair distressed
> And fly this scene of death.

(V.iv.151–2)

She draws a dagger on him, and he flees as the watch enters. Juliet finds the vial: 'O churl, drink all and leave no frindly drop . . .' but hearing the noise:

> Noise again!
> Then I'll be brief. O happy dagger (Kills herself).
> (V.iv.170–1)

Another eighty lines is allowed for the Prince's entry, the friar's explanation and the reconciliation of Capulet and Montague. The death duet is much more extended than Otway's, allowing both lovers some delirium, some rapture and Garrick in a note, says that 'Mr Otway . . . has made use of this affecting circumstance, but it is a matter of wonder that so great a dramatic genius did not work up a scene from it of more nature, terror and distress' and he says that those who have endeavoured to take away for himself the credit by ascribing the scene to Otway 'have unwittingly, from the nature of the accusation, paid him a compliment which he believes they never intended him'.

Otway had himself been an actor at the beginning of his career; Garrick both actor and manager, most cunningly added both scenically and emotionally. The mutual tenderness of the early dialogue however contrasts with the ending – for 'we each die *alone*' – together yet alone here.

Otway had altered Juliet's age to nearly sixteen; Garrick makes her nearly eighteen. Mercutio is allowed the Queen Mab speech in full by Garrick and the Nurse gets a full stint, in verse. Romeo gets his own lines back in the opening of the orchard scene – or at least some of them; for instance the couplet about Juliet's eyes:

> her eyes in heaven
> Would through the airy region stream so bright
> That birds would sing and think it were not night
> (II.i.62–64)

becomes 'that birds would sing and think it were the morn'. Yet it is remarkably faithful, even if Mercutio is severely cut in his exchanges with Romeo and the Nurse. The quarrel is almost complete, but the laments of Juliet were too full of quibbles, though Romeo is allowed

> There's more felicity
> In carrion flies than Romeo.
> (III.v.28–9; cf. Shakespeare III.iii.34–35)

The bridal aubade is given pretty faithfully. Romeo's line 'I must be gone and live or stay and die' is cut as a quibble, Juliet is not allowed to call the light 'a torch bearer to light thee on thy way to Mantua';

'Tis but the pale reflex of Cynthia's brow' is cut from Romeo, and 'I have more care to stay than will to go' Juliet's conceit on the lark who changed eyes with the toad goes out, ten lines being cut to four and her beautiful line 'Then window, let day in, and let life out' and 'Dry sorrow drinks our blood' is followed by an 'adieu' from each (in Shakespeare both are Romeo's). The scene then changes to the interior of Juliet's chamber.

Garrick's play, therefore, marked the bold reassumption of Shakespeare's lines, and his order, except for some parts of Act I, was fairly well followed. Scenic embellishments, consisting chiefly of the gorgeous costumes for the masquerade and the funeral procession, were the chief attractions, rather than changes of scene (the funeral procession had been put on at the rival Barry production first). Romeo continued to dominate, though there were some celebrated Juliets, including Hannah Pritchard 'born to please'; Mrs Siddons did not take the part, she could never have played an ingénue.

The nineteenth century saw two developments; the cutting out of lines felt to be too coarse or offensive to the young persons who were given the family Shakespeare to read, and the development of scenic splendour, historic elaboration, by frequent changes of scene involving lengthy pauses, which in turn led to more cuts.

The cutting of the text in the interests of decency was found also in some translations. A young Kuwaiti student, Nadia al-Bihar, who studied Arab translation was absolutely overwhelmed when she encountered the original. The Arabs are very given to passionate love lyrics and this play was a favourite in Cairo, but so heavily expurgated that poor little Nadia found the bawdry very obtrusive, since she thought she knew the English text well. She wrote an article on this in *Shakespeare in Translation*, III (1976). The Arabic production of 1890, Al-Haddad's *The Martyrs of Love*, opened with the orchard scene; Romeo and Juliet use the same epithets, images and sentiments, and the feud is relegated to a background cause.

Blakemore Evans, in the stage history prefixed to the New Cambridge edition, gives prominence to two young American sisters who played *Romeo and Juliet* in 1845, the elder in the breeches role, as the first to restore Shakespeare's tomb scene. But more than 100 years before, in 1735, Marius junior had been played by Theophilus Cibber's eccentric sister Charlotte Charke. In Cibber's own version she had played the nurse! Garrick and Spranger Barry had played in knee breeches and cocked hat but in 1845 Charlotte Cushman wore a tunic, feathered cap and long hose, as shewn in the New Cambridge edition. The spread of Shakespeare over the theatres of Europe brought to the city of Verona an impulse to locate the historic scenes of the tragedy. Juliet's house and balcony were identified, and Juliet's tomb also became a place of pilgrimage. In 1846 the sarcophagus was being used as a water trough, which indeed it strongly resembles, but as a visitor remarked 'What would we tourists do without these legends!' The moving natural power of the love story invokes this kind of display. On stage the natural and historical background was equally a source of antiquarian interest. The romantic movement made this play a popular subject for paintings; Irving and Beerbohm Tree, the most famous actor managers of the late nineteenth century, were both very lavish. Ballets and operas exploited the pictorial and lyric possibilities of the story and this has continued through the present century. Only gradually did the speed and structural inter-weaving of all the elements in the tragedy produce a swifter and more neutral setting. I remember seeing the youthful Laurence Olivier looking like one of Botticelli's young men, Edith Evans as the nurse, Peggy Ashcroft as Juliet. These were all in the grand tradition.

For Shakespearean critics, the play was becoming glamorous – romantic but *not* tragic and some writers, such as H.B. Charlton, belittled it in the 1940s. Granville Barker's *Preface* (1930), Nicholas Brooke's essay in *Shakespeare's Early Tragedies* (1968) may be set against G.K. Hunter's essay in *Shakespeare Survey* 27 (1974) where he contrasts it with *Titus Andronicus*, paying much more attention to *Titus*. The likeness to the love comedies, the large element of comedy in the first half of the tragedy, made it necessary for the modern stage to deglamourise *Romeo and Juliet*. This was brought about by restressing the importance of the feud, by modern dress performances that made it 'relevant' for the young. The drably dressed Romeo of Zeffirellis' production of 1960 caused a sensation. Jan Kott had missed a trick here – in his *Shakespeare our Contemporary*, (1956) the orchard scene is 'mere bird song' compared with *Troilus and Cressida* – but the image of youth trapped by the brutalities, mistakes and harsh authority of an older generation was thoroughly congenial to the sixties, the years of student revolt, and to the recent rise of Brechtian-Marxist models at the Royal Shakespearean company itself with the direction of Terry Hands and Michael Bogdanov. Derivatives like *West Side Story* follow the same pattern, which might be summed up as Back to Otway! The Brechtian or Marxist slant makes a very popular version for students, the modern equivalent of Shakespeare's young lawyers. Bogdanov's version opened at Stratford in April 1986 and treated the text quite ruth-lessly. The prologue appeared as epilogue, spoken by the Duke as the two golden statues were lit up by the lights of the media and hordes of publicity men stood around. Romeo killed himself with a hypodermic syringe. Tybalt drove a red sports car on to the stage (his Triumph) on to which Mercutio climbed during the duel, fought with modern gang weapons, as his opponent would not risk damaging the paintwork with his chain and spike. Friar Lawrence, a modernist cleric with a cigarette hanging out of his mouth, and the horseplay with the Nurse, were very much that of a stage from which the Lord Chamberlain had abdicated control. In a students' production at Cambridge a few months later, Romeo saw Juliet not at a window but in a bath and in the nude. This is what in the sixties used to be called 'relevance' – making up, as one group said, for the banality of the text! A totally brutal, hostile, gangster world, a core of vulnerable sex-engagement has been after all the recipe for *Hamlet* for some time – at least since Kott and the exuberance of the opening sequences were what took the directors' fancy; so that the conclusion could not be given any weight except to victimise the lovers.

The actors, I am told, were very unhappy at the general thrust of the play; and in November Bogdanov left the company for the Old Vic. The acting at the little new Elizabethan theatre adjoining the main auditorium, The Swan, was much more attractive. This movement is part of the familiar habit of insulting Shakespeare, seeing how much punishment he can take. I can understand that actors must grow stale if they play the classics without respite, and that 'performance theory' may extend itself to complete wrecking of the text in the name of deconstruction. But Shakespeare's writings live again to be reinterpreted in other terms, whilst no one is moved to copy any of the improvers. You may cross a thoroughbred horse with an ass, but the product, a mule, is sterile. The Royal Shakespeare Company is exercising itself with musicals (*Kiss me Kate* is the latest) and with commercial links. Whether this is the cause or effect of government reduction of subsidies I am not sure; but Dr Johnson's words for the opening of the New Theatre in Drury Lane, 1747 by Garrick, may apply today

> The Drama's Laws the Drama's Patrons give,
> For we that live to please, must please to live

or in the blunter form that Garrick used in his own 'Occasional Prologue' for 8 Sept 1750;

> Sacred to Shakespeare was this spot design'd,
> To pierce the heart and humanise the mind.
> But if an empty house, the actor's curse,
> Shows us our Lears and Hamlets lose their force.
> Unwilling we must change the nobler scene
> And in our turn present you Harlequin . . .
> If want comes on, importance must retreat,
> Our first great ruling passion is – to eat.

Notes

1 Dover Wilson's emendation. See *New Cambridge Shakespeare* ed. G. Blakemore Evans (Cambridge, Cambridge University Press, 1984) p. 99.
2 Matthew Wikander, 'Otway and the Exclusion Crisis of 1679.' *Shakespeare Quarterly,* vol 37, No. 3, 1986. Quotations in the text are from *The Works of Mr Thomas Otway,* 3 vols, 1757 (no lineation).
3 The plays of Garrick were most sumptuously edited by H.W. Pedicord and H.W. Bergman (Carbondale, South Illinois University Press, 1981); *Romeo and Juliet* is in Vol. III, fully annotated.

VII.

The Phoenix and Turtle (Cambridge)

Only after the revived taste for Donne and the Metaphysicals did this strangely neglected masterpiece receive its due. Some have called it frigid, a trifle. Middleton Murry in the early 1920s was one of the first to recognise its power, built on paradox yet cunningly avoiding oxymoron. It is exceptionally well attested; it was signed and printed at first in Vatum Chorus (Marston Chapman and Jonson formed the quartet). This issued as with separate title page, in appendix to Robert Chester's *Love's Martyr or Rosalin's Complaint, Allegorically shadowing the truth of love in the constant fate of the Phoenix and Turtle,* published by Edward Blount in 1601. F.T. Prince dismissed Chester as 'rubbish', and another critic describes this collection of the personal bard of Sir John Salusbury of Lleweni, Denbighshire, as 'an attempt to sell the unsaleable'. The new title page reads 'Hereafter follow Diverse Poetical Essaies on the former subject, via the Turtle and Phoenix. Done first by the best and chiefest of our modern writers, with their names subscribed to their particular works; never before extant. And now consecrated by them all generally, to the love and merit of the true noble knight, Sir John Salisburie. Dignum Laude virum, Musa vetat mori.'

Shakespeare's contribution is his highest achievement in what the last century termed the Grand Style or the Sublime. Indeed a paean to Sublimation in many senses, from the chemical to the psychological, its paradoxes lie not only in its theme but in its literary context in Shakespeare's writings. It was the work of the author famous for *Venus and Adonis*, to which it serves as palinode, rather than of the dramatist who in this same year (1601) wrote the most deflationary, the least sublimatory, of his plays, where he built a style from a despair, *Troilus and Cressida*. I don't know that anyone has remarked on the complete dichotomy of these two works. The 'prologue arm'd' of *Troilus and Cressida* would appear to refer to the

armed prologue of Jonson's *Poetaster*, and the quartet who combined so amicably were engaged in the War of the Theatres, some on
one side, some on the other.

A link between Shakespeare's two works is provided by the
Chaucerian connections. In 1598 Thomas Speght's edition of
Chaucer's works made him accessible to a whole generation of poets.
The five acts of Shakespeare's play roughly correspond to Chaucer's
five books; the influence on his poem derives not only from the list of
the birds from *The Parlement of Foules* – all that Ann Thompson[1]
will allow – but also I think from *The Boke of the Duchesse* and
perhaps *The Hous of Fame*. It is a matter of tone and address; the
delicate blend of intimacy and hierarchy, only to be learnt in the
enlarged family atmosphere of the court, was reinforced by those still
lively oral traditions that are lost to us. Chaucer's is poetry for
performance; *The Boke of the Duchesse* was written in 1369 to be
recited in the presence of the bereaved John of Gaunt – who mourned
Blanche sincerely but as a prince was required quickly to make
another marriage. Chaucer, who like his lord was about twenty eight
years of age, would recite his verse from a little pulpit to the ducal
household.

The dream of the bird fable provides a delicate sense of distance
along with the intimacy of inner meaning which is known only to an
immediate circle. Small, eloquent in their song, sensuously quick yet
aerily free from mortal limitations, birds can embody Eros at his
most ardent and least carnal. This is at the other end of the spectrum
from the voluptuousness of *Venus and Adonis*. Paradoxes of intimacy and remoteness arise in a small community close-knit yet
maintaining a precise hierarchy, maintaining 'distance and no space
was seen'.

The specific rite invoked by Shakespeare, as Peter Dronke showed
long ago in a learned article,[2] is partly that of the Bird Requiem or
Bird Mass, deriving from Ovid, used by Skelton in the pretty
burlesque of 'Lament for Phyllip Sparowe'; but also a choir of birds
singing lauds in a tree in Chorus, as in the poem also attributed to
Skelton, *The Armony of Birds*

> wherein did light
> Birds as thick
> as stars in the sky
> Praising our Lord
> Without discord
> In goodly armony

In Skelton's requiem:

> To Jupiter I call
> Of heaven empyreall

That Phillip may fly
Above the starry sky
To tread the pretty wren
That is our Lady's hen:

At the end of *The Parlement of Foules* the full choir in a rondel
celebrates St Valentine

Now welcom somer with thy sonne softe
That hast this wintres weders over-shake,
And driven awey the longe nightes blake!
Seynt Valentyn, that art ful hy on-lofte,
Thus singen smale foules for thy sake . . .
                    (680–84)

(Shakespeare's *Love's Labours' Lost* ends with a song of the Cuckoo
and the Owl.) Chester's extraordinary anthology is Chaucerian in its
presuppositions, since its frame is a medieval debate between Nature
and the Phoenix, reminiscent of Chaucer's *The Parliament of Foules*,
with medieval herbal-, bestiary-, lapidary-sections (plants, trees,
fish, jewels, animals, birds), a dreamlike approach to Paphos' Isle,
where the Phoenix meets the mourning Turtle Dove. On the way a
lengthy history of King Arthur represents perhaps a Spenserian
strain, which the alternative title, *Rosalin's Complaint*, with its
suggestion of Spenser's Rosalind in *The Shepherds' Calendar*, sup-
ports. The narrative line, insofar as there is one, blends celebration
with lament. The Phoenix and Turtle give themselves in turn not to
each other but to 'blessed Phoebus, happy happy light'; they become
one with that 'pure, perfect fire' so that 'one name may rise'. The
Pelican, type of self-sacrifice, watches and celebrates 'a perfect form
of love and amity'.

Genre-criticism and lines of biographic speculation cross and
recross each other, but I shall begin by looking at Shakespeare's
poem in its context of Vatum Chorus. Shakespeare was accustomed
to harmonise with his fellow actors, to absorb or transform their part
in performance, but here he leads the way, being the elder as writer
(though five years younger than Chapman).

For Robert Ellrodt 'truth and beauty vanish from the earth, the
tone is throughout funereal'.[3] The stanza form (quatrains of an
enclosed couplet between two flanking outer lines) was to be used by
Tennyson for *In Memoriam*. The rhythmic force and pulse is slow, is
that of a funeral procession, where the mourners walk in pairs, the
outflankers bearing emblems or trophies, moving to the sound of
muffled drums, tolling bells, the final echo of cannon, as in the great
state London funeral for Philip Sidney. Even today, in our reduced
rituals, a funeral rite creates the strongest of emotional surges and is

so used in centres of political turbulence, from Ireland to the Cape.

Paradoxical euphoria may surge up when a life's full significance is revealed in its close; the bereaved often feel this exaltation. This poem carries religious overtones which have been noted from Fairchild onwards.[4] The paradox uniting Phoenix and Dove is analogous to the union between the second and third persons of the Trinity, which would be familiar to Shakespeare in the hypnotic rhythmic repetitions of the Athanasian Creed, ordained for recital in every church in England on festival days:

> So they lov'd as love in twain,
> Had the essence but in one,
> Two distincts, division none,
> Number there in love was slain.

The creed opens:

> And the Catholick faith is this; that we worship one God in Trinity, and Trinity in Unity:
> Neither confounding the Persons; nor dividing the Substance:
> For there is one Person of the Father, another of the Son and another of the Holy Spirit;
> But the Godhead of the Father, of the Son and of the Holy Spirit is all one; the Glory equal, the Majesty co-eternal.

Christ is also one 'not by conversion of the Godhead into flesh, but by taking of the Manhood into God!'

The very lengthy creed sets up a processional pulse and motion which Shakespeare achieves in much shorter space

> So between them Love did shine
> That the Turtle saw his right,
> Flaming in the Phoenix' sight;
> Either was the other's mine.

Like those of Dante's Beatrice, the eyes of the Phoenix confer a new level of being, but the Turtle and the Phoenix are not equal in greatness, only in purity of intent. In his plays, Shakespeare had reserved and would reserve his plainest monosyllabic style for the core of intense action.

> I must be gone and live or stay and die.
> (*Romeo and Juliet* III.v.11)

Or

> Who would have thought the old man to have had so much blood in him?
> (*Macbeth* V.i.37–8)

(I feel such lines recall some physical experience, perhaps the execution of Lopez, the old Portuguese doctor hanged, drawn and quartered, 7 June 1594) or

> You do me wrong to take me out o' the grave
> (*King Lear* IV.vii.44)

(indeed the whole exchange between Lear and Cordelia.) Or

> Fear no more the heat o' th' sun
> (*Cymbeline* IV.ii.47)

(much used in funerals. I have heard Peggy Ashcroft recite it on one such occasion.)

The Phoenix and Turtle is embedded in action unclear to us; the element of drama is palpable, but interpretation, which would be direct in the performance and to the original and privileged witnesses, is to us ambiguous. Credal affirmation is self-authenticating, provided it is climactic; yet Carleton Brown saw the poem as but 'an ingenious exercise',[5] and for C.H. Herford and M.R. Ridley (as late as 1935) 'a trifle'; 'for them there was no climax in the variety of rhythmic appeal, the triad of modulations: assembly, anthem, threnos. If Walter J. Ong,[6] was moved to quote Eliot's *Four Quartet*, F.T. Prince was moved to cite Mallarmé (and indeed Eliot himself made use of Mallarmé in one of the most enigmatic passages of his work)

> Garlic and sapphires in the mud
> Clot the bedded axletree . . .
> (*Four Quartets* 'Burnt Norton' ii.1–2)

The maximum of resonance and the minimum of particularity is carried in the opening lines

> Let the bird of loudest lay
> On the sole Arabian tree,
> Herald sad and trumpet be.

Chaucer's 'crane, the gyant with his trompe's sound', Shakespeare's own 'cock the trumpet of the morn,' or, as Wilson Knight was convinced,[7] the Phoenix herself, have all been offered as interpretations of the bird; but if Shakespeare had wanted to specify he would have done so. The power to refrain from specific associations at the beginning demands negative capability. The last line of the stanza, 'to whose sound chaste wings obey' might suggest birds or angels. The necessary absence of the specific is a condition of the sacramental.

The trumpet call is followed by the anthem or theme; the final threnos, or lament, is composed by Reason, assenting to the paradoxes that through the death of Phoenix and Turtle, some quality of being 'true' and 'fair' descends upon the mourners. Dronke pointed out that medieval poems of Nature that show an ascent to heaven, permit also a descent with some rarity as a gift for men.

In print, Reason's threnos, separated from the anthem by a richly decorative border, carries a change of rhythm from quatrains to terzains – even slower, weightier and as monosyllabic in their openings. These are the words of Committal; the procession has halted; the conclusion is an urn. It is as if the Mutability Cantoes had ended at the pillars of Eternity, a word used by Shakespeare in the second terzain.

> Death is now the Phoenix nest:
> And the turtle's loyal breast
> To eternitie doth rest.

Shakespeare allows no second Phoenix to be born from the pyre, as does Marston in the next set of verses. Yet the true and the fair will come to 'sigh a prayer', though 'Truth and Beauty buried be.' Prayer, an act at once solitary and yet communal, is an incomplete utterance. The optative and the imperative moods blend, as here. The immediate context, Vatum Chorus, is introduced in two stanzas by Robert Chester, here describing himself as The Author, with a Request to the Phoenix, who is entitled as patron of all his labour

> Accept my home-writ praises of thy love
> And kind acceptance of thy turtle dove.

Written, I believe, in Denbigh, they now celebrate the Phoenix' 'kind acceptance of thy Turtle dove' that is, presumably, some recent graces she has bestowed. Is he, as another turtle, speaking for himself or for Salusbury? The poems, written 'to the love and merit of the true noble knight', are put forward by the main author, who suggests 'some deep read Scholler fam'd for poesy' should sing of her

> Yet I, the least and meanest in degree
> Endeavour'd have to please in pleasing these.

Vatum Chorus then takes over with an invocation to Apollo and the Muses, which some have considered burlesque and which certainly is rejected by Jonson. Drinking to their honourable friend 'in a Castalian bowl, crown'd to the brim' they also invoke 'the ever youthful Bromius' in verses far from transcendent, but they intend to be 'varied from the multitude'. This poem is related by Newdigate to Jonson's *Ode to James Earl of Desmond*.[8] A second pair of stanzas is addressed to Sir John, protesting that the poets indulge no 'mercenary hope'

> But a true Zeal, born in our spirits,

Responsible to your high merits
And an invention, freer than the Times.

Joining in a Castalian bowl was surprisingly friendly; for three of the Quartet were in the autumn of 1601 involved in the War of the Theatres; *Cynthia's Revels* being entered in the Stationers Register 23 March 1601, to be followed by *Satiromastix*, entered 11 November, whilst *Poetaster* followed a month later, both Jonson's plays being for the Chapel Boys. *Love's Martyr* must be later than June 1601, when Salusbury received his knighthood from the Queen.

Shakespeare's company had staged *Satiromastix*; Chapman had moved from collaboration with Jonson for Henslowe to the Children of Paul's, who also staged *Satiromastix*, and in his book Reavley Gair suggests that Marston, who had in 1599 inherited his father's estate, was financing them.[9]

Love's Martyr, therefore, appeared at the height of the three-cornered contest between the Lord Chamberlain's Men and the children's companies, when Shakespeare was also working on *Hamlet* and Marston on *Antonio's Revenge*.

The very feeble stanzas by Ignoto which open the Chorus must have come from someone who was grand enough to be obvious as prime instigator, and are devoted to the Phoenix. They play on 'born' and 'burn' used (it seems) in a metaphoric sense.

Shakespeare follows, then Marston's four verses, describing what Shakespeare so pointedly omits, the birth of a new Creature, created jointly by the Phoenix and Turtle, therefore, surely, something other than another Phoenix. He does not define this same Metaphysical God, Man or Woman but calls for Rapture to raise his Muse above thought, that labours with this birth. He is numbed with wonder at this

divinest Essence,
The soul of heavens labour'd quintessence

and on the new Phoenix which contains nought to be corrupted, he bestows the name Perfection:

By it all Beings deck'd and stained,
Ideas that are idly fained
Only here subsist invested.

(was this a hit at Drayton whose *Idea* had appeared in 1593?)

Marston then changes to Shakespeare's type of quatrain to address Perfection: to produce whom, Nature has been storing up Virtue and Beauty. But in his final Hymn he finds even the name Perfection unworthy of this new birth, 'as firm and constant as Eternity'. Rejecting 'Heavens Mirror' and 'Beauty' as too near the senses, 'Deep Contemplation's wonder' is his final choice, since

> No suburbs, all is mind
> As far from spot as possible defining

adding here a Senecal gloss that the difference between men and gods is that men have a spiritual element but the gods are entirely spiritual in all parts. In one or two critics this has foreshadowed Marvell's *The Definition of Love*:

> My Love is of a birth as rare
> As 'tis for object strange and high:
> It was begotten by despair
> Upon Impossibility.

If Marston will not even ascribe a sex to the new creature, Chapman, in *Peristeros or the Male Turtle*, identifies himself with the Turtle and sees the Phoenix as feminine. 'All love in smooth brows born is tomb'd in wrinkles' yet 'she was to him the analysde world of pleasure'

> Like him, I bound th'instinct of all my powers
> In her that bounds the Empire of desert,
> And Time nor Change (that all things else devoures
> But truth eternis'd in a constant heart)
> Can change me more from her, than her from merit,
> That is my form and gives my being spirit.

In terms of Marston's distinction she is a goddess. For Chapman, as for his patron Ralegh in *Walsinghame* 'true love is a durable fire in the mind ever burning'.

Ben Jonson concludes the Chorus with four poems: a Prelude, a lengthy Epode or Epos, The Phoenix Analysde and Ode (enthusiastike), the last two in quatrains.

First, in jaunty terzains, all the gods, including those of the earlier Vatum Chorus are dismissed as unworthy; he will bring his own true fire. His Epode describes the little kingdom of the inner man. Vice must be expelled, the heart must stand spy for Reason. Love as Desire must be kept out, but not that Love which is 'a golden chain let down from Heaven' which

> In a calm and godlike unity
> Preserves community.

Interrupted by a 'vicious fowl' who denies the possibility of such chaste love, he declares this is neither Abstinence nor Impotence. If the divine Phoenix bestows the wealthy treasure of her love, making his fortunes swim, the Dove will be 'fearful to offend a Dame of this excelling frame'. In a short verse Jonson describes the Phoenix as a woman, though the fairest creature naturally born is but a type of what she is. The final ode extols her wit, judgement and voice, but implying the brightness is not that of earthly beauty:

> Retire, and say her graces
> Are deeper than their faces:
> Yet she's nor nice to show them,
> Nor takes she pride to know them.

A copy of this concluding Ode is found in a Bodleian MS headed 'To L.C. of B,' the kinswoman of Sir John Harrington, who is identified as the author on the title page. This led Bernard Newdigate, on the strength of Jonson's other poems to the Countess of Bedford, in 1937 to identify her as the Phoenix, attesting Jonson's dedication in a copy of *Cynthia's Revels*.

Newdigate is, to my mind, an extreme case of the biographical identification disease (or BIDs). Jonson's poems, I think, establish that the Phoenix and Turtle are not literally married. He retains trace of the assertiveness and contradictoriness that had appeared so strongly in the plays of the War of the Theatres; he, unlike Chapman, does not identify with the Turtle, and he makes no use at all of the legend of the funeral pyre or any of the 'fable'.

Before turning to the biographical aspect, I must add one other feature of the literary context, the volume of 1593, *The Phoenix Nest*, collected poems in honour of Philip Sidney, prefixed by 'The Dead Man's Rite' a vindication of Sidney's uncle, the late Earl of Leicester, from the slanders of the pamphlet known as *Leicester's Commonwealth*, published in 1584: collected by one R.S. of the Inner Temple, Gentleman, it follows the printing of Sidney's own verse in 1593. Marie Axton has shewn Leicester's close connexion with the Inner Temple;[10] and the connexion is, therefore, presumably through him. The anthology includes verses by Lodge, Breton, Peele, the Earl of Oxford, Thomas Warton. There is nothing ascribed to Sidney's closest friends, Dyer and Fulke Greville, but Matthew Roydon's *Elegie or Friends passion for his Astrophill*, something of a forerunner of Vatum Chorus, opens the collection at Nature's assembly. The 'tree that coffins doth adorn' grows in a circle with 'black and doleful Ebony' for an assembly of birds

> Upon the branches of those trees,
>   The aery winged people sat,
> Distinguished in odd degrees,
>   One sort in this, another that,
>   Here Philomel that knows full well,
>   What force and wit in love doth dwell.
>
> The sky bred eagle, royal bird,
>   Percht there upon an oak above,
> The turtle by him never stirr'd,
>   Example of immortal love.

> The swan that sings about to die,
> Leaving Meander, stood thereby.

> And that which was of wonder most,
> The Phoenix left sweet Araby,
> And on a Cedar in this coast
> Built up her tomb of spicery
> As I conjecture by the same
> Prepared to take her dying flame.

A mourner appears to lament immortal Astrophill in the best-known lines

> A sweet attractive kind of grace,
> A full assurance given by looks
> Continual comfort in a face,
> The lineaments of Gospel books

leading into an account of his love for Stella. A storm arises, the birds all lament, the Phoenix sets fire to her nest but her ashes are dispersed in the tempest, so no second Phoenix will ensure. The Eagle ascends with the news to Jove, and so the dreamer wakes (only now do we learn this is a dream vision). The poems which follow are much more of a miscellany on love, including several poems about the Queen.

Roydon, a friend of Chapman and a famous mathematician, may have attracted Shakespeare's attention when he was asked to contribute to a collection which came from another of the Inns of Court, the Middle Temple. The significance of this connection will require a direct entry into the area of biographical interpretation; and I must therefore briefly summarise what is known of Sir John Salusbury, whose life was carefully investigated by Carleton Brown, to whose work little has since been added.

John Salusbury (1566 or 1567–1612) was the second son of John Salusbury, squire of Lleweni in Denbighshire, and his wife Catherine of Berain, who was an illegitimate descendent of the Tudors. After her husband's death she remarried three times bringing a useful network of relatives to her son. John became the heir when in September 1586 his elder brother Thomas, a confessed Catholic, was executed for conspiracy in the Babington Plot. He promptly married Ursula Halsall of Knowsley an illegitimate but acknowledged daughter of the fourth Earl of Derby; they had ten children.

After eight years, in 1595, Salusbury was appointed Squire of the Body to the Queen. A Welshman who was a follower of Cecil might not seem unfitted for this honorary post; but for the brother of an executed traitor it was a special mark of favour, implying trust and intimacy. Under a female monarch duties did not include the bedchamber attendance that made Robert Carey ask it as his only favour when in 1603 he bore the news of accession to James I; but the post gave admittance to the most privileged inner circle of the private apartments, where the trusty Welsh entourage, such as Kate Parry, really had the Queen's close ear. To be a Squire of the Body meant that Salusbury had a cachet of loyalty conferred; and of course theoretically it gave the opportunities for access which, if Salusbury and the Queen *had* been disposed to physical lovemaking, could easily have been arranged. In fact her Squires of the Body were all rather innocuous characters (John Lyly was one, promoted to amuse the waiting concourse of attendants).

The year before this promotion, Salusbury had been made a member of the Middle Temple, and so by the time he received the further honour of knighthood in June 1601, he had had a chance to make the acquaintance of its members. He was also made deputy lieutenant for Denbighshire. All this must have been welcome indeed since, by the summer of 1601, it was clear that the Queen, beginning to show her years, would not be there much longer to patronise the Welsh. In December 1601, Salusbury, now honoured by the publication of his praise, was elected to Parliament as member for Denbigh, but not before he had fought a pitched battle in the churchyard at Wrexham with a rival candidate, Sir John Trevor; and thereafter his fortunes declined. Robert Cecil gave him no opportunity for approaching the new king in 1603; he fell into financial trouble and never returned to court.

Salusbury, a colourful character, fostered masques and plays in Denbigh. He lived on that coast where Sir Gawain travelled in *Sir Gawain and the Green Knight*, where local lords ruled regally.

The MS Peniarth 539OD in the National Library of Wales preserves a collection of plays and masques from Lleweni from c.1600 to 1660, which Reavley Gair worked on and at one time thought of including in a book on provincial academies. Salusbury's own poems are in Carleton Brown's EETS volume (Extra Series No 113, 1914). I think MS Peniarth 539OD might throw light on *Love's Martyr* as a Welsh composition, but the Vatum Chorus was clearly an appendix by Londoners. Of these Marston was himself a member of the Middle Temple and Ben Jonson had strong links for he had recently dedicated *Cynthia's Revels* to the Inns of Court generally and *Poetaster* to Richard Martin, a prominent younger member of the Middle Temple who had been the Christmas Prince in the Revels of 1598–1599, an occasion which saw the expulsion from the society of one of its own poets, John Davies, author of *Astraea*, for an assault on Richard Martin (see my *John Webster*, Chapter II). Jonson dedicated *Poetaster* with the words:

A thankful man owes a courtesy ever . . . I send you this piece of what may live of mine; for whose innocency as for the author's you were once a noble and timely undertaker . . . posterity to owe the reading of that, without offence to your name, which so much ignorance and malice of the times then conspired to have suppressed.

Martin had interceded with Lord Chief Justice Popham on Jonson's behalf in the quarrel. Had he asked Jonson to contribute to Vatum Chorus, perhaps in an attempt to reconcile differences with Marston, Jonson would have felt the obligation of 'a thankful man'? Martin might have been *Ignoto*.

Chapman had been a follower of Essex, whose patronage of the Middle Temple had been abruptly ended by his rebellion and execution earlier in 1601; but Sir Henry Wotton resided there, and so did, from time to time, Walter Ralegh, Chapman's earlier patron and patron of Roydon. Shakespeare's company had played for the Middle Temple and were to do so again.

The occasion, as I have said, was the conferring of a knighthood on Salusbury in June 1601. I would think that the metropolitan connections came through his Inn, a centre of literary activity, and had little to do with his own bard, Chester. But now at last I come to the direct examination of biographic interpretations, particularly the identity of the Turtle and the Phoenix (as reversing the previous order) they are cited on the title page of Vatum Chorus. And I shall confine myself to two recent interpretations, those of Ernst Honigmann in *Shakespeare, the Lost Years*[11] and of Marie Axton in *The Queen's Two Bodies* – though I believe Mrs Axton has also lectured on the subject and may have developed new points. Ever since he edited *King John* for the Arden series in 1954, and dated it in the winter/spring of 1590–91, Honigmann has been engaged in filling in Shakespeare's 'lost years', and in the thirty intervening years he has grown, as might be expected, more convinced and doctrinaire. He has uncovered a number of connections with Lancashire. Shakespeare's membership of the company of Ferdinando Lord Strange, for six brief months fifth Earl of Derby, who played at the Rose in the spring of 1592 giving *Harry the VI* is probable enough. After Derby's death they became the Lord Chamberlain's Men. Honigmann associated a number of other plays with these years, and he accepts that by-no-means-proven theory that when on 12 September 1581 Alexander Hoghton of Lea in his will commended to his brother William Shakeshafte, with some bequests, that this was Shakespeare (then aged 17). In September 1586, when Salusbury married Ursula Halsall, it is Honigmann's contention that Shakespeare wrote *The Phoenix and Turtle*. He would be 22, seven years before he composed *Venus and Adonis*.

It is true that Honigmann has traced a number of Lancashire men with Shakespearean connections – John Cottom, John Weever, Thomas Savage; that his firm conviction about the early start sprang in the first place from his own devotion to Peter Alexander and his theory about *Henry VI* and *Richard III*. But he is steadily adopting more and more unlikely theories, among which I would place his views on *The Phoenix and Turtle*. Ursula's rank as acknowledged if illegitimate child of an Earl of Derby would not give the sort of elevation he supposes above the son of the illegitimate daughter of the Tudors! And after fifteen years of marriage and ten children the absence of progeny (which he thinks was corrected by Marston by referring to their eldest daughter as the new Phoenix) becomes as difficult as the presentation of this piece as 'never before extant'. He thinks this means 'not published'. Above all, however, these biographical pinpointings become more important for him than the poetic experience itself.

This would not greatly matter, if the biographic speculations were not so readily taken up by others. I was very depressed to read in the recently published work of Marie-Thérèse Jones-Davies, doyenne of French Shakespeareans, that she has adopted Honigmann's views without any demur. In *Shakespeare: Le Théâtre du Monde*,[12] she speaks of the poem as 'sa première œuvre composée sans doute plus de dix ans avant sa publication, l'année même du mariage en 1586'. Her new biography is bound to be widely influential in the country of Abel Lefranc where biographical speculations have always flourished – although in her subsequent literary discussion of the poem (pp. 220–23) Mme Jones-Davies makes no use of Honigmann – and I suspect she incorporated him at the last minute.

Honigmann does not appear to have read Marie Axton's Chapter VIII in *The Queen's Two Bodies*, where she identifies the poem as an affirmation of political faith. The Queen is both Phoenix (in her body politic) and Dove; her subjects' loyalty transcends the personal and yet they are mortal; hence each is seen as Phoenix *and* Dove. Those who heard Quentin Skinner's lecture on the emergence of the idea of the State, as transcending all who participate, will realise that this notion was very slow to emerge; there are beginnings in Bodin and in Hobbes, but whilst all were prepared to advise a Prince, or define the duties of citizens in a republic, whilst demogogues' rule or tyrants' were equally abhorrent, the notion that the mutual loyalty of subjects is to prince and prince to an overriding power – the State itself – was left to the unacknowledged legislators like Shakespeare. There were no political definitions; the ageing queen refused to name her successor, and hence the desperate cry of some subjects that she must be immortal, the mask of eternal youth created by Hilliard in painting and by poets – particularly John Davies in his *Hymnes of Astraea* (1599) with his acrostics of Elizabeth Regina. Sir John Salusbury could have known Davies at the Middle Temple; he himself wrote acrostics of an ambiguously erotic kind addressed to his sister-in-law!

Mrs Axton works through Chester's part of the poem, interpreting this in terms of the views of poets in 1601. I have not myself paid enough attention to it to take a stand on this. Wilson Knight also worked through it in his book *The Mutual Flame* where the poem is related to the Sonnets, the Phoenix becomes the fair youth, the dove the poet, and the bi-sexual nature of the Divine Hermaphrodite is finally achieved. Kenneth Muir, in his early *Voyage to Illyria*[13] had also seen the Phoenix as Southampton – this view had been put forward as early as 1893 by von Maunt but encounters the problem that the collection is meant for the honour of Salusbury, after *his* honouring by the Queen; and this implies, I think, that at *some* level they are represented in the Turtle's constancy and the Phoenix' bestowal of her love and favour upon him. Of course levels of meaning are not excluded; the only critic to dwell on this appears to be the Swiss, Hermann Straumann, who in his little booklet *Phönix und Taube* favours the Southampton identification but also stresses *Mehrdeutigkeit* – multiplicity of meaning.[14]

Such, I think, was the creation of small intimate groups. There was the core meaning, clear to the inner circle, perhaps reinforced in performance; but such praise – or satire – was generally applicable, and could be transferred to the new contexts. Chester might well have made Ursula Salusbury a Phoenix in Lleweni and Elizabeth a Phoenix in London, or Jonson have diverted his Epode in the direction of the Countess of Bedford. The transcendent being, the Phoenix-to-be, for Shakespeare was produced by 'Choice being mutual act of all our souls' which made 'merit her election'

> and doth boil
> As 'twere from forth us all, a man distilled
> Out of our virtues
> (*Troilus and Cressida*, I.iii.346–8)

– this transcendent being, the Great Leviathan, was still envisaged politically as a Monarch; though as Marston said not to be defined as God, Man or Woman. Mrs Axton makes some pertinent quotations from contemporary works that deal with the succession and imply the King of Scots as heir. Many were already in correspondence with him, among whom had been Essex. Plays on the succession took the form of dramas about the succession in Henry VIII's time, such as *Thomas Lord Cromwell*. Shakespeare, unable to express any-thing directly in drama by reason of the censorship, produced this enigmatic powerful credo for society debating the issues. Psychology observes that mourning may often be done in advance; the elegy on Sidney gave him the lead – in the legend of the Phoenix dying to be reborn, gave him the theme. None of the other poets used this in their tributes, though Marston comes nearest.

I would then, see the poem generally in the same light as Mrs Axton but I want to add a caveat and a few additional pieces of supporting evidence that have recently emerged from the iconographic studies of Elizabeth in her last years. The caveat rises from the dangers of biographical investigatory disease, whereby the historical basis takes precedence over the poetry itself. For me, the poetry is primary. It doesn't make much odds whether one can identify John Cottom, John Weever or Thomas Savage as people whom Shakespeare encountered, even if they all came from the Catholic strongholds of Lancashire.

The Phoenix was an icon for an old woman. So the septuagenarian Churchyard used her for the Queen in *Churchyard's Challenge* of 1593; also in 1595 in 'A few plain verses of Truth against the flattery of time', to

> call your poets to account
> for breaking of your bounds
> in giving of your fame to those
> fair flowers that soon that soon shall fade
> and clean forget the white red rose
> that God a Phoenix made.

Elizabeth herself used the Phoenix as image in the Armada Jewel which she gave to Francis Drake. It was perhaps a witty reference to the fireship in his naval action. The cult of Elizabeth as divinity began, according to Roy Strong's latest work *Gloriana*,[15] after the end of her last wooing by Alençon, in 1582–4; she was past childbearing, marriage was no longer the answer to the succession. Her deification by Ralegh, Spenser, and in pageantry, with Hilliard's painted Mask of Eternal Youth created rituals which towards the end of the 1590s were felt to be difficult to sustain. The Arthurian continuity of the monarchy gave to Chester's history of King Arthur a Spenserian resonance; and as Mrs Axton notes, the whole volume was reissued in 1611 under the new title of *The Annals of Great Britain or a Most Excellent Monument wherein may be seen all the Antiquities of the Kingdom*; but this was the precise moment when the Arthurian legend was being strongly revived in the Arthurian claims in masque and tourney for Henry, Prince of Wales. It was quite topical. The phoenix image revived in 1604 for King James's Royal Entry in Dekker's device for the pageant at Soper Lane, *Nova Felix Arabia* – but only in the pun; the mourning female figure of

Britannia Arabia was transformed by joy, whilst the boys of St Paul's represented the chirping of a tree full of birds.

In our crucial year of 1601, John Donne, most fashionable of poets, had ruined his career by his secret marriage to his employer's niece, Ann More; but Donne was able to revive the Phoenix image as a double being in 'The Canonization';

> The Phoenix riddle hath more wit
> By us, we two being one, are it
> So, to one neutral thing both sexes fit.

Later he was to describe 'two Phoenixes' in the marriage ode for Princess Elizabeth and the Elector Palatine. The Queen often referred to herself as married to her country and so did James ('the whole isle is my wife'); but he would never have conceded that a greater thing than he was born of the faithful union.

An addition has been recently made to the links between portraits and poetry in the last years of Elizabeth in the article by Mary C. Erler, 'Sir John Davies and the Rainbow Portrait of Queen Elizabeth'.[16] Roy Strong also associated this portrait with Davies' *Hymnes of Astraea*, but I think the credit must go to Dr Erler. In addition to *Astraea*, Davies wrote an entertainment which the Lord Keeper (Donne's alienated employer) gave at Harefield House in August 1602, and another given by Robert Cecil at his house in the Strand in December 1602 – the last that Elizabeth was ever to attend (it is described in Manningham's Diary).[17] It appears that the Rainbow Portrait, still the property of the Cecils at Hatfield House, is closely connected with this entry.

There was a contention between a maid, a wife and a widow. The very curious headdress worn by Elizabeth in the portrait had been identified earlier as that of the Thessalonian Wife, as delineated in J.J. Boissard, *Habitus Variorum orbis gentium* which also depicts a maid and a widow; Frances Yates made this identification in *Astraea* but Mary Erler also finds a Roman triad which is relevant in pose and gesture. She identifies the eyes and ears on the Queen's mantle as representing the Intelligence of state – and Cecil controlled Elizabeth's intelligence service. In the entertainment the Queen was presented with a rich robe by an Emissary of the Emperor of China and this bright sun-coloured mantle may well represent it, a gift from the wisdom of the East and the lands of sunrise. Her flowery bodice represents the eternal spring of her beauty, whilst the face is even younger, more rounded than the Hilliard mask conventionally prescribed. A warm radiant sensory glow emanates from the Queen. Many other symbolic details are interpreted in this portrait, which Dr Erler thinks may be a posthumous deification or glorified memorial of the Queen. She would have been flattered by the image; some of the jewels are identifiable with devices presented to her.

But Shakespeare's Funeral Rite is still to be explained unless, as I have said, the perceptive may do their mourning in advance of the event. This may suggest why the ardent vision broke out at the same time as the harshest disillusion of all that Hector and Troilus believed in. At the Inns of Court there was painful knowledge that behind Davies' vision of the Eternal Spring of Astraea there lurked a gaunt form shaken with rage, grey hair under the auburn wig, an uncertain temper that meant her maids of honour had to be dragooned into their rota of service. Shakespeare's credo of *Quia impossibile est* was not really addressed either to the Queen or to Salusbury. To identify the theme is not to tie it to biographical detail. A decade after she was dead Shakespeare was to write the prophecy of Elizabeth in his last play:

> when
> The bird of wonder dies, the maiden Phoenix,
> Her ashes new create another heir.
> *(King Henry VIII*, V.iv.39–41)

It was, we now see it, a fatally inadequate one. But in public life Shakespeare wrote neither elegies for Elizabeth nor welcomes to James; he was writing *Othello* and *Measure for Measure*, plays of dark questioning.

Yet the Queen herself in her last Golden Speech to Parliament had given voice to the doctrine that the love of the people created the greater harmony of joint government, as she gracefully gave way on the subject of monopolies:

> Though God hath raised me high, yet this I count the glory of my reign that I have reigned with your loves.

Notes

1 Ann Thompson *Shakespeare's Chaucer* (Liverpool, Liverpool University Press, 1978).
2 Peter Dronke 'The Phoenix and Turtle' *Orbis Litterarum* vol. XXIII (1968).
3 Robert Ellrodt 'An anatomy of "The Phoenix and Turtle".' Allardyce Nicoll, (ed.), *Shakespeare Survey* 15, (1962).
4 A.H.N. Fairchild *Englische Studien* XXXIII (1904).
5 Carleton Brown *Poems of Sir John Salusbury and Robert Chester* (London, Early English Text Society, 1914), Extra Series 113.

6 Walter J. Ong 'Metaphor and the Twinned Vision.' *Sewanee Review*, vol. LXIII, Spring 1955.

7 G. Wilson Knight *The Mutual Flame* (London, Methuen, 1955).

8 Bernard H. Newdigate *The Phoenix and Turtle* (Oxford, The Shakespeare Head Press, 1937).

9 W. Reavley Gair *The Children of Paul's* (Cambridge, Cambridge University Press, 1982).

10 Marie Axton *The Queen's Two Bodies* (London, Royal Historical Society, 1977).

11 Ernst Honigmann *Shakespeare, the Lost Years* (Manchester, Manchester University Press, 1985).

12 Marie Thérèse Jones-Davies *Shakespeare: Le Théâtre du Monde* (Paris, Balland, 1987, p. 49. 'It was his first work, composed certainly more than ten years before its publication in 1586, the year of the marriage.'

13 Kenneth Muir and Sean O'Loughlin *Voyage to Illyria* (London, Methuen, 1937).

14 Hermann Straumann *Phönix und Taube* (Zurich, Artemis-Verlag, 1953).

15 Sir Roy Strong, *Gloriana* (London, Thames and Hudson, 1987).

16 In *Modern Philology*, vol. 84 No. 4 (1987), pp. 359–71.

17 Robert Parker Sorlien (ed.) *Manningham's Diary* (Hanover, University of New England Press for the University of Rhode Island Press, 1976).

Shakespeare's London

VIII.

The Politics of Pageantry (London)

The Roman reward for a conqueror, his Triumph, became the term of the London livery companies for the procession that on St Simon and St Jude's Day, 29 October, marked – as it still marks – the installation of the Lord Mayor. The themes for celebration were the greatness of the City and its history; the worthiness of the Lord Mayor's company; the praise and exhortation due to himself from his fellows. Reciprocity of gifts and favours was demonstrated by the Yeomen or Bachelors of the company in supplying the pageant its devices or accompanying speeches, whilst the Lord Mayor and Sheriffs provided the feast at Guildhall, which as early as 1575 cost £600.

The Mayor, chosen from among the governing élite of the Twelve Great Companies, was elected after a sermon had warned all of their duties. Next day the brethren of his livery waited to escort the Lord Mayor to Guildhall for installation, after which they embarked at the Three Cranes in the Vintry for the state voyage to Westminster, where he took his oath before the Barons of the Exchequer. Returning, he landed below St Paul's, where he was met by the full procession, including the pageant, ready in the yard of the Bell Inn. By way of St Paul's churchyard and Cheapside, all set forward for the Guildhall feast returning for evening service at St Paul's and ending with an escort and final speeches before the Lord Mayor's residence. Largess and loyalty combined in a ceremony half carnival, half consecration.

The route was cleared by fencers and 'wildmen' with fireworks; workmen were liberally paid to take down signs or even remove a shop, attendants who were maimed had to be compensated. The almsmen of the livery company paraded in new blue gowns, their schoolboys received breakfast and partook of the feast in return for their speeches; in addition to their pay, the porters who bore the pageant were liberally supplied with drink. The livery had new gowns, half the Bachelors being furred with marten (or 'foynes') and half with lambskin (or 'budge').

Sugar loaves, spices, or, in the case of the Fishmongers, live fish were thrown from the pageant 'ship' to the crowd. The senior company, the Mercers, allowed the fortunate girl who represented the Mercers' Maid, always carried in pageant by their Bachelors, to keep the rich garments and jewels she wore. She had presumably once represented the Virgin Mary. With the clamour of all the bells from London's fifty-seven churches, the royal trumpeters blowing, the gunners of the Tower shooting off their ordnance, the fireworks, the crowd's cheering and impromptu witticisms, any speeches made to the Lord Mayor must have been largely inaudible even to him. As the procession grew in stateliness, he was encountered at different points by different pageants which wheeled into position before him and joined the procession; in the late sixteenth and early seventeenth century, the dramatists from the public playhouses were used to supply the 'devices', which, although agreed with the livery company beforehand, were then printed by the author and offered to the liverymen. Thus definition crystallised the power of the City as it was celebrated; such a manifesto could define attitudes or even initiate policy.

The dramatic growth of London in late Elizabethan and Jacobean times led to increased splendour; and among the Twelve Great Companies, the Drapers, Haberdashers, Mercers, and above all, the very rich Merchant Taylors developed pageantry for the great expansion of the cloth trade, England's chief export. Seven-eighths of England's overseas trade went through the Port of London, of which three-quarters was in wool and cloth. Neptune as presiding deity rivalled Londinium herself. Since the leading citizens were now capitalists and merchant-venturers rather than craftsmen, it is noted in the records of the Merchant Taylors for 1602[1] that a mayor and a sheriff from their company both being merchants, the ship pageant is very properly used; in 1605, the present style of the company is noted as having being given by King Henry VII[2] since:

> they traded, as no men did more
> With forren Realmes by clothes and Merchandize,
> Returning hither other Countries store,
> Of what might best be our commodities.[3]

From the first quarter of the seventeenth century, three of the five Triumphs given for the Merchant Taylors have survived, which show a continuous development of political significance. These are Munday's, Dekker's and Webster's for 1605, 1612 and 1624.

A notice of this company as early as 1553, when Sir Thomas White, founder of St John's College, Oxford, was installed, includes a pageant of their patron saint, St John the Baptist.[4] The Lord Mayor was translated into the stream of mythology and the history of his own company: thus Sir Thomas was to be revived as a benefactor whose memory lived as late as 1624. Any Lord Mayor whose name would bear it was graced with emblematic devices; in 1568, such mighty figures as David, Arion and Amphion harped in the Triumph of Sir Thomas Harper; in 1561, Sir John Roe received a sermon from St John (written by Richard Mulcaster, High Master of the scholars) which was followed by a song, 'Behold the Roe so swift in chace, yet tarrieth still to hear . . .'. This equated him with the Lion and Camel of the company's arms, or the Holy Lamb of their crest, which was liable to turn into the Golden Fleece. Sir John Lemon's lemon tree might be stored for future pageants with these emblematic objects; any mayor with a name as pliable as Webb, Campbell or even Bennett might receive the sort of heraldic greeting that the town of Linlithgow once extended to King James VI, by the use of the Scottish coat of arms, the lion rampant:

> Thrice royal Sir, here I do you beseech,
> Who art a lion, to hear a lion's speech.
> A miracle, for since the days of Aesop,
> No lion till these times his voice dared rise up
> To such a Majesty; then, King of men,
> The King of beasts speaks to thee from his den;
> Who, though he now enclosed be in plaster,
> When he was free, was Lithgow's wise schoolmaster.[5]

A voice from the depths of a plaster lion was evidently a joke, but in late Elizabethan Triumphs the metamorphosis of the Lord Mayor was accompanied by something like the descent of a goddess. The frequent use of the metaphor that the Lord Mayor was married to the City not only echoed the royal image of the monarch being married to the kingdom – Elizabeth spoke of her coronation ring as her wedding ring – it also implied that, like Peleus or Anchises, he had married an immortal.

Two of the Triumphs by George Peele survive in print from the sixteenth century; he succeeded his father, James Peele, clerk of Christ's Hospital, but was also a pageant writer for the Court and contributed to the cult of Elizabeth as Astraea.[6] In his pageant for Sir Wolstan Dixi in 1585, London is seated at the apex of the pageant, under the arms of her royal mistress and surrounded by contributory trades and arts. In *Descensus Astraea*, 1591, he used Elizabeth's title, especially favoured by the lawyers; but in the City the goddess-shepherdess carried a sheep hook, and further mercantile interpretation was given to the pastoral convention by a child who sat spinning at the rear of the pageant – the Lord Mayor being named Webb.

The last mayoral triumph of Elizabeth's reign was devised by Anthony Munday for the Merchant Taylors, with a speech for one of the boys from their school written by their Master. John Webster, father of the dramatist and a member of the company, was paid thirty shillings for the hire of the chariot that drew the children.[7]

Next year, the peaceful accession of James I relieved the suppressed anxieties of a decade. The grand entry for the monarch was still London's celebration, however; James himself was an unknown quantity, though greeted with high hopes as a Protestant monarch who could provide an heir apparent and seemed to guarantee peace by uniting the crowns of England and Scotland. The Lord Mayor became the greatest officer in England at the demise of the Crown, all royal offices being vacated until reconfirmed; he closed Ludgate until he received promise that the Lord Treasurer meant to proclaim the King of Scots. Cecil sent in his Garter insignia as pledge. James's entry had been planned for his Coronation, as had Elizabeth's in 1559; but it was postponed by plague and, when it took place on the Ides of March, 1604, it was, ominously, for the opening of his first Parliament.

Dekker, who took the leading part within the City group, mentions how everyone had joined in the work of measuring and building the seven great triumphal arches, from Fenchurch in the East, where James entered from the Tower, to Temple Bar in the West. 'Such a fire of love and joy was kindled in every brest' that even children would have helped;[8] the rivals Dekker and Jonson, who had just been engaged in theatrical war, combined with young Thomas Middleton, who wrote one speech for Zeal, and Mulcaster, now High Master of St Paul's School, who wrote another, recommending his scholars to James's charity and himself to favour. Jonson published his two contributions separately, adding a panegyric on the opening of Parliament which consisted largely of warnings and admonitions to the King.

All subsequent Triumphs were to derive from this grand entry, London's own exorcism of the gnawing fear of civil strife at a disputed succession, London's own relief, when, like an older medieval city, great and small combined for their pageantry. The livery companies who lined the route from Mark Lane to the conduit in Fleet Street were on this occasion part of the city audience and not on parade; all were unified as in one family. It was as if the disappearance of the Elizabethan legend had released for London a new sense of her own identity. Camden described London as the epitome of the kingdom and, in a speech where the *genius loci* was to have encountered St George and St Andrew on horseback, Dekker borrowed from the works of his fellow Shakespeare, who on this occasion was part of the procession, clad in his royal livery as one of the King's players. Dekker substituted London for Shakespeare's 'royal throne of kings':

> This little world of men; this precious Stone,
> That sets out *Europe* . . .
> This Jewell of the Land; Englands right Eye:
> Altar of Love; and Spheare of Majestie.[9]

This speech was discarded in favour of Jonson's at the great arch of Fenchurch, surmounted by a cutout representation of the entire city. Dekker had shown London as a woman, traditionally; Jonson, more classically, made the *genius* masculine, and the part was taken by Edward Alleyn, in dialogue with the Thames. Jonson's, too, was the final triumphal arch in the form of entrance to a temple; beyond, in the Strand, Westminster presented the tableau of a rainbow and the King was given a speech of apotheosis from the starry Pleiades. Within the City itself, Dekker's relatively unstructured Elizabethan lavishness was held together; at the conduit in Cheapside a device adapted from *Descensus Astraea* showed a miniature drama. Here Britannia-Arabia was transported from mourning to joy by the King's approach, various evil characters seated in the arch were destroyed and a fountain suddenly ran with wine. The maximum number of spectators in the broad thoroughfare could enjoy this transformation in Nova Felix Arabia.

Significantly however, the overt religious appeals to which Elizabeth at her coronation had responded with such dramatic skill – clasping the Bible presented to her to her breast – were here largely confined to the arch erected by the United Provinces of the Netherlands. Seventeen figures representing the states were presented by Dutch merchants and they delivered exhortations about the purity of the reformed faith with the good example set by Elizabeth. The Italian merchants, though but few, expressed their loyalty in another arch, tactfully praising the King as philosopher and poet. The reformed faith was established; future problems were to be constitutional.

Only at the end did Dekker reveal that many of the speeches went unspoken: the King had asked for their omission. Many citizens must have known that James had most reluctantly consented to this entry, on the understanding that he would never be called upon to repeat it. Nowhere did he respond as Elizabeth had done, reciprocating the welcome; in a few months, Shakespeare was to put the royal disclaimer into the mouth of his wise Duke:

> I'll privily away. I love the people,
> But do not like to stage me to their eyes:
> Though it do well, I do not relish well
> Their loud applause and *Aves* vehement.
> (*Measure for Measure* I.i.67–70)

Dekker declared that, as the King left the City, she was '(like an Actor on a Stage) stript out of her borrowed Maiestie' for the royal presence had made the 'Citie appeare great as a Kingdome'. But at a time when Parliament was itself less an institution than an occasional event, the regular, permanent city government really represented the country, especially in resisting royal encroachment, driving hard bargains in return for financial favours; it often appeared, indeed, that the Crown was more dependent on the City than the City on the Crown. Even at this time, one song caused some resentment and Dekker had to explain that 'Troynovant is now no more a city' did not really mean that London was giving up her privileges in becoming for the day a summer arbour, or an eagle's nest or a bridal chamber. It may have been that the boys of Mulcaster's school could lift only the words of the refrain audibly above the roar of the crowd and the din of bells.

Dekker had a fling at the learning of Ben Jonson about his male *genius* of the City;[10] and in future London persisted in being depicted as a female, often crowned with towers, as she had been in the play that had been written by Robert Wilson for the Armada triumph of 1588, *The Three Lords and Three Ladies of London* (1588–90).

Anthony Munday, citizen and draper, remained the usual writer for the mayoral Triumphs, in spite of being caricatured by John Marston as Posthaste (in *Histriomastix*) and by Jonson as Antonio Balladino (in *The Case is Altered*). This '*Pageant* Poet to the City of Millaine' asserts: 'I supply the place sir: when a worse cannot be had, sir!' He favours the use of traditional properties: 'I do use as much stale stuff, though I say it myself, as any man does in this kind, I am sure.' His defence is that he keeps the 'old *Decorum*' and writes plainly for the common people, not to please the gentlemen.[11] The wickerwork City giants and the ship pageant were stale for Jonson, but scholarship was 'stale' for Dekker; the audience did not relish academic commonplaces. If, on a later occasion, Munday showed Robin Hood as son-in-law to Henry Fitz-Alwin, the first Lord Mayor, he joined the ancient figure of woodland freedom, defiance of the law, with an ancient emblem of civic power and legal authority; their conjunction is something better than mere ignorance.

Munday's device for the Merchant Taylor, Sir Leonard Halliday, in 1605 – *The Triumphes of re-united Britania* – gave a heroic role to James, but Elizabeth had already been hailed as 'beauteous Queen of Second Troy' and the City was much more firmly united than the tenuously unified kingdoms. Munday prefixed a summary of British history from the time of Noah, through the period of Albion and the giants, sons of Neptune – two giants drew Britannia's chariot – to civilisation by the Trojan Brute, founder of Troynovant, who at one point was revived from his tomb, with his three sons.[12] Troynovant and Thames, with tributary rivers, sing paeans as the three sons deliver up their divided crowns. Britannia, with the three kingdoms attendant, sat on the Mount, the most prominent of the pageants; but that stale piece, the company's ship, renamed the Royal Exchange, distributed its cargo of spices among the crowd, for the Lord Mayor was to be in 1611 one of the founders of the East India Company and later its Treasurer. The customary eulogies bring Halliday among the immortals, with many quibbles on Halliday and holiday. Fame named all the royal members of the company from the past and remarked that one place is yet unfilled. Neptune and his Queen, parents of the Giant Albion, in their epilogue from the backs of the Lion and the Camel, assuming their modern form, 'wish all good to Leonard Halliday'.

The name of Britannia had furnished the answer to the riddle Jonson had propounded to the Court in his Twelfth Night *Masque of Blackness*, which had brought the twelve Daughters of the Niger to James's revels; this may have carried some overtones of the wealth rolling up the Thames to the Port of London, in a less fanciful and exotic, a more mundane symbolism, than is commonly allowed.

The vacant place in the ranks of royal Merchant Taylors was filled in 1607 at their great feast by the election of the heir apparent, Prince Henry; and a lost Triumph by Munday of the year 1610 presented, for the Merchant Taylors, Merlin in the rock, which reproduced the theme of Prince Henry's Barriers of the same year, where the Prince appeared as an Arthurian knight, and both Merlin and King Arthur were represented.

The next Triumph for the Merchant Taylors, in 1612, was prepared with great care at a cost of £900; for as well as Prince Henry, the Elector Palatine, bridegroom of Princess Elizabeth, was to attend the feast inaugurating the year of Sir John Swinnerton – himself much interested in the press and the theatres.

By its very title, Dekker's *Troia-Nova Triumphans* asserted once more that 'the heap of our sovereign kingdoms are drawn in little and are to be found in this city', but Swinnerton received no less than three separate warnings of the hazards of office. If the problems of rulers had been set forth on the stage, the Lord Mayor was recognised to be as exposed as any prince by the position he filled. These

warnings, it should be remembered, were agreed with the company;
the dramatist was certainly not hazarding a personal opinion. The
first warning came from Neptune, who rode in a sea chariot with
many smaller ships dancing round it, escorting the company's ship
pageant, distributing wine. Virtue gave the second warning;
attended by the Seven Liberal Arts (mothers of trades and profes-
sions) and escorted by armed representatives of the Twelve Great
Companies, she alerts the Lord Mayor to Envy, who was inhabiting
a 'forlorn castle' near to the Little Conduit in Cheapside. Envy's
attack on Virtue is repelled by the bright shield the goddess raises,
but on the return journey from Guildhall the attack is renewed, when
Envy and her castle are destroyed by the twelve knightly companions
discharging their pistols – hardly a knightly weapon. Finally Fame,
from her House which enshrines the royal members of the company,
dead and living, invites Swinnerton to join her band of immortals,
but once more warns him of danger.

Identity is created by Fame; we are in truth what others make of
us. Envy, the second of the Seven Deadly Sins, is secularised, and
shown as poverty-stricken, lean and malignant. In 1604 the political
resentment of the have-nots had been shown in religious terms as
'sedition, a friar' at the Fountain of Virtue – which, like the Castle of
Envy, had been in Cheapside. London was the only city in Britain
with an underworld, a criminal quarter where the Lord Mayor's
power did not extend. Envy had been used by Jonson in *Every Man
out of his Humour* (1600), witches had appeared to give this threat in
The Masque of Queens (1609), and Envy reappeared as Prologue to
his *Catiline* this same year, 1612. Henceforth, she often menaced
Triumphs.

The risks of office were real enough; a week after taking his place,
Sir Leonard Halliday had to deal with the situation arising from the
Gunpowder Plot, and now, even as Swinnerton was greeted with the
final song:

> Honor . . .
> *Waken with my Song* . . .
> *So shall* Swinnerton *nere dye,*
> *But his vertues upward flye* . . .
> *He is living, living ever*',[13]

the Prince of Wales was already very sick. On 6 November, just over
a week later, he died; and with him were buried many of the City's
hopes for a strong Protestant regime. The times were out of joint.

Although Dekker had praised the moderation of the Triumph –
compared presumably with the cost of court masques – yet it ruined
the poet, who for failing all the obligations he had incurred was cast
into a debtor's prison, where he stayed for six years. Among other

creditors, John Webster the elder claimed from Dekker £40 for chariots.

The next year's Triumph went to Thomas Middleton, who for his namesake, Sir Thomas Myddleton, a grocer of strong Puritan convictions, devised the most expensive of all such events, *The Triumphs of Truth*, at a cost of £1300. Based even more firmly on the model of the Moral play, and directed personally to the Lord Mayor, it portrays the conflict of Error and Zeal. This highly religious Triumph was indeed to win support for Middleton, who succeeded the 60-year-old Munday as the regular purveyor; but little of it can have been audible to the bystanders, and it is unique in its address being to the Lord Mayor himself. On his first landing, Error appears accompanied by Envy 'eating of a human heart, mounted on a rhinoceros, attired in red silk, suitable to the bloodiness of her manners, her left pap bare, where a snake fastens . . .'. Truth, her opponent, is copied in the greatest detail from that Truth whom Jonson had depicted in the Barriers for the marriage of the Earl of Essex, prefixed to *Hymenaei* (1606). Truth's Angel and Zeal defend the Mayor; a ship, steered from afar by Truth, contains a baptised king of the Moors – a noteable defeat for Error. Even before his embarkation, London had delivered a sermon to the Lord Mayor; now, placed on a Mount in Cheapside, she is from time to time by Error shrouded in mist. At the very threshold of the Lord Mayor's dwelling, Error is finally destroyed by fire darted from the head of Zeal.

This pageant, by one of the most strongly Puritan of the companies, was succeeded by two by Anthony Munday for the Drapers, which are concerned with the City's struggle against a particular menace. The Cockayne Project, launched in 1614 with royal support, endeavoured to ensure for England a monopoly of finishing the country's cloth before it was exported to the Low Countries. The King's Merchant Venturers, a new company, were given sole rights to export, the rights of the old Merchant Venturers in unfinished cloth being withdrawn. The result was disastrous. The Dutch promptly banned all imports of English cloth, finished or unfinished, and, as they controlled the carrying trade, which England had neither the ships nor the organisation to take over, the country towns producing cloth for the London market, and the weaving and spinning areas, were faced with unemployment whilst the London merchants were ruined. After bankruptcies and riots on a wide scale, the King admitted defeat, the policy of the 'new Draperies' was rescinded and the Merchant Venturers regained their old privileges. *Himatia-Poleos. The Triumphs of olde Draperie, or the rich Cloathing of England* (1614) presents several English wool-producing cities grouped round London; among the figures who repel adversaries are Councell and Discreet Zeale, defending Old Drapery herself, who sits on a high Mount supported by figures engaged in the industry. The next year, *Metropolis Coronata: The Triumphes of Ancient Drapery: or Rich Cloathing of England* celebrated the election of another member of the Drapers' Company as Lord Mayor, doubtless to meet the growing trade crisis. This was largely a water show (it was the exports that had been hit) and the main theme, Jason's search for the Golden Fleece; Neptune, Fame, Time and various Lord Mayors of olden days are travelling in a boat shaped like a whale. On land, the pageant ship is named for the Lord Mayor, the *Jewel*, 'appearing to bee lately returned, from trafficking Wool and Cloth with other remòte Countries' (Sig.B2 v). London sits crowned and surrounded by the Twelve Great Companies, but the final song is entrusted to Robin Hood, that lawless provincial. One of the chief opponents of the Cockayne Project was the former Lord Mayor, Sir Thomas Myddelton, whose family spoke bitterly in Parliament against it. Eventually however, Cockayne was himself to become Lord Mayor.

In 1614, in the preface and dedication of his *Odyssey*, George Chapman had sneered at 'popular vapours' like the Lord Mayor's Show; but the game of 'vapours', as Ben Jonson that same year was to demonstrate in *Bartholomew Fair*, consisted in contradicting the last speakers. Here, the City defied the Crown.

Old Anthony Munday, who had been attacked by Middleton, although he had had some share in the Triumph of 1613, came back a last time for the Fishmongers' Triumph of 1615, showing how William Walworth, Lord Mayor, had suppressed revolt in the time of Richard II. This, too, was a topical gesture, for the unemployed weavers were beginning to riot. In the pageant of 1617, Middleton introduced a comic Spaniard, who spoke in Spanish, and two ugly Spanish women. This was the first note of an increasingly anti-Spanish mood that prevailed in the City, derived as much from trade rivalry as from religious zeal, and leading to new differences with the Crown.

In 1618, the execution of Sir Walter Ralegh, James's sacrifice to the Spaniards, was deliberately fixed for the day of the Lord Mayor's Triumph, so that popular interest might be distracted. In 1620, the Puritan company of the Haberdashers very surprisingly resurrected their patron saint, Catherine of Alexandria, while in 1623 the Drapers' Triumph for Sir Martin Lumley celebrated openly the City's rejoicing at the return of the Prince of Wales from Spain without the Spanish bride he had gone to woo. Their traditional canopy of three crowns and a cloud pierced by a sunbeam is interpreted as the mist of heresy pierced by a gospel ray:

> More to assure it to succeeding men,
> We have the crown of Britain's hope agen,
> Illustrious Charles our prince.[14]

Such was the popular rejoicing that Ben Jonson, who had written a court masque on the same theme, *Neptune's Triumph for the Return of Albion*, found that Spanish protests had prevented its performance.

This Lord Mayor's *The Triumphs of Integrity* implicitly criticised the Crown by complimenting Lumley on having risen from humble origins, as superior to those who:

> stand fix'd,
> As if 'twere competent virtue for whole life
> To be begot a lord; 'tis virtuous strife
> That makes the complete Christian.[15]

This was reinforced by the figures of Tamburlaine and Pertinax — who overthrew monarchs.

By 1624 unofficial hostilities against Spain had started, especially from the armed merchantmen of the Port of London. Middleton's audacious comedy, *A Game at Chess* in August that year, drove him into hiding, but it is quite likely that the allegory against Spain was supported by highly placed persons at Court.[16] His temporary disappearance, however, gave the last Lord Mayor's Triumph of King James's reign to John Webster, the tragic poet, Merchant Taylor, who devised his *Monuments of Honour* for the installation of Sir John Gore (a relative of the Davenant family, stepfather to the actor Nicholas Tooley).[17] This Triumph introduces several motifs from recent celebrations, but adds also to the union of the living past with the present in a strong note of protest. Like his predecessors, Webster, in publishing his piece, which he proclaims is 'invented and written' by himself, associates with it 'the great care and alacrity of the right Worshipful the Master and Wardens' and their committees 'both for the curious and judging election of the Subject' and for providing the setting 'answerable to the Invention'. (Gerard Christmas, who for years had provided the carpentry and the sea Triumphs, was official painter to the Navy.)

The sea Triumph opens with the usual rhetorical enquiries from Thetis to Oceanus:

> *What brave Sea-Musicke bids us Welcome, harke!*
> *Sure this is* Venice, *and the day Saint* Marke
> *In which the* Duke *and* Senats *their course hold*
> *To wed our* Empire *with a Ring of Gold.*[18]

By this comparison with the Republic, London is invested with sovereign power. The second sea pageant presents a fair globe encircled by seven English navigators, including Drake, Frobisher, Hawkins and Humphrey Gilbert, for the London merchants were the heirs of the West Country privateers; by 1624 many merchants who had never been to sea were engaged in this profitable business. The company's venerable ship pageant brings, hanging in her shrouds, the Golden Fleece. Troynovant is seated in the Temple of Honour in Paul's Churchyard, attended by five other cities, including Venice; in the lower level of the Temple sit five eminent poets and scholars, all associated with London, and including Sir Thomas More and Sir Philip Sidney.[19] Troynovant presents the

> *worthy men*
> *Who do eternize brave acts by their pen . . .*
> *These beyond death a fame to Monarckes give,*
> *And these make Cities and Societies live.*[20]

A knight in armour, wearing the company's colours, identifies himself as Sir John Hawkswood, who gained fame in the Italian wars, but who firmly proclaims his humble origin. He is followed by Queen Anne of Bohemia, consort of Richard II, riding alone. She had been admitted to the company, but her ensign would suggest to the crowd the contemporary Queen of Bohemia, their beloved Princess Elizabeth, symbol of the Protestant cause in Europe and a centre in the City for anti-Spanish feeling, since the Spaniards had overrun her territory. Two knights of St John who had defended Malta and Rhodes against the Turk follow her.

The patron of the company was St John the Baptist, and Webster had carefully sought out connections with the old Priory St John in Clerkenwell, as well as finding Hawkswood. Repeating from last year's triumph that virtue may ennoble humble men, he used the company's motto, *Concordia parvae res crescunt,* recited in chorus by the English kings who were free of the Merchant Taylors, and who are now seated in the Chariot of Fame. These include King Richard III, previously omitted, but restored by Webster as 'a bad man but a good king'.[21] The resurrected figure of Sir Thomas White, in the Monument of Charity and Learning, revives a Lord Mayor who held his Triumph 71 years earlier. The Lord Mayor, holding office for one year only, could not be deified as the monarch was deified in the court masque, but he became part of a historical continuum, a succession; in the living union of past and present he acquired his immortality. Hence the 'monuments' – a word restricted to those erected for the dead – culminated in the Monument of Honour, the Mount, which always made the grandest display. If Sir Thomas represented historically as the patron of learning the Seven Liberal Arts, a rock of jewels represented the City's opposition to Spain. For on it, raised on a pedestal of pure gold, stood the figure of Henry, Prince of Wales, dead twelve years since – Henry, the Protestant champion, reincarnation of the chivalry of Sir Philip Sidney and steadfast opponent of the Spanish alliance proposed for himself. He had indeed been a member of the company; but the silent rebuke of this figure, especially when coupled with Anne of Bohemia, was emphasised when he was distinguished in the final speech to the Lord Mayor as:

> *Worthy Prince* Henry, fame's best president,
> Cald to a higher Court of Parliament.[22]

For City and Parliament were drawing together in opposition to the Crown. He is immortal; as dusk fell, the Prince of Wales's feathers on the four pyramids that marked Henry's earthly decease were lit up, and his jewels glowed. The poet who had written his funeral elegy, where 'Sorrow' masked in 'pleasure[']s] garment'[23] was using the celebration both for mourning and for assertion of living values. *Non norunt haec monumenta mori* ('These monuments do not know how to die') appeared as motto on his title page.

The way forward could be found in such tentative combinations of powerful images, for these did not involve the difficulty of putting new political statements into direct words. Tentative, uncommitted, they made their silent appeal to the common people and gave a united affirmation to ideas that as yet 'dodged conception' – the unfocused lines of those politics to be hammered out by lawyers and Parliament men in the coming decades. As early as 1604, the fragility of affirmations made in the Triumphs had been noted by Dekker: 'Behold how glorious a flower happiness is, and how fading. The minutes that lackey at the heels of Time run not faster than do our joys.' Webster echoed those sentiments in the verses he also offered in 1604 for the triumphal arches that marked James's entry.[24] Yet, he added, by printing these devices, they had been given 'new life when they were dead'. So, too, were historic figures from the past.

Webster's own tragic structures, where he had renounced the classic Messenger and Chorus, were a precedent for his now renouncing the 'tediousness' of quoting classical precedents from Rome, which might weary the Lord Mayor and would assuredly 'puzzle the understanding of the Common people'. Dekker, not Jonson, provided him with a model.

Webster himself, in wishing prosperity to the Lord Mayor, ironically enough introduced another year of disaster. The plague broke out with greater virulence than at any time since 1603; the Lord Mayor's house was itself infected and for a time his deputy discharged his functions. This catastrophe coincided with the death in

March 1625 of King James; Charles I was thus enabled to forgo any coronation entry. The citizens who had begun to erect triumphal arches took them down. The new monarch never entered Troynovant in state.

If he were not acting in Webster's pageant, a 16-year-old youth, now in the highest form at St Paul's, would certainly be marching. He was the future author of *The Tenure of Kings and Magistrates,* John Milton.

Notes

1 *Malone Society Collections,* III, pp. 58–9. A full list of all recorded and all surviving Triumphs is given here, pp. xliv–xlvi.
2 Formerly they had been known as Taylors and Linen Armourers – providing padded harness for knights and their steeds. See following note.
3 A. Munday, *The Triumphes of re-united Britania,* Sig. C2r. Later in the stanza he writes: 'Henry the seventh . . . To Merchant Taylors did exchange their name'.
4 J.G. Nichols (ed.), *The Diary of Henry Machyn* (London, Camden Society, 1848), p. 47.
5 Quoted by D. Harris Willson in his *King James VI and I* (London, The Bedford Historical Series, 1959), pp. 392–93.
6 See 'Queen Elizabeth as Astraea' in Frances A. Yates, *Astraea* (London and Boston, Routledge & Kegan Paul, 1975), pp. 29–87, for a full discussion of the political and imperial implications of this title.
7 *Malone Society Collections,* III, p. 60.
8 Fredson Bowers (ed.), *The Dramatic Works of Thomas Dekker,* II (Cambridge, Cambridge University Press, 1955), p. 258.
9 *Ibid.* p. 256.
10 'To make a false florish here with the borrowed weapons of all the old Maisters of the noble Science of Poesie . . . were to play the Executioner and lay our Cities household God on the rack. . . . Such feates of Activitie are stale, and common among Schollers before whome it is protested we come not now (in a Pageant) to Play a Maisters prize for *Nunc ego ventosae Plebis suffragia venor*', *Ibid.* pp. 254–55.
11 C.H. Herford, Percy and Evelyn M. Simpson (eds), *Ben Jonson* III (Oxford, Oxford University Press, 1925) I.i.29.30–1, 48–50.
12 Compare the awakening of Bohun from his tomb in Robert Greene's *The Scottish History of James the Fourth,* ed. Norman Sanders (London, Methuen The Revels Plays, 1970), pp. 4–10.
13 Bowers, *Op. cit.* III, pp. 243–45, ll. 461, 495, 501–2. 506.
14 A.H. Bullen (ed.), *The Works of Thomas Middleton,* III (8 vols printed by editor, London, 1886, rare: reprinted New York, Ames Press, 1964).
15 *Ibid.*

16 See Margot Heinemann's *Puritanism and Theatre* (Cambridge, Cambridge University Press, 1980), chapter X.

17 Information from Mary Edmond.

18 F.L. Lucas (ed.), *The Complete Works of John Webster*, III (London, Chatto & Windus, 1927), p. 318.

19 See M.C. Bradbrook, *John Webster, Citizen and Dramatist* (London, Weidenfeld, 1980) pp. 180–82.

20 Lucas *Op. cit.* p. 320.

21 See Bradbrook, *Op. cit.* p. 178, for similar sentiments elsewhere.

22 Lucas, *Op. cit.* pp. 326–27.

23 Lucas, *Ibid.* p. 279.

24 Lucas, *Ibid.* p. 259.

IX.

Publication and Performance in Blackfriars' Drama (Toronto)

The permanence of printing may always be challenged by the penetrative force of performance. Jonson put printing first; Webster balanced performance and publication; Heywood constantly protested his reluctance to commit drama to cold print. The writer's aim will be modified by his relations with the crafts of printer and actor. Jonson had early acting experience, but was by nature a director; Webster, an exceptionally sympathetic but relatively independent citizen; Heywood, like Shakespeare, a fully professional actor and playwright who spent most of his very long working life with one company. At the court of Queen Elizabeth, small material reward came from print to Gascoigne, Spenser, or Lyly; and nobler writers who took a direct part in the social 'game' of courtly wooing, a Dyer or a Ralegh, went no further towards publication than to hang their verse on trees. As for print, they would as lief the town crier spoke their lines.

The printing of epigrams and characters, from the mock courts of Christmas Princes at the Inns of Court, came towards the turn of the century. In the reopened chorister's theatres of St Paul's and Blackfriars, verbal tilting became more lethal as the Christmas games of the lawyers were institutionalised. Law supplied playwrights, audience, and some finance. If Education might teach good manners by exposing Folly, satire became a duty and denunciation a proof of zeal. The lawyers had mainly satirised one another. Practice in whitewashing a client and blackening an opponent might be considered part of their training and no ill feeling need remain out of court. But London was the centre of the printing trade (the Stationers' company were perfectly ruthless in destroying a university press that threatened their monopoly). The printing of plays started as a regular practice with the choristers' plays, the young lawyers' wish to display their own eloquence, the companies' need to advertise and lack of the financial power to control their authors (as did Henslowe of the Bankside).

Until the middle of the sixteenth century, as Glynne Wickham has recently observed, plays were occasional events associated with particular festivals of the church year or with private festivities such as a wedding.[1] The 'device' for such entertainments gave a speech for the occasion to a symbolic figure whose garments and attributes 'deliver the nature of the person . . . and the word the present office' (as Ben Jonson put it in describing the pageants for King James's entry to London). Commenting on this, Wickham observes:

> The concept is a difficult one to define precisely in words, largely because the visual element formed so crucial a part of it. Moreover, it incorporated a striking paradox; for while the visual component was designed to arrest attention and boldly to proclaim an idea, the form in which it was cast was often designed, like a riddle, to conceal a secret.   (page 66)

The 'secret' was often some personal application; if it was in praise of the Chief Spectator, it could be a personal plea (as in some of Gascoigne's shows for Queen Elizabeth), or it could be an open secret which spectators were expected to share.

Peele's *Device of the Pageant born before Wolstan Dixi* (1585) opens the way for the pageant by a speech of homage from a Moor riding on a lynx – at once an heraldic beast of the Skinners' company and, in the imagery of the five senses, emblem of keen sight. Boys representing arts and trades, the City herself, assorted Virtues, and the River Thames extol the Lord Mayor and the queen, with additions from torch-bearing nymphs. No riddles here; but when in the Accession Day tilt a decade later Peele wrote on the familiar school theme of choosing a course of life, the characters representing Hermit, Secretary of State, and Soldier were covertly identified.[2] In Lyly's comedies, the queen provided the only unambiguous figure.

Icons for public entertainments all over Europe remained extremely conservative.[3] The sophisticated for private sports sought devices – witty and new. In Ben Jonson's *The Case is Altered,* Antonio Balladino (Anthony Munday) protests, 'I do use as much stale stuff, though I say it myself, as any man does in this kind, I am sure.' He does not write to please gentlemen. Nor did Dekker, who protested at Jonson's making the genius of the City for King James's royal entry masculine, in the Roman fashion. Though played by Alleyn, this genius lacked the appeal of the maiden city, married to the hero of the day; cities, like ships, should be feminine. Ben Jonson moved into print as a dramatist when he moved from the public to the choristers' theatres. *Every Man out of his Humour* (1599), which had failed in public, was published with a dedication to the Inns of

Court. Dedications were usually addressed to individuals in hope of reward; Jonson made his name in the theatres where the lawyers dominated, putting his general appeal to the kind of audience he wanted. In the 'Characters prefixed to the Action' he identified himself with their kinds of composition and instructed both readers and players in the mode of approach. Writing for boys, he could take the role of dominie, which was highly congenial to him; but in *Cynthia's Revels*, dedicated to the 'fountain of manners', the court itself, and the most strictly verbal of his early comedies, Jonson plied the tawse upon the great, in a manner not calculated to win their favour. Gentlemen are satirised in Act I, ladies in Act II; the games played include Substantive and Adjective, a Thing Done and Who Did It, a Challenge at Courtship (of the kind that Sir Toby Belch tried to teach Sir Andrew Aguecheek), and finally a Litany of Repentance. At the end, he probably used an effigy of Queen Elizabeth as a 'device' to transform the envious Macilente. A play of characters needs little action; it is a procession, a verbal parade, and therefore is as clear in print as in action.

In the opening scene, Sogliardo, 'an essential clown . . . enamour'd of the name of gentleman,' is coached to be 'a Gentleman of the Time.' He must buy new clothes, swear fashionable oaths, be melancholy at meals and 'humourous' at plays; 'Ruffle your brow like a new boot, laugh at nothing but your own jests, or else as the noblemen laugh'. He should send letters of commendation to himself (a trick practised as late as 1700 by Witwoud in *The Way of the World*) and hire servants who can maintain themselves by petty theft.

Here was satiric introduction for ignorant country youths, who had been dependent on *The Book of Riddles* or *The Hundred Merry Tales* for conversation. The game of characters was played widely – Shakespeare shows Portia and Nerissa amusing themselves at the expense of the suitors in *The Merchant of Venice* (I.ii), while the 'device' of the caskets itself consists of the riddling outer objects and the 'word', with accompanying image, each conceals. In Ben Jonson, the characters function as a group; a whole society was defined from a single point of view, that of a judicious spectator, summing up the evidence. The young lawyers were being rehearsed for a place on the bench. The little microcosm chosen, whether court, city, or lawyers' inn, reflected a moral judgement on a purely social situation.[4]

In performance, interaction of characters could be formal or minimal, which suited the choristers. Jonson uses social rituals like the drinking game in *Every Man out of his Humour* (V.iv).

His next play for the choristers, *Poetaster* (1601), antagonised the army, the law, and the stage: years later, Ben Jonson was to boast to

Drummond of Hawthornden that he had written it against the lawyer-dramatist John Marston, though in his 'Apologetical Dialogue' his disclaimer was 'I named no names'. When Julia and Ovid play at being gods in order to satirise her father the emperor, Jonson comes near the dangerous heart of these private games; for the parting of these lovers, he turned however to the public stage for the popular 'device' of the second balcony scene in *Romeo and Juliet*. As a personal acknowledgement this play was dedicated to the Middle Temple's Christmas Prince, Richard Martin, who had interceded with Lord Chief Justice Popham on Jonson's behalf.

In their reply, *Satiromastix*, the players shrewdly exploited the inconsistency between Jonson's lofty contempt for 'Opinion' and his very obvious attempts to advertise himself. This same inconsistency is found among the lawyer-poets, especially in Marston's masterpiece *The Malcontent* (1604), which he offered to his former opponent, Ben Jonson, proclaiming himself now both friend and admirer. Marston had begun to print very early, but had insured himself against scorn by dedicating his first play to Nobody. The two sides of the malcontent himself, the noble banished duke, Altofront, and his disguised self, the bitter fool, owe a great deal to Hamlet and his antic disposition, but they also resemble the two sides of a satirist. The character Malevole is given at the start as a 'monster' (I.iii.16–20). The part, played by boys, attracted Burbage, and the men's company took it over. The play was in print and they were entitled to do so; Marston and Webster supplied some additions. The company, led by Burbage and Shakespeare, had learnt what Kenneth Muir termed 'Shakespeare's Open Secret'.[5] Performance itself had shown that the apparent inconsistencies, contradictions, unexplained changes could add depth and integrity to the actor's role; and from the leading part might extend to the whole play. Interplay between the 'delightful Proteus', Burbage, and the rest grew out of a company where the playwright was also a supporting actor. The non-verbal aspects were drawn from a text rich in all the complicated energies it generated. The gaps allow the actor to 'breathe' inside his part; it is not possible to pluck out the heart of Hamlet's mystery. And in the dynamics of performance, as Melchiori has observed in translating the text, 'gestures, colours, the physical presence of the actors, sounds, music, noises (take a slap for example) all play their part.'[6] Recently the dynamics of contradiction have been traced in the philosophy of Shakespeare's time.[7]

These could be simplified in the 'perspective picture', a device which showed an anamorphic image of death turning into love, mirth into grief; such might serve to suggest much deeper mysteries, as when Cleopatra sees Antony as one way like a Gorgon, the other way a Mars. The old opposition of image and 'word' had become fused; the malcontent as played by Burbage must have been in sharpest contrast to the successful choristers' version. Ironic play on this fact is essential to the induction which was among the earliest printed works of John Webster. The playgoers who sit in judgement are also 'characterised' − that is, satirised. It is notable that Shakespeare himself uses the definition of 'characterists' ironically − as when Iago satirizes the Good Housewife − in front of Emilia; or Cornwall draws the character of a blunt man to discredit Kent.[8] To understand such 'open' writing, what was printed had to be reconstructed as full performance by the reader, though implicitly given.

The Malcontent achieved three editions in the course of 1604. The fame of the London theatres had built up a market for plays so that even statesmen like the Earl of Devonshire could amass a good library for 'recreation'. Before the reign of Elizabeth, 27 plays only had been printed; no less than 103 of the 168 printed in her reign had appeared after 1590.[9] Ben Jonson's new claim for the dignity of the form was being justified.

Shakespeare's gentle art of feeding his conception of the play in performance to the actor-reader through the implications of his language gave to the audience that kind of involvement usually generated by special occasions − such as the appeals in the choruses of *King Henry V*, and that which the Essex conspiracy tried to exploit by a command performance of *King Richard II*. Shakespeare sometimes seems to have authorised a 'witty' text, like *Titus Andronicus* (1594) or *Love's Labour Lost* (1598), but most were retained by his company, unless some unscrupulous 'stolen and surreptitious copies' appeared.

Webster's second incursion into print in the year 1604 was the 'Ode' he contributed to Stephen Harrison's *The Arches of Triumph*, a set of fine engravings celebrating the seven arches built for the *Magnificent Entertainment* of King James's entry to London. Webster makes three significant points; whilst memories of joys are transient, memories of sorrow abide; the stone arches permanently commemorating cruel Roman wars are compared with Harrison's painted woodwork. Yet the common joys of that great national celebration, in which the city represented the whole kingdom's relief that civil war had been averted, have been captured, 'giving them new life when they were dead.'[10] Life, the quality for which actors were praised, could be preserved even for those parts of the occasion which were not verbal; the work of his 'good countryman and friend' challenges that which Folly imputes only to strangers (London as Troynovant perhaps assisted in this bold claim).

> Perfection must be bold, with front upright,
> Though Envy gnash her teeth, whilst she would bite.

This final 'device' or icon of Webster's own creation was to be contradicted two years later when, in publishing the text of his court masque, *Hymenaei*, Jonson confessed that Envy could not be eliminated:

> Only the envy was that it lasted not still, or, now it is past, cannot by imagination, much less by description, be recovered to a part of that spirit it had in the gliding by.

Later he was to quarrel with his collaborator, Inigo Jones, whom he wished to demote to coadjutor. At the court, where the chief performers did not speak but royalty appeared in some divine epiphany to dance, there was little chance that the 'word', spoken by their servants, would win priority, although the text was probably printed as a sort of programme and given to the king – this certainly happened to the mayoral Triumphs, where the playwright employed for the 'device' now contracted with the Livery company for printing some five hundred copies.

The next of Shakespeare's tragedies to appear in print came from the press of a young man who was Webster's contemporary, friend and fellow parishioner of St Sepulchre's, who might also be seen as the first craftsman from the printing house to collaborate with actor and playwright. Nicholas Okes, apprenticed at Christmas 1595 to Shakespeare's fellow townsman, Richard Field, who had just printed *The Rape of Lucrece* (Nicholas was to reprint it a dozen years later), set up business in 1606 at the sign of the Hand near Holborn Bridge with one press, two assistants and a scanty supply of type. Through the close work of Peter Blayney, we now know that Okes specialised in the printing of single plays; more is known about the detailed working of his press during the first two years of his trading than of any other printer of the time.[11] It is too early to estimate the general bibliographical effect of Blayney's work; but Okes's quarto of *King Lear* (1608) was to leave a deep impress upon the mind of John Webster. The world of madmen, where identity is lost, touches the world of the 'characterist' only when Mad Tom describes his other 'self', a 'serving man proud of heart'. In those scenes where Lear, his Fool, and Mad Tom achieve a unity of the outcasts, we reach a world that is also the obverse of that of the satirist and of the royal masquers (who were all dressed alike, a band of supernatural unity). It supplied Webster with a new tragic vision, which was to combine with his training among the lawyers in a masterpiece that Okes published four years later, *The White Devil* (1612).

The year 1608, which saw the closing of the choristers' theatres and the publication of *King Lear*, saw also the first translation of Theophrastus, supposed model for the characterists. The ambitious Puritan cleric Joseph Hall, who had begun his career by a quarrel with Marston, added to this volume his own offering of incense at the shrine of James I, in his character of a Good Magistrate:

> He is the ground of the good laws; the refuge of misery; the comet of the guilty; the paymaster of good deserts; the champion of justice; the patron of poets; the tutor of the church; the father of his country; and as it were another God upon earth.[12]

This voice, emerging among abrasive epithets, 'stabbing similes', and sharp epigrams of a satirist, has the effect of a masquer appearing after a grotesque antimasque – strangely and perhaps unintentionally dramatic.

Another portrait of James had caused the closure of the choristers' theatres, and on the public stages the court masque had become the device for presenting depravity, *The Revenger's Tragedy* being a play of the king's own company.

The King's men also staged Jonson's *Volpone*; the alternation of godlike powers revealed in the court masque with city vice revealed in 'Venice' was later to be introduced into the masque itself by the new 'device' of the antimasque, first supplied by Jonson in 1609.

It is only recently that the 'clashing tones' and 'horrid laughter' of Webster's tragedies have been recognised as achieving a complex unity through performance.[13] The disjunctions and changes of tone and direction which critics found disruptive make these the most actable of Jacobean plays after Shakespeare's, and they are now frequently revived. Webster, though not an actor, was the first in publishing his text to praise the leading actor by name; later he was the first also to append the names of the actors to their role.[14] He had begun his career in collaboration with Heywood, Dekker, and other popular writers. (Dekker's account of the *Magnificent Entertainment* of 1604 includes sentiments in the commentary that are very close to Webster's 'Ode'.) Later he was to work with the clown William Rowley, leader of the Queen's men (who also worked with Middleton and Heywood). Yet Webster had been entered at the Middle Temple and collaborated with Marston; as the son of a wealthy coachmaker he was poised uncertainly between citizen and legal 'wit'.

In the very carefully phrased note 'To the Reader' prefixed to *The White Devil* (1612), Webster recorded his good opinion of playwrights whom he distinguished for style, works, and composition (Chapman, Jonson, Beaumont and Fletcher) and the 'right happy and copious industry' of his friends 'Master Shakespeare, Master Dekker and Master Heywood'. Industry was the word for craftsmen; these were men writing for performance, whose works were to be met only in the theatre. Dekker had hopefully praised his friend's 'brave triumphs of industry and poetry' before *The White Devil* made its debut upon the boards of the Red Bull Theatre.[15]

Webster, heroically attempting to unite the sophisticated style of the Inns of Court playwrights in their intimate roofed playhouses with the spectacle and dramatic range of the open stages, had worked slowly; he confessed: 'I do not write with a goosequill winged with two feathers' — as in the 'Apologetical Dialogue' appended to *Poetaster*, Jonson, charged that he will scarce bring forth a play a year, had replied 'Tis true! I would they could not say that I did that!' The pains of a writer for print did not chime with the quick extemporising expected on the boards. In *Satiromastix* Jonson had been shown painfully beating out an ode to spontaneity; a detractor was later to characterise Webster scratching his head, twisting his mouth, like a figure from an antimasque at Blackfriars.[16]

Webster's own 'full heightened style' is so burnished that every word sparkles, most of them, like Chapman's, being adapted and transformed from reading in modern writers. His story too, like Chapman's, is taken from modern history, an innovation in tragedy. The scene of railing between Ludovico and Flamineo (III.iii) is in the style of Marston his ally, like his 'stabbing similes' and his disjunctive leaps. On the other hand, he had not neglected spectacle. The six ambassadors who attend Vittoria's trial appear later at the election of the pope wearing the insignia of noble Orders – the Garter, the St Michel, the Saint Esprit, whose holy emblems might have drawn the rebuke that later Sir Henry Wotton was to administer on the copying of noble insignia in Shakespeare's *King Henry VIII* (1613): 'sufficient . . . to make greatness very familiar if not ridiculous'. The gorgeous scene at the wedding tourney (with the Medici disguised as a Moor, his companions in religious habits) must have been very expensive to produce. Yet the ferocious and surrealist fable, the deep uncertainty of the very natures of Vittoria, Monticelso, or Florence, leave at the core of the play a Shakespearian mystery.

Webster blamed the weather and the audience for his play's failure, rather inconsequently comparing groundlings to those ignorant readers who go to bookshops in search of new books, not good ones. He himself, with the help of Nicholas Okes, sent it to those same bookshops, complaining that he would really have preferred to write classical closet drama; but the public won't even consider that. Disappointment and proud self-justification give Webster a distinctly Jonsonian accent here. His next tragedy, *The Duchess of*

Malfi, succeeded with the King's men and was therefore, withheld from publication.

His best-selling work was the anonymous thirty-two characters contributed to the sixth edition of Sir Thomas Overbury's *A Wife* (1615), which carried as subtitle, 'Many witty characters and conceited news written by himself and other learned Gentlemen his friends'. This best seller was to furnish the model for one of the most popular forms of the century. It was 'Overbury', not Joseph Hall, who provided a definition of what a character was – squared out 'by our English level'. Not a hieroglyph, *imprese* or emblem, but

> it is a picture (real or personal) quaintly drawn in various colours all of them heightened by one shadowing. It is a quick and soft touch of many strings, all shutting up in one musical close; it is wit's descant on any plainsong.

This has about as much resemblance to Theophrastus as Renaissance popular drama to classical plays.

When Webster and Overbury's other friends in the Middle Temple collectively built up his posthumous work, they were using the old confident form of surveying and judging the social scene to probe an infamous history of black magic and brutal murder, which all the plots of revenge plays could scarcely outgo. The net was already closing on those who in 1613 had poisoned Overbury, then a prisoner in the Tower of London. Suspicion pointed at the Lord Chamberlain, patron of all poets for court performance, and his wife – the Earl and Countess of Somerset. Next year they stood trial before the House of Lords and were convicted of a crime which cast its shadow even upon the Crown itself.[17]

A Wife had been reputedly given to the earl by Overbury as an ideal that would deter him from pursuing Frances Howard, then Countess of Essex; this had roused her murderous rage. Webster had also presented the king's favourite with his elegy for Prince Henry, *A Monumental Column*, as an example of good life. *A Wife* was therefore an item in that court news which for three years buzzed round the earl and countess; and in editing this volume (or at all events contributing the biggest share to the enlarged edition), Webster was joining such famous contributors, as Sir Henry Wotton, who wrote 'The Character of a Happy Life,' and John Donne, 'The Character of a Dunce'. His successful tragedy, *The Duchess of Malfi*, had not only opened with three character sketches of the main figures; it had continued in a dark atmosphere of rumour and hidden menace which reflects the atmosphere of the English court; it had incorporated and transformed some material from *A Monumental*

Column. The duchess faces immolation as 'a loving wife' (IV.i.73–4), but her secret death in prison is stigmatised as 'murder'. The fourth act, with its unearthly rituals, its chorus of madmen, makes Shakespearian demands on audience and actors for which the 'characters' of the opening scene had served only as prologue. It may be that Webster felt when the truth was exposed that life had overtaken art; he wrote no more in this vein for the stage. Jonson, too, after 1616 retired from the public stages; he also published his collected *Works* in folio, carefully expunging from *Hymenaei*, written a decade earlier to celebrate her first nuptials, the name of Frances Howard.

Among his contributions to this prestigious volume of Overburian 'characters' Webster included the 'Character of an Excellent Actor' and the nostalgic 'Character of a Fair and Happy Milkmaid', echoing the elegaic note of his tragedy.[18] It is the note of mourning; the milkmaid hopes to be buried in the spring.

Webster praises the 'life', the energy of good actors; their 'full and significant action of the body' charms the audience, till a man of thought might apprehend 'the Ghosts of our ancient Heroes walked again', whilst their speaking improves the art of the poet: 'for what in the poet is but ditty, in him is both ditty and music',

> He is much affected to Painting, and 'tis question whether that make him an excellent Player, or his Playing an exquisite Painter.[19]

The pictures here given of the court include the game of Conceited Newes, which Jonson had satirised some years before in his epigram on 'The Court Pucelle,' whose chamber is

> the very pit
> Where fight the prime cocks of the game for a wit[20]

one set of news being contradicted by the next. Webster's own 'Character of a Courtier' observes, 'The substance of his discourse is news ... he is not, if he be out of court; but like a fish breathes destruction, if out of his element'. Among the 'News from Court' in Webster's edition of 'Overbury' is the daring affirmation:

> That men's loves are their affliction. That titles of honour are rattles to still ambition. That to be a King is Fame's butt, and fear's quiver. That the souls of women and lovers are wrapped in the portmanque of their senses.

Somerset had been given his earldom to make him a fit match for the Countess of Essex; 'Fame's butt ... fear's quiver,' quibbling on the damage inflicted on the king and his notorious fear of physical attack, offers the complete refutation to Joseph Hall's encomium. The next edition of 'Overbury' contained elegies on the now-acknowledged fact of his murder, a denunciation of 'the clean contrary wife', and a salute to Overbury's marriage to immortality, through his poem.

The last work which Webster published through his friend Nicholas Okes was *Monuments of Honour,* a mayoral Triumph which contained more criticism of the Crown, in 'wits descant' on the traditional plainsong of the old devices.[21] In the year previous to this, 1623, the year of Shakespeare's First Folio, he had given Okes the text of *The Duchess of Malfi,* for which young John Ford of the Middle Temple wrote verses of commendation based on Jonson's tribute to Shakespeare. After placing Shakespeare above the Greeks and Romans, Jonson wrote:

> Thou art a Moniment without a tomb
> And art alive still, while thy book doth live,
> And we have wits to read, and praise to give.

Ford wrote of Webster:

> Crown him a poet whom nor Rome nor Greece
> Transcend in all theirs, for a masterpiece:
> In which, while words and matter change, and men
> Act one another, he, from whose clear pen
> They all took life, to memory hath lent
> A lasting fame, to raise his monument.

Middleton, the London pageant poet, Rowley, leader of the Queen's men and Webster's collaborator, also assured Webster the sort of 'monument' that he had offered the Lord Mayor, that his friends had offered Overbury – the monument of print.

Another member of the Queen's men succeeded Webster and Middleton in the devising of city triumphs; this was Thomas Heywood, longest-lived and most productive playwright of his time, who has now sunk into neglect. His plays have not been edited since 1874; his other works have not been edited at all. This, however, might not have disturbed him, for print was not his medium.

For 39 years, from 1602 till his death in 1641, Heywood was an actor and sharer in the company successively under the patronage of the Earl of Worcester, Queen Anne, the queen of Bohemia, and Queen Henrietta; he must have given the kind of continuity that John Heminges gave to Shakespeare's company. Webster calls him 'beloved friend'; their elegies for Prince Henry had been bound up together with Tourneur's and printed, of course, by Nicholas Okes. Heywood's was dedicated to Worcester.

The son of a Lincolnshire parson, descended from minor gentry of Mottram, Cheshire, Heywood became as completely a Londoner as Peele, Munday, or Dekker. No stories clustered round him; he, however, could describe all the dramatists by their familiar names – Will, Ben, Kit, and the rest – and write a *General (though Summary) Description of all the Poets both foreign and modern*, with their 'portraits', which was never printed. He repeatedly protested that he did not seek publication, but if his plays were taken down in shorthand and wretchedly set out, he would print by agreement with his company.[22] In his *Apology for Actors* (1613), where he speaks on behalf of his friends and is supported by their commendations, he thanks Nicholas Okes for being 'so careful and industrious, so serious and laborious to do the author all rights of the press' while castigating William Jaggard for unauthorised printing of two of his songs in an edition of *The Passionate Pilgrim* attributed entirely to William Shakespeare – with which, Heywood said, Shakespeare was 'much offended'. Elsewhere he complained of a schoolmaster in West Ham who had appropriated his Latin translations.[23]

In a prefatory note before *The English Traveller*, published in 1633 when he was nearly sixty, Heywood is more explicit than any other playwright of his day. He states that he had a hand 'or main finger' in 220 plays (the number surviving is now twenty). His plays 'are not exposed unto the world in volumes to bear the titles of works (as others)' for three reasons. First, some 'by shifting and change of companies' are lost; others are held by actors who want the exclusive right; lastly, Heywood has no ambition to be 'in this kind voluminously read'.

The English Traveller was for Heywood an exceptional play; as the prologue says, 'He only tries if once bare lines will bear it'. There is no spectacle, no combat, marriage, not so much as song, dance, or masque. It reworks a theme he had used all his life, the deceived husband or lover who forgives his erring spouse or mistress. From Matthew Shore in the early *King Edward IV*, through the hero of *A Woman Killed with Kindness* (1604) to the delicate portraits of Geraldine and Old Wincot in *The English Traveller*, he was to proceed to the great triumph of *Love's Mistress* (1634), the story of Cupid and Psyche, which was the queen's birthday offering to the king and staged for the court by Inigo Jones. This was far above the level to which Heywood usually aspired, but it is a misnomer to call his work 'bourgeois tragedy'; the family feels its corporate unity shattered by the lady's betrayal; in the plot, all the servants play a significant role; their loyalty is that of the country household. Among the swampy miscellanies which Heywood compiled in his later years, *The Hierarchy of the Blessed Angels*, dedicated to the

Catholic queen, reduces the whole universe to a household centre.

In addition to these miscellanies, some of which were in folio, Heywood wrote four mayoral Triumphs during the 1630s for which his motto on the title page was *Redeunt Spectacula* (in this, he deputised for Ben Jonson who, as city chronologer, should have been writing them).

The basic reason for Heywood's not publishing his dramas was none of the three given in *An Apology for Actors* but rather that Heywood thought pictorially, in so far as he 'thought' at all. He enjoyed that instinctive sympathy and rapport with his audience and his fellow actors which is the theatre's especial gift. Modern critics like T.S. Eliot and L.C. Knights, who ignore the dimension given by performance, dismiss him.[24] For Heywood a play, though dynamic, had the dual components of the 'device'. *An Apology for Actors* emphasizes the need to *see* a play:

> To see, as I have seen, Hercules in his own shape hunting the Boar, knocking down the Bull, taming the Hart, fighting with the Hydra, murdering Geryon, slaughtering Diomed, wounding the Stimphalides, killing the Centaurs, pashing the Lion, squeezing the Dragon, dragging Cerberus in chains, and lastly on his Pyramides writing *Nil Ultra*, O these were sights to make an Alexander.
>
> (pp. 20–1)

The argument from example had been Philip Sidney's, but Heywood not only rejoiced in the effectiveness of 'inexplicable dumb shows and noise' which Sidney rejected; as dramatist of the Red Bull, he also rejoiced in the mixture of hornpipes and funerals. His printed texts are but as scores for orchestra, or scenarios – Lamb termed him a prose Shakespeare – but what he lacks is precisely the poet's power to integrate the 'activities' with the actual texture of the writing itself.

He does not argue the case for acting but presents the grand theatres of the ancient world, the careers of ancient actors, as a herald might blazon a noble ancestry. Webster says he has erected 'monumental theatres' from ancient ruins. In the theatre he intuitively adopts a structure that is absent from his other writing. *The Four Prentices of London*, his early and notorious romance (Beaumont was to parody it in *The Knight of the Burning Pestle*) does not work like a dream play of pure enchantment, such as Peele's *The Old Wives' Tale*. It is true that Godfrey of Bulloigne, one of the Nine Worthies, and his three brothers begin their adventures in exile as London prentices, that one shipwreck lands them as far apart as the very bounds of Europe – to meet as crowned kings and conquerors of Jerusalem. Yet the adventures are worked out with the logic of modern science fiction and in the same manner as the balanced plots and sub-plots of his later plays. There is not only a balance between the main story and the melodramatic sub-plot of *A Woman Killed with Kindness*, but both are perhaps meant to contrast with the exotic violence of the King's men's great success of the same year, *Othello*. In presenting a double bill at court before Queen Anne and the Prince of Wales in 1612, *The Rape of Lucrece* was combined with *The Silver Age* – that is, the story of Amphytrion, the innocent adultery that ensured the birth of Hercules, an implicit contrast with the story of the rape. In these matters Heywood acquired increasing skill, without forgoing his earlier theatrical material. In *Love's Mistress*, the clown purloins what he takes to be Psyche's Box of Beauty (it is a replica, substituted by Cupid) and paints his face, unconsciously, with black spots, recalling the spotted Conscience of Robert Wilson's *Three Lords and Three Ladies of London* (1588). As the leading men of Heywood's company were clowns, he had always to find them a part; but if this sometimes means that the plays read as if written for as well as by Bully Bottom, the stage effect can be different.

In Heywood the actor controlled the writer; structure evolved for performance. In the passage quoted from *An Apology for Actors*, the excitement of the actor remembering the adventures of Hercules as he had both written and played them in *The Silver Age* and *The Brazen Age* can be felt in the climactic build of the sentence. Although Heywood objected to thefts by printers, he himself had no scruples in borrowing from the plays he heard only in the theatre, more especially those of Shakespeare, which evidently stuck in his memory.

The Rape of Lucrece (1607) makes the clashing tones of Webster sound positively harmonious by contrast. Nicholas Okes had re-printed Shakespeare's rhetorical poem that same year – perhaps it was used in the theatre for exercises, as the Sonnets are used today by the Royal Shakespeare Company.

The poem contains a bashful servant whom Lucrece sends to summon her husband after the rape. In Heywood, the clown, who is given the Shakespearian name of Pompey, is shown revealing in a three-man catch what he must not say; and this immediately pre-cedes the tragic death scene of Lucrece.

Valerius: Did he take fair Lucrece by the toe?
Horatius: Toe, man?
Valerius: Ay, man.
Clown: Ha, ha, ha, ha, man.
Horatius: And further did he strive to go?
Clown: Go, man?

Horatius: Ay, man.
Clown: Ha, ha, ha, ha, man fa derry down, ha fa derry down.

This perhaps does not differ from the jig which followed *Julius Caesar* at the Globe; the crowd may not have distinguished it from the Clown in *Antony and Cleopatra* or the Porter in *Macbeth*. When 'the stranger who acted Valerius' added new songs, Heywood printed them, including that Latin ditty, 'The Cries of Rome,' which advertised 'Salt, salt, white Worcestershire salt!' *The Rape of Lucrece* also contained Scevola thrusting his hand in the fire, Horatius at the bridge, and a final duel in which Tarquin and Brutus kill each other. Perhaps the most serious lines in the play are those in which three nobles discuss the misgovernment of the Tarquins and Lucrece's husband advises 'harmless sports' as a protection in bad times. 'So shall we seem offenceless and live safe.' In *An Apology for Actors* (where this story is cited as a remedy against lust) Cicero is quoted as telling the ruler that plays kept the subject harmlessly employed, when otherwise they might be tempted into sedition. Tullia, who shows distinct traits of both Goneril and Lady Macbeth, at one point exclaims, 'There is no earth in me, I am all air and fire!' *The Four Ages*, a secular equivalent of the craft cycles which runs to five plays, starting with the birth of Jupiter, includes the reworking of material from earlier plays and more lines from the Globe. Saturn's wife, preparing to sacrifice the infant Jupiter at her husband's command, exclaims, 'I'll kiss thee ere I kill thee'; Medea invokes a

> Goddess of witchcraft and dark ceremony
> To whom the elves of hills, of brooks, of groves,
> Of standing lakes and caverns vaulted deep
> Are minister, three-headed Hecate.

Neither *Othello* nor *The Tempest* was yet in print; Sinon's 'A horse, a horse!' capped by Pyrrhus's 'Ten kingdoms for a horse to enter Troy!' might be justified since the cry of Richard III had become common property. The conclusion of the series — which required the co-operation of the two companies, owing to the size of the cast — shows the death of all participants in the Trojan War except Ulysses and Aeneas, who is instructed (in another borrowing) by the Ghost of Hector —

> *Heu, fuge, nata dea; teque his pater eripe flammis*

— to set out for the founding of Rome and London, the New Troy. Heywood's reshaping of earlier theatrical devices may have been a reason for avoiding print, but it did not prevent his response to new styles. When in 1615 he published *The Four Prentices of London*, where, to the blare of drums and trumpets, the grand old circus parade moves in strict if gaudy symmetry, he apologised for 'my first practice . . . as plays were then, some fifteen or sixteen years ago, it was then in the fashion'. Since those days he had progressed to Medea hanging in the heavens surrounded with 'strange fiery works', and nearly twenty years later, in *Love's Mistress*, he was to provide a stage equivalent for Quarles's *Emblems*, the loves of Amor and Anima, published that same year.

The sub-plot of *The English Traveller* combines a Plautine story with a beast fable (Reynard the Fox fixes a coxcomb on the head of the Old Lion, subverting the Lion's whelp) and these with the popular theme of the London Prodigal, which he had treated before in *The Wise Woman of Hogsdon*. He can write a duel for two railers (Sinon and Thersites in *The Iron Age*, who greet each other as 'urchin' and 'toad'), but he was never in his life guilty of a witticism.[25] Saturn becomes only a king of Crete; Plutus comes not from Tartarus but Tartary, with a train of camels. In the four mayoral Triumphs of the thirties, Heywood put London always at the centre and was tacitly critical of the court simply by ignoring it. He could revive for the Puritan Haberdashers their patron St Katherine; he worked happily with Gerard Christmas, the king's painter for the navy, and collaborated with him in designing the figures and scroll-work for *The Sovereign of the Seas*, publishing in 1637 *A True Description of His Majesty's Royal Ship*. Christmas prepared the devices for the mayoral Triumphs; that of 1635 featured a big water show and parodied the royal masque of the previous year, *Coelum Britannicum*. The last Triumph, *London's Peaceable Estate* (1640), celebrated the city's overseas plantations in Ireland, Virginia and the Bermudas; the River Nile provided almost Websterian fable; but there was also direct and poignant warning of the dangers ahead – which the court had recognised from another point of view in *Salmacida Spolia*, the last masque. Nicholas Okes was succeeded by John; they continued to print Heywood, who, fortunately for himself, was buried in his parish church of St James, Clerkenwell, before the king raised his standard at Nottingham and the Londoners closed the theatres. Nicholas was buried in St Bartholomew the Less 11 April 1645.

The range of Jonson's work demands to be seen as a whole; it is only as background that Webster's minor works (including *The Devil's Law Case*) deserve to be set beside his two masterpieces; but with Heywood there is a case for looking at what his age most applauded and which today presents the most difficult reading. For it is in his spectacular work rather than in *A Woman Killed with Kindness* and *The English Traveller* that the collaboration with Okes and Rowley, or with Webster, may with labour be reconstructed.[26] When a detractor taunted Webster as 'the playwright-cartwright', he was demoting the member of the powerful Merchant Taylors' company, but it was a craftsman's fellowship who erected the monument of the First Folio 'only to keep the memory of so worthy a friend and fellow alive, as was our Shakespeare'. Webster and Heywood shared the spirit that prompted this enterprise – which none the less, without the example of Ben Jonson's Folio, might not have appeared. (The only other folio of plays to appear was that of Beaumont and Fletcher in 1647; for the succeeding age, these made up English drama.) The collective origins that inhibited print in Shakespeare's case, but his alone, also eventually ensured publication.

Notes

1 Glynne Wickham, *Early English Stages* III (London, Routledge & Kegan Paul, 1981) p. xvii.
2 See David H. Horne (ed.), *The Life and Minor Works of George Peele* (New Haven, Yale University Press, 1952) pp. 178–81.
3 George R. Kernodle, *From Art to Theatre* (Chicago, Chicago University Press, 1944) p. 105. The *Ballet Comique de la Reyne* and Bruno's *Spaccie delle Bestie Triomphante*, both of 1582, supplied the bases for two Caroline masques of 1632 and 1634.
4 The most famous of character books, John Earle's *Microcosmographie* (1628), was followed by, among others, Wye Saltonstall's *Picturae Loquantes* (1631).
5 *Shakespeare Survey* 34 (1981)
6 Giorgio Melchiori, 'Translating Shakespeare: An Italian View' *Shakespeare Translation* 5, Tokyo 1978, p. 20.
7 See Norman Rabkin, *Shakespeare and the Common Understanding* (Berkeley, California University Press, 1976) and Robert Grudin, *Mighty Opposites: Shakespeare and Contrariety* (Berkeley, California University Press, 1979).
8 The 'Character of a Blunt Man' is one of Earle's most penetrating satires.
9 H.S. Bennett, *English Books and Readers 1558–1603* (Cambridge, Cambridge University Press, 1964) p. 255.
10 See M.C. Bradbrook 'The Politics of Pageantry' *Poetry and Drama: Essays in Honour of Harold Brooks* A. Coleman and A. Hammond (eds), (London, Methuen, 1981). See above, pp. 98–9.
11 Peter W.M. Blayney, *The Texts of 'King Lear' and Their Origin;* vol. 1 *Nicholas Okes and the First Quarto* (Cambridge, Cambridge University Press, 1982). Okes was the son of a horner (i.e. a man who pasted a sheet of paper with the alphabet and the Lord's Prayer on a board and covered it with sheeting of horn, as a child's first reader). He was possibly the

grandson of Nicholas Okes, lute player, who in 1561 received payment for his part in a Lord Mayor's Triumph (*Malone Society Collections* III.41).

12 Hall's *Vergidemiae,* which initiated the quarrel with Marston, appeared in 1597.

13 See Jacqueline Pearson, *Tragedy and Tragicomedy in the Plays of John Webster* (Manchester, Manchester University Press, 1980) and Nicholas Brooke, *Horrid Laughter* (London, Macmillan, 1979) chapter IV, which is particularly concerned with production. Compare Michael Scott, *The Plays of John Marston* (London, Macmillan, 1978).

14 Praise of Richard Perkins comes at the end of *The White Devil;* he played Flamineo. The actors' names precede *The Duchess of Malfi.*

15 In 1609 two of Shakespeare's fashionable works had been pirated – the Sonnets; and *Troilus and Cressida,* published by a pair of young stationers. W.R. Elton thinks Marston may have procured the copy from his inn. Dekker's praise comes in his dedication of *If it be Not Good.*

16 Henry Fitzjeffrey of Lincoln's Inn; printed in *Certain Elegies done by Sundry Excellent Wits* as 'Notes from Blackfriars' (1618). See M.C. Bradbrook *John Webster, Citizen and Dramatist* (London, Weidenfeld & Nicolson, 1980) Chapter VIII, p. 169, for Webster's quarrel with the lawyers about acting.

17 For the Overbury murder, see William McElwee, *The Murder of Sir Thomas Overbury* (London, Faber & Faber, 1952) and Beatrice White, *Cast of Ravens* (New York, Braziller, 1965). Sir Nicholas Overbury, Thomas's father, was a bencher of the Middle Temple. The fullest edition of *A Wife* is that by James E. Savage *The Conceited Newes of Sir Thomas Overbury and his Friends* (Gainesville Florida, Florida University Press, 1968).

18 *The White Devil* V.iv.95–104; *The Duchess of Malfi* III.v.18–21; IV.ii.12–14. The character was further known from its use in Izaac Walton's *Compleat Angler.*

19 The painters and limners of the period who congregated near Webster's home have recently been studied by Mary Edmond (The Walpole Society, vol. 47, 1978–80). Many were rather what we should call decorative painters than picture makers; like Shakespeare and Burbage, devisers of *imprese* for tourneys, etc.

20 For this poem, see Herford and Simpson (eds), *The Works of Ben Jonson* VIII, (Oxford, Oxford University Press, 1952) p. 222. Savage identifies the Pucelle with Cicely Bulstrode and the author of the 'Foreign News' with Sir Henry Wotton. Lady Southwell contributed to the ninth edition.

21 See the works cited in nn 10 and 16 above. See also p. 105ff.

22 See the prologue to *If you Know not Me, you Know Nobody,* the preface to *The Rape of Lucrece,* the prologue to *A Challenge for Beauty.* The epilogue to *The Royal King and the Loyal Subject* repeats the apology of the preface to *The Four Prentices of London:* 'This play is old' . . . but then,

> What's now out of date, who is't can tell
> But it may come in fashion and suit well?

23 See A.M. Clark, *Thomas Heywood, Dramatist and Miscellanist* (Oxford, Oxford University Press, 1930) pp. 80–2.

24 'The sensibility is merely that of ordinary persons in ordinary life . . . of those of Heywood's plays which are worth reading, each is worth reading for itself.' T.S. Eliot *Elizabethan Essays* (London, Faber, 1934) p. 107. Knights uses a Leavisite approach to Heywood in chapter VIII of his *Drama and Society in the Age of Jonson* (London, Faber, 1937). See also note 26.

25 Heywood is guiltless of the 'stabbing simile', that favourite tool of the satirist, of Marston and Webster – which also survived as late as Witwoud in *The Way of the World*. Millamant is driven to cry, 'Truce to your similitudes!' (II.i).

26 See my article 'Thomas Heywood: Shakespeare's Shadow' *Collected Papers* Vol. III (Brighton, Harvester Press, 1983).

The Constellated Globe

X.

The Bankside in Elizabethan Times

Henslowe and the Rose Theatre

In Henslowe's Rose, the neighbourhood shaped the tradition. This was the City's spillover; a play area, a region of taverns, brothels and prisons. Two hundred years before, from Southwark, with its shipyards and its breweries, the rumbustious Harry Bailly had led the Canterbury Pilgrims from the Tabard Inn. The City now controlled the western end of Bankside, Bridge Ward, which commanded the south gate of London Bridge; the Liberty of the Clink, originally the manor of the Bishop of Worcester, still belonged largely to the church and here some of the duties of magistrates were entrusted to churchwardens. Eventually as churchwarden, Henslowe was himself, for example, responsible for plague returns and on these depended the orders for closing theatres. The little ribbon of streets, less broad than the river itself, ran from St Saviour's, giving on to open fields and meeting the Manor of Paris Garden. Here from 1560 the Master of the Royal Game had kept bears and mastiffs and here too in Southwark High Street bulls were baited by order of the City before slaughter. No less than five prisons stood on Bankside, run with relative mildness compared with the dreaded City fastness of Newgate, or the royal fortress of the Tower. Prisoners from the Clink, the Counter, the Marshalsea, the Queen's Bench and the White Lion might walk abroad with their keepers; some indeed might patronise a playhouse. The trades of shipbuilding, brewing and tanning supplied London; disbanded soldiers, seamen wandering from channel ports filled the taverns, and fugitives from the justice of the City hid in this region where, west of Waverley House, the home of Lord Montague, Henslowe's first patron, stood the palace of the Bishop.

Philip Henslowe's father had been Master of the Game to Lord

Montague at Brill Park in Hampshire; and if in that piously Catholic household, he had been christened for King Philip that would place his birth in the years 1554–1559. On the testimony of his son-in-law he married in 1580 Agnes Woodward, widow of a wealthy dyer to whom he had been apprenticed; she must have been senior to himself. Henslowe carried on the dyeing, he dealt in the starch so fashionable for ruffs, kept up mining and farming in his old home, brought his brother and nephew to London and might still invoke Lord Montague to stand his good lord in local disputes. He secured over thirty properties on Bankside including taverns, tenements, an ordinary and a brothel.

In August 1584 Lupold von Aedel, a traveller from Pomerania, visited the newly reopened bear ring. In January of the previous year, the galleries of an older bear ring had collapsed, killing eight people; but in spite of denunciations from the pulpit of this judgement of God upon the sinful suburb, it was rebuilt a little to the south of the former site, as shown in the engraving of 1593 by John Norden, a surveyor who knew the district well. Von Aedel's description prefigures a theatre; in the manner of that built by Burbage in Shoreditch, it had three galleries.

> There is a round building, three stories high, in which are kept about a hundred large English dogs . . . the dogs were made to fight singly with three bears.

They were followed by a horse and a bull; but as prelude to the grand finale, a 'show of men and women entered . . . from a separate compartment, singing, dancing, conversing and fighting with each other' after which white bread was tossed to the crowd who scrambled for it, then:

> Right over the middle of the place a rose was fixed, this rose being set on fire by a rocket; suddenly many apples and pears fell out of it down upon the people standing below. Whilst the people were scrambling for the apples, some rockets were made to fall down upon them, out of the rose, which caused a great fright but amused the spectators. After this, rockets and fireworks came flying out of all corners and that was the end of the play.

Largess of fruit or bread or wine was a feature of the Lord Mayor's annual pageant, but must have encouraged the pickpockets – as indeed was shewn in the play that was to open the last of the Bankside playhouses, the Hope, in 1614 – Ben Jonson's *Bartholomew Fair*, where a rich simpleton loses his possessions in such a scramble. Even today the mechanisms of lighting up fireworks by a travelling rocket may be seen in Florence at the Easter festivities at the Duomo.

The actors who came forth 'singing, dancing, conversing and fighting with each other' may have been engaged in a jig; their animal energy would be as infectious to a foreigner as to the locals.

Very shortly afterwards Henslowe rented from a powerful city church, St Mildred's Bread Street, in March 1585 at a rent of £7 a year for 31 years, the ground on which he built the Rose Theatre. In a later illustration by John Norden, it was labelled The Star; the first name had been the original one of this site, but a revolving rose could easily turn into a blazing star, which became a popular theatrical spectacle. Henslowe entered into contract with a member of the Grocers' Company already resident on the site to build a playhouse in which the grocer was to have sole right of victualling – which for visitors from across the Thames, out for the day, might be very important. No more is heard of this man, John Cholmley; perhaps he merely wanted to secure right of entry or – as later at another playhouse, the Boar's Head – the stronger interloper played cuckoo in the nest. By Simon and Jude's day 1587, local inhabitants were complaining of Sunday playing at the Rose. Henslowe may have begun by thinking of bear baiting since he had a hereditary interest and later himself became Master of the Royal Game. But the history of the Rose was begun when on 22 October 1592 Henslowe's stepdaughter, Joan Woodward, married the great actor Edward Alleyn. Henslowe was amongst the wealthiest men in the Clink, his rates assessed at £10 a year; the household was pious and Protestant, Henslowe a governor of the local school. Alleyn, born 1 September 1566, so about a dozen years his junior, soon showed his business sense and was eventually to surpass his father-in-law as founder of a school and an almshouse, where their joint papers survive. Henslowe's *Diary*, preserved at Dulwich in the College of God's Gift, had begun in February 1592 as a sort of account book and general memorandum; it continued sporadically till 1603.

Here in opening, Henslowe noted in February 1592 extensive improvements, totalling £108, for his new tenants, The Lord Strange's Men, of whom Alleyn was leader though his personal allegiance was to the Lord Admiral, Charles Howard of Effingham. And so, though he may have begun by thinking of bear baiting, Henslowe swung towards players. His *Diary,* concerned at first only with daily takings, in the later part is concerned with actors and authors, costumes, payments for commissioning plays. Later in return for advances he directly bound both players and playwrights as his servants. He purchased the Old Bear Ring and also a little theatre at Newington Butts, a mile to the South, which had originally been built in his garden by one of Lord Warwick's Men, Jeremy Savage.

In his Diary Henslowe entered the couplet:

> When I lent I was a friend,
> When I asked I was unkind.

The actors of Jacobean times alleged that he had made and broken companies; but his record does not bear out the image of the grasping and unscrupulous exploiter of talent. If sometimes he exacted bonds, at other times he was ready to take a man's word. In times of plague he seems to have acted as pawnbroker for local women, perhaps the madams of the brothels, taking small pledges. He headed his letters and his accounts with 'Jesus' or other ejaculations. Three months before the wedding, Alleyn was driven to touring by the long closure for plague, and the correspondence whilst the Rose was shut between June 1592 and May 1594, shows a close domestic attachment. Greg observed: 'Of Henslowe's knowledge or ignorance of stagecraft we have absolutely no means of judging' (*Diary*, vol. II (1908), p. 112) but a man who had Edward Alleyn as a son-in-law and partner for a quarter of a century could not have remained without sound knowledge both of the dramas and the players. Alleyn had a finger in every pie and to this placid and conservative household he brought a fiery temper, a flamboyance of address, an apprentice or two, and such fame that a letter addressed to him needed no further superscription. Within the shifting, unstable population of the district, with its many masterless men, Henslowe and the Rose imported a touch of City stability and solidarity, to which Alleyn attached himself. The son of a Bishopsgate inn holder, he had been orphaned early, and took to a player's wandering, but his brother kept the inn and also held there a stock of theatrical properties. Alleyn's imposing height, his magnificent voice and presence combined with an interest in quick-change acts; he created the great Marlovian heroes and was famous also as Kyd's mad, playacting, quick-change Hieronymo.

The Liberty of the Clink defined a social mood as well as a legal boundary 'In populous city pent'; jostling down narrow alleys to the dozen riverside stairs, men in slashed breeches and padded doublets, women in farthingales were ejaculated by the wherries and scullboats of the watermen upon the fringes of the South Bank. Liberation must have swept them along, recreation have lured more powerfully than by walking through Bishopsgate into the marshes of Moorfields or Shoreditch. In time of plague, it was noted, the brothels did a roaring trade, but theatres were deserted.

The Lord Strange's Men, who had been listed in a Privy Council license of May 1593, included William Kemp, Thomas Pope, John Heminges, Augustine Phillips, George Bryant 'being all of one company'. Here were Shakespeare's friends and perhaps as a hired man not a sharer, Shakespeare himself, already famous as the author of immensely popular plays on King Henry VI. Ferdinando Lord Strange was a patron of letters; in September he succeeded his father as Earl of Derby, but died the following April. His Countess, that Alice Spencer of Althrop whom Spenser had celebrated, for a while in May 1594 lent her patronage to the group. The Lord Chamberlain's Men played in tandem with the Admiral's Men – for Alleyn's Lord now lent his name – in a short season at Newington Butts from 3 June; there had been a brief opening of the Rose in the Christmas season, when *Titus Andronicus* was given, to be printed later in the year as having been performed by Strange's, Sussex's and Pembroke's Men. The last company had broken up in September 1593, as Henslowe wrote to Alleyn, being forced to pawn their books and apparel.

However, a secure playhouse and a famous leader did not appeal to some of the most experienced players, though Henslowe retained senior actors such as Thomas Downton and Richard Jones. To the Theatre in Shoreditch went under the title of the Lord Chamberlain's Men, Heminges and Phillips, Pope and Kemp; with them too, and soon to be a sharer, went William Shakespeare. A decade after von Aedel's visit to the bear ring, the distinctive style of the Rose emerged, and for the next five years the two companies began that distinction between types of playing which eventually was defined by different localities as well as by different troupes, almost in the modern manner.

The Lord Admiral belonged to the great Catholic clan of the Howards but had married into the Lord Chamberlain's staunchly Protestant family; and was his brother-in-law. The players settled down near the theatres, some became respected citizens and, paradoxically, these skittish wanderers turned into men of business as Henslowe turned into their manager and banker. He and Alleyn lent each other money, Alleyn eventually becoming the bolder and certainly, as the Lord of Dulwich Manor, the grander partner. Some of the players held shares in the stock of the theatre, but not in the theatre itself.

Lord Strange's troupe had originally been famous for Symons, a tumbler, and its brief predominance may have been due to the clowns Kemp and Pope, the first of whom had already travelled abroad. The energy and expertise of players who later came to the Rose, sent from this centre of showmanship Richard Jones and others who like human rockets shot in display all over the northern part of Europe. In a breakaway a third company was formed; first at the Boar's Head in Whitechapel and then at the Red Bull they were to carry on the tradition of spectacular entertainment led by clowns.

With the seamen who went downstream, now went the players and in the decade of the 1590s were to fan out to Livornia and Styria with their 'singing, dancing, conversing and fighting'. The apprenticeship may have been at the Rose, but the volatile strollers enhanced the older tradition of wandering troupes, now declining in England. Provincial companies, whether amateur or professional, then took a much lower place.

This is also the period of the main entries in Henslowe's *Diary*, which together with a 'plot' or scenario, and an actor's part on a scroll gives the best glimpse into his daily working. The Elizabethan stage is reconstructed from the documents of the Rose, the texts of Shakespeare from the Theatre, and records of litigation or of travel. The 'plot' and the 'part' suggest that actors had little notion of the play as a whole; it was read over to the sharers, but the plot was hung in the tiring house and the scrolls distributed. When roles were doubled, changes of costume might help, costume being the outstanding expense in many plays.

Plays were put on rapidly although favourites were kept in repertory. Four or five writers were given a plot and prepared individual scenes, so that varying views of the same character or even the same event might be given. Anthony Munday was one of Henslowe's team – but in *The Book of Sir Thomas More* for example he collaborated with at least four others, mostly from Henslowe's team of writers.

Henslowe evidently held on to the books which he paid for on the nomination of the acting companies, for they were often transferred to other groups. The repertory of the Rose as he recorded it is largely lost, although some plays may have been printed under alternative titles – *John a Kent and John a Cumber* by Anthony Munday may be *The Wise Men of West Chester*, surviving in the country which it depicted, in a single manuscript; *Fair Em the Miller's Daughter of Manchester* (1590) played by Lord Strange's Men (but not for Henslowe) may have succeeded in Stanley's territory in Lancashire.

Philip Henslowe survives today in terms of his financial links, so that his relationships, therefore, appear as based on money. The connecting record comes in terms of debtor and creditor, banker and client, capitalist and craftsman. Alleyn's role, like Henslowe's, became increasingly managerial; Henslowe treated the playwrights as he treated the actors, striving to bind both by indentures. All were inclined to fickleness. If a writer were commissioned to write a mayoral pageant, for instance, he would hopefully furnish on credit and might find himself in a debtor's prison, as Dekker did for six years. Like his predecessor in pageantry, George Peele, Dekker was reduced to begging; but while Peele begged of Lord Burleigh, Dekker begged of Alleyn.

In effect Alleyn and Henslowe became the true patrons of players and playwrights. They became shrewd talent spotters. It is no longer necessary to defend Henslowe against moral strictures of scholars as in the nineteenth century; his mind was subdued to what it worked in, like his Dyer's hand (a phrase Shakespeare may have learned on the Bankside). Only this enabled him to survive the first challenge to his theatre. It was to come from a neighbour whose wealth was much greater and his morals much inferior to Henslowe's – Francis Langley, Lord of the Manor of Paris Garden.

Langley and the Swan Theatre

Another traveller and another document ensure the significance of the Swan. In 1595 Johannes de Witt wrote a description of London accompanied with a sketch of the interior, according to his note the grandest of four London theatres, capable each of holding three thousand spectators. Its outer walls were of flint, its wooden pillars painted to represent marble, it stood in the Manor of Paris Gardens, closer than the Rose to Paris Garden stairs, ready to entrap fashionable clients coming by water from the Court, or from the Middle and Inner Temple.

Francis Langley, its builder, Lord of the Manor, had no knowledge of the theatre; in comparison with him, Burbage who concealed about his person parts of the daily takings, or Henslowe, were benevolent despots. Born in 1548, he had been adopted by his uncle and admitted as a Draper. A wealthy city Goldsmith, after becoming Lord Mayor, his uncle died in 1576. In 1585 Francis obtained the office of City Alnager or inspector of woollen cloth for export. If Henslowe was hard financially, Langley was criminal; and after harrassing unfortunate merchants by extortion, intimidation and fraud, in 1599 he was to be deprived of office.

But he had grown rich, bought property which he mortgaged in 1589 to buy the Lordship of the ancient Manor, whence he could see crowds crossing to visit the newly opened Rose. In February 1594 when the plague was abating, by mortgaging all his Cheapside property, he raised £1650 to build new tenements and the splendid Swan – completed some time in 1595. A flying swan was the badge of the Lord Chamberlain and perhaps Langley hoped to lure his men from their northern theatre, where they were in difficulty with their ground landlord about renewal of the lease.

The fury of Henslowe and Alleyn must have been roused when in
1595 their takings showed a significant drop, to spiral downward
still farther next year. A connection with the Lord Chamberlain's
men is hinted in October 1596. Langley craved sureties of the peace
against William Gardiner, a justice of the peace for Surrey with
whom he already had a violent quarrel, and against his stepson,
William Waite; a counterwrit was laid by Waite against William
Shakespeare and two women unknown. Shakespeare by February
1597 was resident in the Liberty of the Clink; had there been an
approach to him by the owner of the Swan? The pacific Shakespeare
seems to have retaliated with portraits of Gardiner and Waite as
Shallow and Slender in *The Merry Wives of Windsor* in the spring of
1597 – and were the two ladies associated with him the Merry Wives
themselves?

By February 1597 Langley had succeeded in luring players from
the Rose, who gave bonds to appear at the Swan and nowhere else;
Richard Jones, Gabriel Spencer, Thomas Downton and William Bird
played there as Lord Pembroke's Men, reviving the company that
had gone bankrupt in 1593. One player with Pembroke's Livery
could by exemplification claim that title. Pembroke, at this time
President of Wales, could not have been active at Court in his men's
interest; Langley later claimed to have spent £200 in 'making ready'
with costumes and possibly playbooks. He also borrowed money off
Robert Shaa, another way of attaching this actor.

In six months the venture had collapsed with the arrest in August of
Spencer, Shaa and Ben Jonson by the notorious Topcliffe, hunter of
recusants for Cecil. 'A lewd play . . . containing very slanderous and
seditious matter' had been seen at the Swan. Thomas Nashe, who
claimed to have written only Act I (and the plot), fled to his native
Yarmouth, and occupied himself in writing in praise of the Red
Herring. William Ingram in his study of Langley, discovered more
red herrings in this affair. In the first week of August, an anonymous
informer gave warning to Topcliffe of 'a seditious play called *The
Isle of Dogs*' – who on 10 August sent the informer to his master
Robert Cecil, to report, asking that he be rewarded and describing
his poverty and his great need. The case did not stand up to
investigation and the prisoners were released in early October. They
returned to Henslowe who put all except Spencer under bond to play
at the Rose. Langley then sued them, but as the Master of the Revels
had not licensed the Swan, his playhouse remained, at least theoretically, shut. If the question 'Who benefits?' is asked, the answer is
clearly Henslowe and Alleyn. The anonymous poor and debt-laden
informer had rendered them singular service, perhaps not without
reward.

Whilst wealthier than his rival, Langley was without expert knowledge of play procedures which long acquaintance had given to Henslowe and Alleyn, who would see exactly what strings to pull. They often disregarded a Privy Council order and got away with playing in Lent, or before restraints were lifted. The customary pleas in the previous July from the Lord Mayor about the enormity of players and demand for their restraint do not affect this case, being put forward before, and not caused by, the play.

On 19 February 1598 the Privy Council authorised two companies, the Lord Chamberlain's and the Lord Admiral's, and these alone, to play in London at their accustomed playhouses north and south of the river. Playing in City Inns had been earlier forbidden and this the City could enforce. Although the order was not of such overwhelming force as is sometimes suggested, it represented a triumph. I cannot imagine that by this order to 'pluck down' stages, galleries and rooms, the Privy Council meant to order the demolition of buildings. Seating and staging could be readily dismantled – this was to be demonstrated when the internal structure of the theatre was removed to the Bankside to furnish the Globe. To remove enough planks to make a stage unusable ensured that no one unauthorised could perform there; to put out of action the kind of frames erected in the tiltyard or the standings erected for the Lord Mayor's show was a familiar event. The noble peers were not carpenters but they knew what happened at Hampton Court at Shrovetide; even today many a college at Oxford or Cambridge may pack away the hall stage in an old garage or garden shed. The Inns of Court must have done the same. The boards may now have been replaced by stack-a-bye chairs, but in signing such an order, Howard and Hunsdon were not being unduly ferocious, in terms that nowadays would involve compensation. Their order is comprehensible; the theatres were to be 'voided' like tables in hall after dinner.

Langley had other ways of making money; he was raising loans, oppressing the merchants of Bartholomew Fair, and fighting with the churchwardens over payment of tithes. Edward Alleyn sold his stock in the Admiral's Men whilst retaining a special share without responsibilities; a sleeping partner, who did not appear on stage. Henslowe was angling for the Mastership of the Royal Game, turning again to bears. Alleyn was on the way to Dulwich Manor, and Shakespeare in 1597 bought New Place in Stratford, having already acquired his coat of arms. It was as a gentleman that Shakespeare moved to Bankside and possibly made some first encounter with Langley. In February of 1597 old James Burbage died; two months later the lease of his theatre expired. The company moved to the little Curtain adjacent; they had already agreed to have nothing to do with Langley, although the Swan must have looked very tempting.

The Globe and Lord Chamberlain's Men of Bankside

If *The Merry Wives of Windsor* carried a 'gleek' against Mr Justice Gardiner and his stepson, William Waite, Shakespeare and his company could be forgiven for a momentary siding with Langley. James Burbage's attempt to get a footing in the Blackfriars in the previous year had failed; the little theatre there, which had been used by the Children of the Chapel had functioned only once a week, but in the Great Parliament Chamber which had been bought for £600, the Lord Chamberlain's Men would obviously play every weekday. This theatre would have had only a total capacity of 600–700, even with the galleries added by Burbage, as against the capacity of around four times that number in the arena (see below p. 171).

The company stayed at the Curtain, near neighbour to the theatre, where they staged not only Shakespeare's new plays but in September 1598 Jonson's *Every Man in his Humour* – a moderate success, an answer to the Henslowe production in May of the previous year of Chapman's *Humourous Day's Mirth*.

Ben Jonson on 22nd September killed the fellow actor, Gabriel Spencer, who had shared prison with him, in a duel at Shoreditch. Spencer was one of Henslowe's star actors and Ben Jonson one of his hired poets; the murder was tersely recorded by Henslowe in a letter to Alleyn as committed by Benjamin Johnson Bricklayer – a recollection of the indictment. Jonson (found guilty but saved by benefit of clergy), produced a second success for the rival's theatre.

Henslowe was also losing actors to a newly formed third adult company playing at the Boar's Head in Whitechapel, near the deserted theatre. His chief rivals, however, were uncomfortably close when on 16 October 1599 he gave Downton £10 to pay the quartet who had written *Sir John Oldcastle,* an attempt to meet the resounding success of Shakespeare's *King Henry IV.* For Shakespeare was part sharer in the new theatre, the Globe, which had opened on Bankside only a month before.

The Lord Chamberlain's Flying Swan had indeed taken flight and from Shoreditch had landed in Henslowe's backyard. The plot of land leased 'in the occupation of the William Shakespeare and others', saw an erection which was the work of an actor's syndicate formed by Richard Burbage, whose capital was tied up in the unusable Blackfriars Theatre, now leased to choristers.

The moves and counter moves resemble nothing so much as the squabbles of birds over control of their territory. Langley was soon taking an interest in The Boar's Head and Alleyn also moved over to the North Bank, but farther to the West. His Fortune Theatre, modelled on the Globe, was finished 8 May 1600; its cost only £520 in all, less than half the price of the new Globe but probably more than the cost of the Boar's Head to all parties (which may have been £500).

This, like the Boar's Head, was a square building, probably a converted inn, and its name, The Fortune, frankly acknowledged its speculative nature. The Lord Admiral's Men migrated; but the Rose continued in use – and so, it would appear, occasionally did the Swan. But 'the glory of the Bank' was now the Globe.

Its opening was written up by yet another traveller, Thomas Platter, from Basle. He had recorded his interest in the graded admission charges and control of entry at a theatre in Bishopsgate – the Curtain – but on 21 September 1599 he went with a party across the water where in 'the straw thatched house we saw the tragedy of the first Emperor, Julius Caesar, very appropriately performed with approximately fifteen characters'.

The five years between the reopening of theatres after the plague, in 1594, and the opening of the Globe had proved crucial for London actors. The two rival centres of Shoreditch and Bankside were set up soon after Henslowe had first attracted men from their provincial retreats. Henslowe was shaken by Langley at the Swan, Burbage by the need to find a venue; the first was resolved by Providence or design, the second by combining actor-owner functions, whilst the leading actor at the Rose assumed a more distant and managerial function. Ben Jonson and then Heywood split off from Henslowe, who was left as dramatists with Munday, Haughton, Chettle, Porter, Dekker and, rather surprisingly, Chapman. But thanks to Henslowe's papers and de Witt's sketch, more is known of Bankside than of anything north of the river. The brightly painted merchant vessels of a new enterprise, flags at the turret and trumpets sounding, set out to conquer the City, which, in spite of routine opposition from the Mayor and Aldermen, welcomed its conquerors.

The Repertory of the Rose

The second play Jonson wrote for the Lord Chamberlain's Men, *Every Man out of His Humour* (1599), he published in 1600. After he wrote for them less, because any play was company property once it had been paid for, but print destroyed that monopoly. Memorial reconstruction by actors would not be easy since their general idea of a play would be very dim; 'stolen and surreptitious copies' were rare. Alleyn took no heed to preserve the author's version, probably in the confidence of a great star, he relied on his own performance; the texts of Marlowe that eventually and belatedly came from his stock were very corrupt. Lines did not count as much as the power of Alleyn, 'able to make a bad matter good'. Only one printed play can be associated with the Swan, and that from a later date. *A Chaste Maid in Cheapside* (1613), Middleton's blistering indictment of City morals, was played by the Lady Elizabeth's Men and comes quite near to Langley's state of life – but was presented after his death.

The Rose with its lost plays, always starred at first Edward Alleyn; as well as Tamburlaine, there was Tamer Cham, and the roaring parts of Peele. The repertory of the brief Christmas seasons of 1592–3 and 1593–4 includes Greene's *Orlando Furioso* and his *Friar Bacon and Friar Bungay*, Marlowe's *Jew of Malta*, and *Muly Morocco*, probably Peele's *The Battle of Alcazar*; later Kyd's *The Spanish Tragedy* and *A Knack to Know a Knave* (printed 1595), *Titus Andronicus* and *Harry the VI*; another list for February–June 1592 included Lodge's atrocity play about the sack of Antwerp, *A Looking Glass for London and England*, extremely noisy and spectacular. The 'suit of glass' for 'Longshanks', Peele's *Edward I*, is listed in the properties. It was, presumably, sewn all over with mirrors.

The playwriting syndicates who worked for Henslowe would use familiar models and the actors might formulate details for stock roles. Two late and successful comedies from the Rose, supply contrasts with the Shakespearean tradition of the nineties. The first, not infrequently revived today, Dekker's *The Shoemaker's Holiday* was exceptionally printed in 1600, a year after its commission; the second, Henry Porter's *Two Angry Women of Abingdon*, was printed the same year and evoked two lost sequels, but may have been written as much as ten years earlier.

The frolic shoemaker, Simon Eyre, dominates Dekker's master-piece; his torrentially brisk patter with repeated catchphrases is in the same style as the speech of the frolic innkeeper in *Sir John Oldcastle*, commissioned by Henslowe to counterbalance Shakes-peare's *King Henry IV* and to which Dekker was later commissioned to make additions.

Simon Eyre is the distant ancestor of Dickens' Sam and Tony Weller. He administers rather rough treatment to his spouse Margery, a former tripe seller with aspirations to gentility, who is the 'Bessy' of this Morris Dance, always unconscious of her bawdry till she has uttered it and then apologising with her catchword 'But let that pass'.

Eyre's fortune is made by a shrewd city deal which he makes with the captain of a foreign ship, thanks to one of his journeymen, who is a nobleman in disguise and a former student at Wittenburg. From him Eyre borrows the earnest money to acquire freight which must be quickly disposed of and resells the cargo at great profit before full payment is due; this wheeling and dealing raises him eventually to be Alderman and Lord Mayor, when he begs of the king privileges of markets and holidays. To show a Lord Mayor frolicking like a player even in the presence of kings, was a daring challenge when the City had threatened not long before to suppress players.

Shoemakers had featured as madcaps in Jonson's *The Case is Altered* (1597–8) but Juniper is not the centre of the play: Shakespeare made use of another in the opening scene of *Julius Caesar* when Dekker's play was on the boards. In the spring of 1599, a Lord Mayor had been committed to the Fleet for opposing his daughter's marriage to a peer; in this play Eyre's predecessor Oatley takes this line with his daughter Rose, in love with Eyre's princely prentice Lacey, heir to the Earl of Lincoln. Two love stories among the shoemakers concern this romantic pair (who are reminiscent of the disguised Lacy Earl of Lincoln and the Fair Maid of Fressingfield in Greene's *Friar Bacon and Friar Bungay*) and secondly Simon Eyre's journeyman Ralph who has married the maid of the household, Jane.

Pressed on his wedding day to serve in the French wars, Ralph cannot be released; whilst Lacy, deserting his command for love of Rose, appears disguised as a Dutch shoemaker and uses the money given him to lead the expedition to finance his new master's financial gamble. Eventually he is not only pardoned by the king – who though nameless is clearly the future victor of Agincourt – but given a knighthood, the equivalent of a combat medal and, in spite of parental pleas, by royal fiat wins his bride.

Jane is boisterously admonished by Simon Eyre in the kind of whip-smacking rhythms he uses to his wife:

> This fine hand, this white hand, these pretty fingers must spin, must card, must work, work, you bombast cotton-candle queen, work for your living with a pox to you.

> (I.i.208–10)

Driven away by Margery's dislike of her 'airs' Jane sets up as seamstress but when wooed in her shop by a merchant who tells her of her husband's reported death, her cries 'For God's sake leave me ... for God's sake leave me to myself alone ... once more. Begone, I say, else I will go' (III.iv.99–114) are softened only by our awareness that Ralph has returned, though lamed, and is now seeking her. I do not remember any other character before Hamlet who voiced this need for solitude in bereavement.

The merchant who has turned from wooing Rose to wooing Jane, commissions her wedding shoes from one which Ralph instantly recognises as his own work, and so the shoemakers win a victory over the merchant by taking Jane from him in his wedding procession and claiming all the finery he has bestowed as well. The folk motif of recognising his own bridal gift softens the implicit protest of this social contrast; whilst the most radical action is the instant walkout of the journeymen, threatened if Eyre does not give the unknown Dutchman (Lacey) employment – the more impressive in view of the antialien demonstrations that had lain behind *Sir Thomas More* half a dozen years before. The name Dekker, of course, suggests Dutch extraction; and he knew the language.

The tragic balladlike fidelity of the poor is contrasted with Lacey who had learnt shoemaking in Wittenberg (from a cousin of Hans Sachs perhaps?) when he had prodigally overspent; to pardon a reckless spendthrift was clearly popular with the younger section of the audience, and is seen in many city comedies, including Shakespeare's *The Merry Wives of Windsor*. Social gradations, nicely kept, could be paralleled from life; the Earl of Lincoln represents the players' patrons; the Lord Mayor, with his country manor house, Langley; Simon Eyre, member of a minor craft guild who enriched himself by judicious bargains, Henslowe himself.

Eyre is full of pious oaths, including one currently fashionable with Jonson's Braggart Soldier, 'By the foot of Pharoah'; his wife quotes scripture (catastrophically). The author's address to 'all good fellows', whom Eyre terms Mesopotamians and Assyrians, commends the mirth of this play as having pleased her Highness – 'being indeed in no way offensive'. The granting of a trade concession to the shoemakers for a market is just what this favoured group of players too could boast, thanks to their designation by the Privy Council.

The final sequence, fast and packed with action, equals the earlier bursts of fireworks; *The Shoemaker's Holiday*, an idyll of the City, comes nearest to transmitting the atmosphere of the Rose, in a form that can be staged today.

Two Angry Women of Abingdon probably originated at Oxford; its author could have been the Henry Porter who matriculated from Brazenose in 1579; he worked with both Jonson and Chapman and was respectfully termed 'master' by Henslowe, who exacted a 'faithful promise' to write only for the Rose. This play, a great success, must have been cut, for its text is almost as long as *Hamlet* and at first shows overindulgence in the comic servants' parts; it becomes a nocturnal pursuit of runaway lovers through the mazes of a wood, the two angry mothers ending with a fight for a torch. The farce is akin to the lovers' blind man's buff of *A Midsummer's Night's Dream*, or the pursuit in *The Tale of a Tub* (or rooftop chases in early cinema). Neatness and logical precision in the farcical gyrations suggest a classical plot, but it evidently appealed in the same way as Chapman's comedies, such as *The Blind Beggar of Alexandria* (1596), which parodies Marlovian favourites in an action for a quick-change artist.

The most significant recovery from Henslowe's workshop is not with his papers; *The Book of Sir Thomas More* is written in five hands including that of Munday, his principal plotter as chief. Dekker, Heywood, Chettle and it is thought Shakespeare, added sections; the tiny part of the Messenger (scene ix) is ascribed in another hand to Thomas Goodal, who appears in the plot of *The Seven Deadly Sins* with men from Lord Strange's players.

Sir Thomas More, most famous of London worthies, with his pranks and his uncomprehending wife, foreshadows Simon Eyre. Even his relation to the King is similar, the tragic end being curtly stated and totally unexplained; the play is aimed at a London audience.

The latest editors, V. Gabrielli and G. Melchiori, date the play by pointing to the antialien riots of prentices in the spring of 1592, the antialien inscriptions on the Dutch church in March 1593, of which they find echoes in the 'Shakespearean' speech. *Titus Andronicus*, marked as 'ne' (i.e. 'new') by Henslowe, was given three performances in the brief winter season, 27 December 1593 to 6 February 1594, and published later that year as having been played by Strange's, Sussex's and Pembroke's Men. Perhaps Shakespeare was briefly available to write a plea for the poor aliens, in danger of banishment − a fate too like that of the poor players. The speech contradicts the main tenor of the opening scenes which show the Lombards arbitrarily commandeering goods and wives of Londoners. The contributions of Dekker and Heywood are among their earliest; but Shakespeare would, presumably, not have contributed after his taking up shares with the Lord Chamberlain's Men in the summer of 1594; and the merriment is not unsuited to the desperate gaiety shewn in plague times, that Dekker enlarged on in his plague pamphlets. Thomas Goodal was a Mercer and seems to have dropped out of acting or perhaps died in the plague years. Lord Strange's Men were on tour with Alleyn.

This riddling story serves to show the incompatibility of Henslowe's old fashioned work with Shakespeare's art. The average time taken by Henslowe's playwrights to write a play was between a fortnight and a month. The average output of Shakespeare, despite his well-attested facility, was two plays a year. The internal consistency, already shown in *Titus Andronicus*, must have shown too in the acting, educating those who played, making for a distinctive acting style.

Henslowe was not concerned to be consistent about aliens. William Haughton's *Englishmen for my Money* (1598) is distinctly chauvinistic, whereas *The Shoemaker's Holiday* is notably liberal. The foreigners, von Wedel, de Witt and Platter certainly were impressed by what they met on the Bankside. Perhaps they had already seen English actors at home.

Note

This chapter could have had several hundred footnotes but I am not giving the many references that might be cited. E.K. Chambers, *The Elizabethan Stage*, 4 vols (Oxford, Oxford University Press, 1923); W.W. Greg (ed.), *Dramatic Documents from the Elizabethan Playhouses*, 2 vols (Oxford, Oxford University Press, 1931); A Harbage (rev. S. Schoenbaum) *Annals of English Drama 957–1700* (London, Methuen, 1964) and Glynne Wickham, *Early English Stages*, vol. III, (London, Routledge & Kegan Paul, 1981) are so well known that it should be enough to say that they give the foundation of the argument.

Carol Chillington Rutter, *Documents of the Rose Playhouse* (Manchester, Revels Plays Companion Library, 1984) collects documents chronologically, based on R.A. Foakes and R.T. Rickert (eds), *Henslowe's Diary* (Cambridge, Cambridge University Press, 1961) with new consultation of the text.

William Ingram, *A London Life in the Brazen Age, Francis Langley 1548–1602* (Cambridge Mass, Harvard University Press, 1978) deals with the Swan Theatre and gives much new material.

Thomas Dekker, *The Shoemaker's Holiday* ed. R.L. Smallwood and Stanley Wells (Manchester, Revels Plays 1979) provides additional material to that in Bowers' and Hoy's edition of Dekker's Plays (Cambridge, Cambridge University Press, 6 vols 1961–79). *Sir Thomas More* is forthcoming from the Revels Plays ed. Vittorio Gabrieli and Giorgio Melchiori, who produced an Italian edition (Bari, Biblioteca Italiana di Testi Inglesi, 1981).

Andrew Gurr, *Playgoing in Shakespeare's London* (Cambridge, Cambridge University Press, 1987) represents another part of the play's background which expanded the perspective I have used, and shows the difficult and delicate operation of putting together the evidence for such a study.

XI.

The Brownes, the Greenes and the Red Bull

Two Robert Brownes

The triumphant dominance of English actors in Germany and neighbouring lands has not been brought into the social history of London theatre, although chronicled by E.K. Chambers, as well as by Cohn, Herz, Harris, Brennecke and Creizenach, who by now are out of date. Recently, however, new explorations have been made by Willem Schrickx and Jerzy Limon, tracing routes and local records of leading groups.

In England, theatre historians have been concerned with digging out the facts about the Boar's Head and other places on the North Bank from legal records and little has been done to relate these two fields. Herbert Berry, *The Boar's Head Playhouse* (1986) made a start. From the fragmentary evidence, it would appear, the first overseas troupes came from Henslowe's and Alleyn's circle at the Rose, but later family connections were with the Boar's Head and the Red Bull, offshoots of the spectacular tradition.

The actors were a clannish and close-knit society, based on family ties, given to intermarriage. Overseas troupes needed a strong leader who knew his way about and was recognised by noble patrons, themselves often linked in close family networks. For in Europe traditions fading in England revived, or were reverted to – dependence on noble patronage and residence in the festive seasons, travel in summer. As our actors till the end of the sixteenth century played in English, their 'activities' – tumbling, swordsmanship and broad clowning, especially bawdy clowning, became their distinguishing features, with splendid costumes and plenty of music and noise. That is, the older features of the spectacular tradition were emphasised; the leader was often a clown and the repertory was based on Henslowe's.

The name appearing most frequently in the 1590s is that of Robert Browne, and in Jacobean times that of John Greene. These not uncommon names were connected in London by marriage, though sometimes apparently split by family disagreement. Whilst the evidence is far from clear, there were two Robert Brownes, one based in Stepney and one in Southwark; among their descendants, running down to the mid-seventeenth century, I have found in all six Robert Brownes. The interpretation must be conjectural; but as the investigators of the European connection have been concerned with itineraries, the London investigations with legal identities, an initial attempt to relate the two may lead to correction and improvement by others.

Robert Browne (of Stepney?) appears in 1583 in company with the 16-year old Edward Alleyn at Leicester as a member of Worcester's Men. Edward 'Alleyn's mother, widow of a Bishopsgate innholder, had remarried a Haberdasher named John Browne. Robert Browne of Stepney was associated with a Haberdasher with overseas trading interests, Oliver Woodliffe, in the ownership of the Boar's Head playhouse; his son, another Robert, was after his death apprenticed to a Haberdasher. The trade gilds, especially the smaller ones, were another form of clan association and it is not improbable that Browne was Edward Alleyn's stepbrother. This would account for the interest in him shown in Alleyn's correspondence – not always a friendly one.

Robert Browne was married at St Leonard's Shoreditch, the actors' parish church, on 28 November 1589, to Anne Bristowe of Holywell, who may have been related to James Bristowe, Henslowe's 'boy' who makes frequent appearances in the diary. The entire family, except for Browne himself, was wiped out in the great plague of 1593; a son Augustine (possibly a godson of Augustine Phillips) baptised 28 December 1590, was buried 5 September, then John Hinch, possibly a servant, and Robert Browne junior on 15 September, and on 17, '— Browne, wife of Robert Browne of Stebinheath' i.e. Stepney. No one remained to record Anne's name; but Henslowe wrote to his son-in-law, on tour:

> For other news I can tell you none but that Robert Browne's wife in Shoreditch and all her children and household be dead, and her doors shut up.[1]

Ten years later, in another plague year, Robert Browne himself was to die, disillusioned subtenant of the Boar's Head in Whitechapel. When on 16 October 1603 he was buried in St Mary Matfellon, Joan Alleyn on 21 October wrote to her husband, again on tour:

All the companies be come home and well, for all we know, but that Browne of the Boar's Head is dead and died very poor, he went not into the country at all.[2]

He had married a girl – 17 in 1595 according to later testimony – Suzanne or Susan, who could have been Susan Gaskin to whom Thomas Pope the actor left £100 because he had brought her up. She was granted probate since her husband died intestate and soon married Thomas Greene, clown and leader of the troupe at the Boar's Head and later at the Red Bull. Children of Robert and Suzanne Browne baptised at St Mary Matfellon included William, future actor, baptised 25 April 1602; Elizabeth, baptised 13 February, buried 24 July 1603; Anne, posthumous, baptised 22 January 1604. From William's will it appears an elder son Robert and a daughter Susan were also born.

Suzanne would take her husband's shares in the company and theatre with her when she married Greene; after his death in 1612 she harassed and eventually divided the players, by then at the Red Bull.

In Southwark another Robert Browne, actor, was assessed for taxes as of St Saviour's parish; he was termed 'gentleman', a style assumed by actors who were not entitled to be citizens. In Shoreditch, however, on 15 March 1593 he married Cicely Saunders (an Everett Sanders appeared with Robert Browne overseas in 1592) but some children were baptised in Southwark – Robert, son of Robert Browne a stage player, 19 October 1595, Elizabeth, 2 December 1599. On 2 April 1598 he lent £10 under bond to Ben Jonson and, in Hilary Term 1599, after an action in the Queen's Bench brought by him, Jonson was jailed in the Marshalsea and Browne awarded £1 damages. Yet a daughter Jane, baptised at St Leonard's on 13 January 1600 is described as of Stepney. The connection between Robert Browne of Stepney and Robert Browne of Southwark has never been worked out; it is assumed, for instance by Willem Schrickx, that the Robert Browne who is first met travelling overseas is Robert Browne of Southwark and that the same Robert Browne appeared in 1620 at the court of Elizabeth of Bohemia, the winter queen, in Prague. From his first appearance he appears prominent. Such prolonged travel, particularly in the very active kind of productions that were required, seems unlikely; actors usually retired before fifty, and in 1620 the Browne who first appeared with Edward Alleyn as a member of Worcester's Men, if the same age as Alleyn, would have been 53. Robert Browne of Southwark is too old to have been Robert Browne of Stepney's son; but given the conservative naming habits both families shared, he might have been a nephew, perhaps son of the Edward Browne who was also at Leicester in 1583. Alleyn, Henslowe and Shakespeare all helped their nephews.

In 1589, when Richard Jones relinquished his share in goods held jointly with Edward Alleyn and Robert Browne, Alleyn was already famous. Next year Robert Browne made his first overseas appearance as a player at Leyden; on 10 February 1592, the Lord Admiral issued a passport for him to go overseas with John Bradstreet, Thomas Sackville and Richard Jones. By way of Zealand they arrived at the court of Duke Heinrich Julius at Wolfenbuttel and a distinguished tradition began. I think Robert Browne of Stepney was overseas probably at the August fair in Frankfurt when in September his wife and children perished. The remarriage of Robert Browne of Stepney and the marriage of Robert Browne of Southwark produced families, whose later histories will emerge in Jacobean times. From the scanty record it would appear that the first was of particular interest to Alleyn but not on good terms, whilst the second appears, from occasional notes to Alleyn, to have been confident and respectful. My explanation would be that the first Robert Browne began the career overseas but was replaced by the second, his namesake, at the time when the first became too much involved in the London theatres and too old to sustain a double career; at about the time, that is, when Alleyn sold his shares in the Rose. His overseas leadership had given him the capital to start up in imitation of Alleyn and Henslowe, which may account for the note of triumph in Mrs Alleyn's writing that he died very poor – had he not once been rich, there would have been no point here; but he left a powerful legacy of future trouble in his formidable widow who, outliving her second husband, married a third and ruled the roost till her death as late as 1649.

But when Robert Browne of Southwark married Cicely Saunders, there was a Robert Browne in Hesse Cassel.

The English Players in Europe

In North Germany English actors took the leading role that Italian musicians took in the English court. In Denmark, Brunswick and Hesse Cassel, they resided on handsome board wages; in 1587 in Saxony, the wages were 100 thalers (about £30) a year. In summer they toured to the great fair at Frankfurt, and in such cities as Leyden, Utrecht, Cologne and Strasbourg; in the south Augsberg, Ulm, Nuremberg were visited. Bradstreet and Sackville became burghers of standing, settling as Breitstrasse and Sachsweil. The players might need three wagons for their goods, though conditions varied from castles to town halls – some towns even built theatres, as at Dantzig – elsewhere they played in schools, any available halls, inns and, at fairs, in booth theatres. The Duke of Brunswick and the Landgrave of Hesse Cassel built their own theatres eventually; the Landgrave, Maurice the Learned, himself wrote comedies.

Die truppe Kemp appeared in 1579, Brownesche Truppe in 1590, according to Hertz. As the actors played in English they ranged from farce to atrocity, but the chief role was the clown's. At Brunswick Sackville became John Possett, George Vincent became Pickle-herring; these names rose to be generic.

Some verses written in German in 1597 on Frankfurt fair describe the fool Jan with huge shoes and slops (Tarlton's costume – and that of Charlie Chaplin), eating voraciously and pattering bawdy. The tumbler who leapt high in the air, displaying in his tights enough to kindle passions of all women, could also lead. The chronicles of the City of Munster describe in 1599 the arrival of 11 Englishmen, all young and lively fellows, led by an elderly man who managed everything. On five days they acted five comedies; between the acts, or whilst they changed their costumes, a clown 'made many antics and pranks in German'; they also sang and danced. The charge was a shilling, so under license of the town council they must have made a good sum. At Nuremberg and Augsberg theatres were built in the South, whilst at Ulm the players used 'the shoehouse'; but it was not unknown for burghers to complain of indecency and withold per-mission.

Maurice of Hesse Cassel proved a good lord to Robert Browne, sending him into England on commissions in April 1595 and again in 1597; in 1596 he was in Prague, but in 1598 he took leave for Heidelberg.

The players had their ups and downs. Richard Jones, a musician and fellow of Alleyn and of Robert Browne, surrendered to Alleyn his share in their joint stock of apparel, books and instruments on 3 January 1588–9, for the very large sum of £37.10s, yet in an undated letter he asks Alleyn for a loan of £3 to get his suit and cloak out of pawn to go abroad 'with Mr Browne and the company' – but he adds 'not by his means, for he is put to half a share and to stop here, for they are all against him going'.[3] In 1620 his second wife, Harris Jones, wrote to Alleyn, whilst waiting to join her husband in Warsaw, to ask his help.

However, as Thomas Dekker was to put it, 'We can be bankrupts (say the players) on this side, and gentlemen of a company beyond the seas'.[4]

In 1592 Fynes Moryson gave a most disparaging account of the

English players he saw at Frankfurt, which nevertheless pays an involuntary tribute to their acting skills:

> I remember that when some of our cast and despised players came from England into Germany and played at Frankfurt in the time of the Mart, having neither a complete number of actors nor any good apparel, nor any ornament of the stage, yet the Germans, not understanding a word they said, flocked wonderfully to see their gesture and action, rather than hear them, pronouncing English which they understood not, and pronouncing pieces and patches of English plays, which myself and some English men there present could not hear without great tediousness.

It is evident that the dialogue was made up of remembered imperfect scraps from actors' memorial resources; apparel and ornaments are expected by the travellers· such a group may be compared with the eleven young men who appeared at Munster seven years later under their elderly leader.

The chief advantage to continental players of the better kind lay in close connection with the royal and ducal courts. This archaic status of the actor, vestigial in England, remained in Brunswick, Hesse Cassel and at the courts of Denmark and the Vasas. Players were given annual contracts. This would enable Robert Browne and Richard Jones to maintain a brave stance when they returned to London as 'servants to his Highness the Landgrave of Hesse Cassel' whilst perhaps abroad they used their status as servants of the Lord High Admiral to inflate their demands to their new patrons. The extraordinary tones of flattery with which they addressed the burghers can be found in Limon's extracts from the State Archives at Dantzig — 'Herr Burgomaster, Noble, Honourable, Famous and Wise, Praiseworthy Magnificences' opens one request — which was turned down.[5]

Jones and Browne, unlike others, never seem to have severed their connections with the London stage. Jones is mentioned frequently in Henslowe's *Diary*. Kemp, who also worked with Alleyn 1589–1592, first went abroad as the Earl of Leicester's player at Elsinore in 1586 and appeared with his troupe at Dantzig in 1597, although he also played in Shakespeare's *Much Ado About Nothing* generally dated 1598. He left the Lord Chamberlain's Company in 1599, selling his shares, and in February 1600 performed his dance to Norwich, after which at some point he claimed to have danced over the Alps.

Kemp was the embodiment of the successful clown and his fame was international. He was a swordsman and wrote his own comedies as well singing, dancing, 'gurning' (making faces through a curtain, or in a horse collar). He ended up with the breakaway group that returned from the Boar's Head in 1602 to act at the Rose for

Henslowe; the burial of a William Kempe was recorded in plague time at St Saviour's on 2 November 1603. His tradition remained abroad among the actors.

Here there are occasional liftings of the curtain to show some particular scene; much the most detailed is contained in a letter about the visit of John Greene and his troupe to Graz in Styria during the winter of 1607–08, written by the Archduchess Maria Magdalena.

John Green had appeared in Browne's troupe, at Lille in 1603 and at Frankfurt in 1606, together with another well-known English actor, Robert Ledbetter, but by spring 1607 he had succeeded to the leadership. He may have been the brother of Thomas Greene, the clown, and leader of the Boar's Head team, who remembered a brother John in his will (with a third brother Jeffrey). If so, he was by 1607–8 also the brother-in-law of Suzanne, widow of Robert Browne of Shoreditch. His repertory was taken from the Henslowe-Alleyn stock and was very old fashioned by Jacobean standards. But his greatest success, *Nobody and Somebody*, had belonged to the Queen's Men and was entered in the Stationers' Register for March 16th, i.e. Queen Anne's Men.

Had the letter written on 28 February 1608 by the Archduchess Maria Magdalena of Habsburg concerned the Globe, the Fortune or the Blackfriars, it would have been celebrated as a prime English theatrical source for actors. She was 18 years old, betrothed to Cosimo de Medici, Duke of Florence, writing to her brother the future Emperor Ferdinand II. She had become a fan of John Green 'the fellow with the long red hair who always played the small violin'; a long postscript recounts with fond partiality a mortal quarrel in which he engaged. Drinking and swearing eternal friendship in a tavern with a Frenchman and a German, Greene refused to return a ring their hostess, 'that bad villainess', had bestowed on him; next morning the men fought with rapier and dagger. Greene disarmed the Frenchman but when the fight resumed, the Frenchman ran beserk; Greene stabbed him through the right eye into the brain, whilst before riding off, a companion of the Frenchman stabbed Greene in the breast. The Archduchess's account ends with her royal mother (a formidable matriarch) taking the wounded man into her own palace. The rest, no doubt fearing reprisals, wished to depart. They went to the Spanish Netherlands.

Such violence was not unprecedented; as early as 1579 four English musicians and actors arrived at the Danish court, residing till in 1586 one Thomas Bull killed a fellow countryman in a quarrel about a girl. He was beheaded. In spite of his wound in 1608 Greene recovered and his activities continued till 1626 when he is heard of in

Dresden and Frankfurt. It is not impossible however that his name became attached to a company and remained after he had withdrawn, for companies of 'English comedians' were increasingly made up of Germans, who retained the style.

In the year of the festivities at Graz, Robert Browne of Southwark was bequeathed by the famous comedian Will Sly his share in the Globe, with remembrances to his wife Cicely and daughter Jane. Jane married Robert Reynolds, of the Queen's Men, the most famous of all overseas comic actors who wrote comedies of Pickleherring. In 1610 Browne turns up with Richard Jones as one of the patentees of the King's Revels company; in April 1612 he wrote to Alleyn to recommend a young actor named Rose who had joined the troupe at the Fortune, and to beg the place of a gatherer there for Rose's wife, assuring Alleyn that both were trustworthy, the husband being 'an old servant of mine' (a Rowland Rose, servant to Samwell had been at the old Boar's Head). In 1620 Richard Jones's wife wrote to Alleyn from Danzig where she was waiting to join her husband, about her property, the Leopard's Head in Shoreditch, which had been part of her dowry. Limon claims the town theatre of Danzig (built by 1612) copied the Fortune Theatre.

It was not till 1624 that Richard Jones, having tried to reinstate himself in England, confessed to the Duke of Pomerania that he was 'an old man and tired of travelling' and, therefore, wanted to settle there, but at the death of his patron in 1626 he returned to London, the year of Alleyn's death on 25 November. Bentley records him at Worcester in 1630, where with two others he was indicted for forging a licence to exhibit a show.

Thus, the indomitables disappeared in the first years of King Charles; Robert Browne of Southwark had died in 1622, and his widow Cicely married again, for she is named executrix in the will of her son Robert, who died in the next year, 1623, as Cicely Robins. He lived in Clerkenwell, the new actors' district, but asked for burial in Shoreditch. William, the actor son of Robert Browne of Stepney, made his will 23 October 1634, which is printed by Bentley, leaving all management to his mother Suzanne. It asked for burial in St James's Clerkenwell 'near to my father Greene'. But his elder brother, the third Robert Browne, the Haberdasher, survived till 1666. It was he whom 'father Greene' had apprenticed to William Holden in May 1611.

The actors' troupes that expanded in Germany during the early seventeenth century – including by 1615, John Spencer's, Robert Archer's, Ralph Reeves' – were outshone by such famous musicians as Farnaby the younger, John Bull and Dowland. Some may have secured patronage through the family links of the Stuarts – James's queen, playloving Anne, was sister to the King of Denmark, to the Duchess of Brunswick and to the Electress of Saxony. Troupes would be lent for a family occasion, like a wedding. The Habsburgs, of course, were everywhere; and like the musicians, John Greene was a Catholic, or at least professed to be one. The Archduchess Maria Magdalena records that he went to confession after his affray and he is depicted on a presentation Manuscript of *Nobody and Somebody*, now in the Vienna State archives, with his long red hair and carrying a rosary. He signs the fulsome dedication 'JohGrene, Nob. Anglus'. John Spencer's company was recorded as being converted en masse at Cologne in 1616; there were 24 members of the group who were persuaded by a Franciscan.[6]

Spencer holds the record for public takings in a single day at Regenberg in 1613, 500 florins.

One of the most valuable features of the Archduchess's letter is the listing of the plays performed. These were all by 1608 extremely old-fashioned and consisted of well-worn favourites from the Henslowe-Alleyn repertory. Of the old play *Dives and Lazarus* she reassures her brother:

> I can't begin to tell your Dearness how beautiful this was, for there wasn't a bit of lovemaking in it, they moved me so deeply, they acted so well. Surely they must be good actors.

This play is mentioned among the repertory of the players in *The Book of Sir Thomas More*, and later appeared as a motion, or puppet show. In 1593 Robert Browne had been playing *Gammer Gurton's Needle*, a farce from 1553. Maria Magdalena also mentions in 1608 'a play about a king of England who is in love with a goldsmith's wife' – Heywood's *King Edward IV*; 'a play about a noble lady of Antwerp' – *Friar Rush; Old Fortunatus; Dr Faustus;* 'a play of a Jew'; one on 'a king of Cyprus and the Duke of Venice' (printed in German in 1620); *The Virgin Martyr* and, in honour of the Medici, *The Great Duke of Florence,* but above all, recently printed, the old *Nobody and Somebody,* which proved adaptable to local satire. This was the play chosen by Greene for his grand presentation copy to the presiding lord, the Archduke Maximilian, brother to the Archduchess.

This play may be the lost *Albere Galles* of Henslowe (1602), but when printed in 1606 was described as being from the Queen's Men so it was evidently in repertory at the Boar's Head. It is out of the same stable as Robert Wilson's *The Cobbler's Prophecy* and *Edmund Ironside* – the farcical story of an imaginary early English king, mixing secular morality and satire on court and country. It appears as a burlesque of *King Henry VI*, Henry becoming Elidure, his termagent Queen replacing Queen Margaret, his ludicrous younger brothers replacing the warring factions of Lancaster and York. The villain Archigalle is supported by Sychophant, who is kin to Wilson's villain Dissimulation, and whose one good deed is to reconcile the warring queens of Elidure and Archigalle into Unity.

The continental text exists in three versions, which read like very bad Quartoes. The constant play upon Nobody and Somebody would be tedious unless these morality figures had some topical application through a cunning manipulator. In the English text of 1605 the frontispiece presents two Harlequin figures, each carrying a bat, one with breeches from neck to knee, the other with doublet from neck to knee. Complaints are spread against Nobody for relieving the poor, helping distressed prisoners and so on, whilst Somebody attributes all his worst deeds to Nobody; but 'Somebody will at length be proved a knave'.

In 1602 John Marston had dedicated his *Antonio and Mellida* to 'the only rewarder and most just promoter of virtuous merits, the most honourably renowned Nobody, bounteous Maecenas of poetry and Lord Protector of oppressed innocence'. In *The Fawn* he was to praise ironically German clowns, saying of the court fool of Urbino 'Nay, tis a pure fool, I can tell you; he was bred up in Germany' (II.i.321). A version of this play appeared in Germany the same year and was still being played by John Greene in his last appearance in 1626.

The growing control of London players and playhouses between 1597 and the new restriction of licensing to royalty under the Stuarts, must have accelerated a move to the alternative European market, seen in the arrival of Spencer, Greene and others round 1606, with the extension of their travels, the cultivation of plays in German, and growing regularity of programmes and tour routes.

The effect of foreign troupes upon London playwrights and productions must in 1608 have been quite strong. For example, *The Revenger's Tragedy* (1607), if by Cyril Tourneur, could have been influenced in its markedly archaic and moralistic basis – the gulling of the Duchess's son could have come out of *Nobody and Somebody* – by Tourneur's residence at Brill as a member of Vere's garrison. The songs, added much later to Heywood's *Rape of Lucrece*, were noted as being by 'a stranger'. A *Rape of Lucrece* was played at Danzig in 1619 by an amalgamated troupe of Browne and Greene. In 1621 at Dresden *The Massacre at Paris*, *Tamburlaine* and *Nobody and Somebody* were given.[7] Some plays were published in German texts in 1620 (see *Annals* pp. 202–03). The best known in this country is the later, eighteenth-century version of *Hamlet*, *Der*

Bestraft Brudermord, where, in a scene unknown to Shakespeare but which perhaps came from the *Ur-Hamlet*, the prince stationed prisoner between two of the pirates who have captured him and are about to shoot him, at the critical moment ducks so that they shoot each other, a stage trick mocked in *King John* (II.i.413).

Greene played in German; the early texts in English had exploited the open-air style of Peele and Marlowe, that repetitive patterned speech where words are put over against the noise of crowds and battle scenes on stage. 'Doublets' became a special feature, as Brennecke observed:

> One device which seems to have been used . . . was that of immediately following a word with its synonym. The idea seems to have been that if the audience could not catch the meaning the first time, possibly it could when repeated with, a variant.[8]

Peele would simply repeat the phrase itself with variations, as 'damned be her charms, damned be her cursed charms'; this style had suited Alleyn. The German *Titus Andronicus*, based on Shakespeare but even more horrific, contained such doublets as 'concord and harmony', 'elect me and accept me', 'dissension and strife'. Shakespeare had indeed used doublets but developed the form into such memorable uses as 'the dark backward and abysm of time' and 'the expectancy and rose of the fair state'.

It would appear that the travelling players in *Hamlet*, who come to Elsinore from 'the city', might well represent, not country touring in England but, touring overseas; and that the best of the overseas actors became prosperous and famous. But to Shakespeare, 'their residence, both in reputation and profit, was better', as Hamlet says (II.ii.328–29).

Robert Browne and Thomas Greene of the Boar's Head and Red Bull

The story of the Boar's Head Theatre in Whitechapel (1595–1605) is preserved by the legal records of a struggle for what was evidently a rich prize. The shape and dimensions of this inn-yard theatre can also be reconstructed, but the relation of the story to the overseas players has not been taken up.

The eastern suburbs beyond Aldgate received sailors from ships anchored below London Bridge and overseas visitors, eager for entertainment after voyaging. The area was well supplied with inns and inn yards were easy to control; the inn itself could accommodate the players and their properties as well as spectators in the rooms off galleries surrounding the yard. John Alleyn, brother of Edward, who kept the family inn in Bishopsgate, a servant himself of the Lord Admiral, held a stock of instruments and apparel. Kemp also kept an inn. The Boar's Head has been located more or less exactly on the site of Petticoat Lane; in its oblong yard wagons bringing up wool cloth from East Anglia for export had once lodged. Plays were recorded at the Boar's Head as early as 1557, and in Stepney in 1567. John Brayne, Burbage's brother-in-law, a grocer of Bucklersbury, had set up a stage in the yard of the Red Lion, eight years before he collaborated with Burbage for the theatre at Shoreditch. Their quarrel foreshadows that at the Boar's Head; those prepared to invest money in theatre needed collaboration, but the history could be stormy.

A theatre was begun in the yard of the Boar's Head when plays restarted in 1594 and the Shoreditch Theatre became the home of the Lord Chamberlain's Men. A haberdasher with overseas trade connections, Oliver Woodliffe, who with his wife took a 21 years' lease from Lady Day 1595, persuaded Richard Samwell, the innkeeper, to supervise the erection of the playhouse. In April 1598 Samwell took over the inn and in August 1599, by verbal contract, the theatre, only in three months' time to sublet the theatre to Robert Browne.

The Privy Council's action in closing City inns to players, two years earlier in 1597, had enhanced the value of a site just beyond the boundary. Woodliffe, who still lived in the inn and retained a small part of it, during 1598 had been abroad on business; but when he returned in 1599 to find Samwell had turned to Robert Browne for assistance, he himself turned to none other than Francis Langley, who, defeated at the Swan, was ready for another venture. Robert Browne had advanced £200 towards erecting the enlarged galleries in the yard and improving the stage; for the lease he paid £360, less what he had advanced, and moved his company of players in, as well as residing himself. Thus, three of the disputants were in residence there. Their families joined in the affrays that followed, even babes in arms were present. Woodliffe was fraudulent in disposing of his lease first to Samwell, then to Langley. The question turned on the ownership of the yard and the galleries that now stood there. Woodliffe and Langley harrassed Samwell by every legal trick they knew but they did not disturb Browne, Samwell's subtenant, since his players were the source of coveted revenue. A vast network of cross-suits and physical forays followed, which have been disentangled by Herbert Berry.[9] Queen's Bench, Chancery, the Court of Requests and Star Chamber were all involved.

The reasons for suggesting that Robert Browne of the Boar's Head

was the player who first went overseas are the large sum of money he
was prepared to put down, his association with Woodliffe's trade
gild, the Haberdashers' (to which his son was apprenticed and to
which, if he were Alleyn's stepbrother, his father had belonged), the
knowledge which an overseas player might be presumed to have of
the potentialities of the area – the players now followed merchants to
German ports – Konigsberg, Elbing, Danzig, Wolgast in the Baltic,
as well as the more accessible regions of Brunswick and Saxony.
Thus, such a player would be able to attract clientele. In 1597 Robert
Browne ceased to be employed by the Landgrave of Hesse Cassel, but
an actor named Robert Browne was at Frankfurt in August of 1599,
three months before the bargain with Samwell at the Boar's Head.

The disappearance of the Lord Chamberlain's Men to the Globe
had left the home market of the eastern and northeastern suburbs
open. The excitement in the London theatres was at its greatest
round Christmas. Whilst Alleyn in December 1599 was proposing to
move his troupe to the Fortune, away from Bankside, Browne began
recruiting from them. John Duke, an experienced player, and Thomas Heywood, a popular actor-dramatist, came over and Browne
bound them by the same kind of indenture that Langley had introduced at the Swan to play only for him. Browne succeeded in getting
invitations to Court in the winter of 1599–1600 and also in 1600–
1601. He gained the patronage of William Earl of Derby, brother
and successor to Ferdinando, Lord Strange, the fifth Earl, an earlier
patron. A letter (undated) from the Countess to her uncle, Robert
Cecil, Secretary of the Privy Council, pleads for the intrusive third
troupe, by the Order of 19 February 1958 rendered illegal in
London:

> Being importuned by my lord to entreat your favour that his man Browne
> with his company may not be barred from their accustomed playing
> whereof they have consumed the better part of their substance, if so vain a
> matter would not seem troublesome to you, I could desire that your
> furtherance might be a means to uphold them, for that my lord taketh
> delight in them, it will keep him from more prodigal courses.[10]

In June 1599 the Earl of Derby had been reported to be 'busy penning
. . . for the common players', but in November 1599 it was heard
that 'Lord Derby hath put up the children of Paul's to his great pains
and charge'. By 22 June 1600, the Privy Council forbade all performances in common inns and restricted acting to twice weekly.

The Countess of Derby was the daughter of the Earl of Oxford and
his name was next used; the Privy Council restored the ban on 22
June 1600, especially any plays in common inns. But early in 1601

Browne rented the Boar's Head to a group known as Lord Worcester's Men, formed by amalgamation with Oxford's. The Earl of
Worcester, like Oxford an old man, had been Browne's patron long
ago in 1593. He had now succeeded the disgraced Earl of Essex as
Master of the Horse, becoming thereby a member of the Privy
Council, so his name was worth invoking for official recognition,
and it was as Lord Worcester's Men that the troupe was licensed by
the Privy Council in March 1602. This third troupe had been strictly
included both in February 1598 and in June 1600; on the second
occasion performance is limited to twice a week in each house. There
were now six theatres in all (Globe, Rose, Swan on Bankside, Boar's
Head, Curtain and Fortune on the north bank) as well as the two
revived hall theatres for choristers.

Browne had enlarged the galleries at the Boar's Head, improved
the original freestanding stage and, presumably, bought an expensive wardrobe, aiming at becoming the kind of actor-manager that
the Alleyn-Henslowe combination stood for. Langley seized the
chance to muscle in, offering Woodliffe £400, but also extracting
from him a bond in return; he paid down £100 cash.

But Browne and the players quarrelled. By autumn of 1601 they
had started a Chancery suit against him, which smouldered till May
1602, when Browne had Duke and Heywood attached by the Sheriff
of London. The Lord Keeper threw this quarrel out as 'no meet
matter for this court' but Worcester's Men, as they had now by
licence liberty to play, moved off to Henslowe's Rose.

At one point in this bewildering series of moves, in February 1602,
the Sheriff of Surrey was ordered to attach Robert Browne at the suit
of Oliver Woodliffe; this would suggest that Robert Browne of
Southwark was somehow involved, for Browne clung to the Boar's
Head, although this troupe had moved off, thus destroying the value
of the northern playhouse. Two months later Browne's son was
baptised in the parish church of Whitechapel, so the redoubtable
Suzanne must have been still in residence. Samwell, the most vic-
timised of the four, expertly harrassed in constant arrests by the
venial officers of the Marshalsea, after bringing a suit against his old
partner Browne, had died before the summer of 1601. Langley, who
had been forced to sell his Manor of Paris Garden, was buried in St
Saviour's, Southwark 9 July 1602 and a year later, on 30 July 1603 at
St Mary Matfellon, Oliver Woodliffe. The plague had struck London, theatres had been closed in March 1603 on the death of the
Queen. All that Woodliffe had been entitled to from the theatre was
half the gallery receipts from those built against the long western
wing of the courtyard, which he reckoned at about £200 a year. In
reply to a request from Woodliffe, Browne said that between

Michaelmas 1602 and March 1603 this would not amount to £6 in all.

At this point Worcester's Men made a brief appearance overseas. 'We are like so many starved snakes . . . nobody comes at us, not a gentleman' as Histrio laments in *Poetaster* (III.i). It is thought that Browne fell into the hands of a moneylender, Israel Jordan; no wonder he died poor, as Mrs Alleyn unfeelingly reports. But he did not go into the country, she added; he clung to the Boar's Head, with the fascination of a gambler who has staked all, until he succumbed to the plague and joined his enemy in the charnel house of St Mary Matfellon 16 October 1603, before the start of the Christmas season. The lawsuits lapsed as all contestants were dead. Worcester's, now Queen Anne's Men, soon returned to the Boar's Head, which they said they liked better than the Rose; the posthumous daughter of Robert and Suzanne Browne was christened Anne for the Queen and Suzanne married the leader of the troupe, the 'lean clown' Thomas Greene, thus taking back to the players any claims she might have.

The Queen's Men became a stable company and outpaced Alleyn's troupe at the Fortune, now Prince Henry's Men, whom, however, they pursued when in 1606 they moved to a new theatre also, it appears, in a converted innyard. The Red Bull, in the parish of St James, Clerkenwell, became their home for eleven years. Thomas Heywood was their dramatist, a full sharer was the innkeeper, one Aaron Holland. But probably, as at the Globe, the players were in control themselves.

Two plays only from the Boar's Head survive in print – *The Thracian Wonder* and *How a Man May choose a Good Wife from a Bad*, together with some quotations and a handful from the Red Bull – late texts of Marlowe's plays among them. Only four plays out of five hundred printed in the reign of Charles I come from the Red Bull.

Worcester's Men appeared at Frankfurt for Easter 1603 in the company of Robert Browne, who had been there for the Fair in 1601, 1602; he was to appear there again in 1606 and 1607 after which his appearances cease, for a full decade. Never again was he employed by the noble men; and it may be that his name remained for a troupe no longer under his control. Names were used as labels of prestige; even at home in 1607 Thomas Greene paid the old clown John Shanks to desist from using the name of Queen Anne's Men for a group with which he was touring, which he could do by exemplification – that is, producing the copy of the original licence carried by each original member mentioned as enrolled. The descendents of both Robert Brownes came together in the Red Bull's parish, St James Clerkenwell, in the time of Charles I. Their boldly spectacular style, learnt on the continent, was re-emplanted here; farce, jigs, plays of adventure of travel were staple. The troupe became more famous for this style than the old Alleyn-Henslowe group at the Fortune, of whom the records are even more meagre, since all their playbooks were destroyed in a disastrous fire in 1622. After 1608, nothing is heard of the Boar's Head.

The fraternity of the actors appears on every hand; in 1602, or thereabouts, when Henslowe revived *Tamar Cham* its 'plot' includes in the final procession as supers 'Old Browne' and 'Ned Browne' – who sounds like a boy, but Edward was one of the family names (and was the name of Lord Worcester himself).

Sly's bequest to Robert Bròwne of Southwark, his wife and daughter, came in 1608; the testimonies to Thomas Greene include that of his stepson, William Browne, who in 1634 wished to be buried next to 'my father Greene'; he also left twenty shillings to his fellow actors to buy mourning ribbons 'in remembrance of me'. In 1611 John Cooke wrote a play named for the clown, *Greene's Tu Quoque*. The catch phrase ('You're another') is of the same kind as Lavatch's serviceable phrases in *All's Well* 'O, Lord Sir' and 'Spare not me'.

Red Bull plays reached Germany; such were Heywood's on classical themes: *The Iron Age*, on The Destruction of Troy and *The Silver Age* on Amphytrion – spectacles that could shrink to motions at fairs.

The Red Bull was the only London playhouse which was not demolished in the Civil War; the only one to evolve a distinctive style and a stable tradition out of the effervescent late Elizabethan situation. It was recalled by Dryden:

> here a course of mirth, there another of sadness and passion, and a third of honour and a duel; thus, in two hours and a half we run through all the fits of Bedlam . . . our poets present you the play and the farce together; and our stages still retain somewhat of the original civility of the Red Bull . . .
> *Atque ursum et pugiles media inter carmina poscunt.*
>
> (*Essay of Dramatic Poesy*)

As a schoolboy the Restoration playwright Thomas Killigrew frequented the Red Bull and, when the actors cried 'Who will be a devil and he shall see the play for nothing', would volunteer to run round throwing fireworks and so got to see plays (Pepys' *Diary* October 1660).

Their affection balances the quarrels about the Boar's Head, where Francis Langley expertly harrassed his opponent with fictitious debts, though Samwell held out for a full year; Browne understood far less the harsh world of London sharks, which almost calls to mind the Chancery fog of Dickens's *Bleak House*, than the merchants Woodliffe and Langley, who eventually outplayed him. The experienced actor was needed to hold a troupe together, but in these unstable conditions he could not do so.

Later still, Browne's residuary claims were to prove the downfall of the Red Bull troupe, as C.J. Sisson showed long ago.[11] Browne of Stepney was able and experimental and led the way for others more fortunate than himself. The continental players probably reached their apogee in the decade 1605–15; they persisted even after the Thirty Years' War in 1620 drove them out of some accustomed territories. Two or three troupes are heard of as late as 1658, long after the theatres of London had been closed by the Parliamentarians. Indeed, theatres were about to reopen in welcome to the patronage of the Merry Monarch, Charles II.

Shakespeare's own company, the Lord Chamberlain's Men, had played in the Cross Keys Inn, in Gracechurch Street which was their winter quarters in the years 1594–95. It was probably smaller than the Boar's Head, its yard being in the City walls, but, presumably, it had a moveable stage, normal galleries and a view from the rooms. The Lord Chamberlain had gained special leave for his company from the City Fathers, who had been forbidding plays in the inns since the mid-century; one such Act led in 1576 to the building of the theatre; the death of the Lord Chamberlain in 1596 banished the players from the Cross Keys. Blackfriars, bought in 1596, may have been seen as an improvement on the Cross Keys. The story of this company, however, is a more complicated and oft-told tale.

Notes

Herbert Berry, *The Boar's Head Playhouse* (London and Washington D.C., Associated University Presses and Folger Shakespeare Library, 1986) summarises his previous work and takes issue in Appendix 9, on the subject of the two Robert Brownes with Willem Schrickx, who has written in *Shakespeare Survey* on several occasions. My own views differ from both. Jerzy Limon, *Gentlemen of a Company* (Cambridge, Cambridge University Press, 1985) on foreign travel, deals with northern and eastern Europe.

1 R.A. Foakes and R.T. Rickert (eds), *Henslowe's Diary* (Cambridge, Cambridge University Press, 1961), p. 277.
2 *Ibid.* p. 297.
3 *Ibid.* p. 274.
4 Jerzy Limon, *Op. cit.* p. 5.
5 *Ibid.* pp. 52–53.
6 *Ibid.* p. 122.

7 Continental plays are listed in Harbage and Schoenbaum's *Annals of English Drama* (London, Methuen 1964) (supplementary list k) and include more of Marlowe, *Orlando Furioso*, Heywood, *Hamlet*, *The Spanish Tragedy*, *Romeo and Juliet*, 'Pyramus and Thisbe', *Julius Caesar*, *Lear*, *The Merchant of Venice*, *Titus Andronicus*.

8 E. Brennecke, *Shakespeare in Germany* (Chicago, Chicago University Press, 1964).

9 Herbert Berry, *Op. cit.*

10 E.K. Chambers, *The Elizabethan Stage*, 4 vols (Oxford, Oxford University Press, 1923), vol. II Lord Derby's Men.

11 C.J. Sisson, 'The Red Bull Company and the Importunate Widow'. *Shakespeare Survey*, 7, 1954.

XII.

The Main Collaborators: Shakespeare and his Company

James Burbage Sons and Co.

For the last hundred years Shakespeare's theatre has been surveyed in detail. The books are a library in themselves. But the company which surrounded him as his human environment remain shadowy. Richard Burbage, his leading man and guider of the enterprise, the clowns Kemp and Armin have been studied, and everyone knows the names of Heminges and Condell, editors of the First Folio – but no more than the names.

However faintly, the image of that little society may be guessed by its persistence over sixty and more years from the 1570s to 1642. Other groups surrounding it were of comparative but minor sort; persistence is not a feature of play groups. The others emphasize its structure, but also demonstrate its distinction – which was built up by Burbage and Shakespeare. Richard's brother Cuthbert and Shakespeare's brother Edmund were important and unimportant members, yet these names suggest the spirit of community in the enterprise that supported the writer and which must have been further enhanced by familiar supporters in the audience. Even the dimmest vision of that dynamic activity that generated the plays' life makes them different from other Elizabethan writing, even that of Shakespeare in his narrative poetry. Relations of the narratives with the early plays are obvious; *Titus Andronicus* and *The Rape of Lucrece*, like William and Edmund Shakespeare, are siblings. But a line may be traced from *Titus Andronicus* to *King Lear*, whilst *The Rape of Lucrece* remains with the laments of other poets, with Spenser and the Spenserians. The wanderings of Spenser's knights in his greatest poem show only a shadow world; Shakespeare's world of being is born and every day until now is reborn, and every time differently – as it was differently created in the spirit to that original group – engendered by the possibilities within it.

The mutual kindling of Shakespeare and Burbage can be guessed by the new life that today springs, not only from Gielgud, Olivier or Sher, but from students in Spain or Shanghai. The internal perform-ance enjoyed by every reader is essential to every audience; by suggesting the original conditions in human terms. It is necessary to remember the alternative groups and their practice. Shakespeare, a fountain of life, released the spring within others for a collaborative venture, where no one can say 'This is mine' or 'That is yours'. Even the best plays surviving from the other companies indicate the immense gap; and there are few of any kind.

Shakespeare's power to give his actors something to work on, even in the smallest speaking parts (consider Constable Antony Dull), if due to his own position as a supporting actor (as were Ben Jonson, Heywood and Brome), developed uniquely through his membership of a uniquely stable company, grouped round the Burbage family, and more especially round Richard Burbage (1567–1619), the lead-ing actor from the early 1590s and, after his father's death in 1597, theatre owner; but unlike his great competitor, Edward Alleyn of the Rose, all his life a working member of the company.

The formation of James Burbage Sons and Co. (which would be the modern style of the Lord Chamberlain's Men) meant that from July 1594 Shakespeare as a sharer became 'subdued to what he worked in, like the dyer's hand'.

James Burbage from 1567 had been investing in London theatres, when the Red Lion in Stepney was made an inn-yard theatre. Its upper platform was provided by a moveable 'turret' planted on stage, like the 'castle' wheeled into a hall, or for a street pageant, which had been found from the fourteenth century. The Red Lion had been financed by his brother-in-law, John Brayne, who also backed the Shoreditch Theatre in 1576 which stood near Burbage's home in Shoreditch, in the grounds of a former Benedictine nunnery. In 1584 he claimed protection against the City as 'Lord Hunsdon's Man'. Perhaps he had helped the Lord Chamberlain to erect tempor-ary stages; by trade he was a joiner.

The core of what later became his company had been in the service of Ferdinando Lord Strange, who for six months succeeded his father as Earl of Derby and then mysteriously died in April 1594, just as the London theatres were reopening after two years' closure for plague. For a brief season they had joined with Alleyn and Henslowe's company at a little theatre in Newington Butts, a mile to the South of the Thames, where they gave *Titus Andronicus*, *The Taming of the Shrew* and a version of *Hamlet* (possibly Kyd's) for a few weeks in

June 1594. Previously, with Strange's Men on 21 April 1591, Henslowe had gained the large daily share of 33 shillings for 'Harey the VI'; Richard Burbage had acted with great success as Richard III. From May 1593 the company included two famous clowns, Will Kemp and Thomas Pope, with John Heminges, Augustine Phillips and George Bryant. Lord Strange's Men had been traditionally given to 'activities'. They regrouped after Derby's death as Lord Hunsdon's Men, with James Burbage at the centre. Such patronage gave them the most powerful protection, for, as Lord Chamberlain, Hunsdon was in control of all court entertainment through the Master of the Revels. Thus, Hunsdon was really a more accessible advocate than the Queen herself, as being more directly concerned with ordering and arranging. A friend at court, a leading member of the Privy Council, ensured the company's stability. Most companies were volatile in membership and shifting in venue. Though James Burbage appears to have been a quarrelsome and not very scrupulous man, the gradual tightening of control of London players during the 1590s favoured this particular fellowship.

At Christmas 1594 Shakespeare, Kemp and Richard Burbage had been payees for the court performances, but John Heminges then took over this responsibility, remaining payee and business manager till his death in 1630. Heminges had married the widow of a famous early actor, Knell; his son William succeeded as playwright. He became a sidesman of St Mary Aldermanbury; about 1601 he retired from acting but remained with the group and was trusted by the Master of the Revels. It is thought he played old men, but the part that seems best designed for him is that of the Earl of Kent.

Kemp, Pope, Phillips, Bryant and Cowley had been with Derby's Men. It was essential for a company to have at least one famous clown and, if possible, a duo. Kemp and Pope played comic leads; Pope also took military roles and had travelled abroad. He lived in St Saviour's parish and, though unmarried, appeared to have taken several apprentices, to whom at his death in February 1604 he left both armour and his wearing apparel. He appeared as joint payee with Heminges from time to time. Augustine Phillips, who died a year after Pope, in an exceptionally detailed will remembered the members of the company, beginning with Shakespeare and ending with his two apprentices. He had appeared before the Privy Council in 1601 to clear the company of suspicion in their playing of *King Richard II* on the eve of the Essex rebellion. His sister Elizabeth had married Pope's apprentice, Gough. Whilst Kemp departed in 1599 and Bryant joined the Royal Household some time before 1598, close-knit ties of intermarriage and neighbourhood held many. Shakespeare never settled in this way. In 1596, the year in which his family obtained a coat of arms (and the year in which Shakespeare's only son died), he left the parish of St Helen's Bishopsgate and moved to the Bankside, an advance guard for the company's collective move to the Globe three years later.

In 1602–4, however, he was lodging with a Huguenot family of Mountjoy in the northwest corner of the City, at Silver Street in the parish of St Olave's, Cripplegate. This was also an actors' quarter and not far from St Mary Aldermanbury where lived Heminges and Condell, the two sharers who edited his plays after his death and who, together with Burbage, were remembered in his last will. Shakespeare was approached by the Mountjoys in the delicate matter of their daughter's betrothal to their apprentice and the fixing of the dowry. It does not appear that Shakespeare took apprentices; but his youngest brother joined him as a player.

It was again in the autumn of 1596 that William Wayte, a stepson of William Gardiner, Surrey justice of the peace, had sworn the peace against William Shakespeare and two women in Southwark, conjectured to be part of some quarrel connected with the theatres (see above p. 140). Gardiner was an enemy of the notorious Francis Langley, the builder of the Swan Theatre on Bankside – had Langley been trying to entice the Lord Chamberlain's Men to his new house, knowing they had problems with the lease of the ground for the Shoreditch Theatre? The rent they had paid was £14 a year and it was for little more (£14.10s a year) that in December 1598 the company gained a 31-year ground-lease for the land on which they constructed the Globe.

Their steady rise in confidence through a period of uncertainty is apparent. The death of the Lord Chamberlain on 22 July 1596 had dealt a severe blow, since his son, who continued as patron, was not immediately elected to his father's office. According to Nashe, they were in uncertainty till March 1597, when the second Lord Hunsdon became Lord Chamberlain. That same year saw the beginning of the quarrel between James Burbage and his ground landlord; the lease of the theatre was due to expire in April 1597, by which time James Burbage was dead. Shoreditch was left to his eldest son, Cuthbert, Blackfriars to Richard. Here, in the 1580s, choristers had played Lyly's comedies; in February 1596, James Burbage had bought for £600 from Sir William More the Great Hall, used once as a parliament chamber for the cause of Henry VIII's divorce. Burbage erected seats for a theatre, but the noble inhabitants of the place banned it by appeal to the Privy Council against a 'common playhouse' – eventually leading Richard to offer it in 1599 for a later generation of choristers.

The build-up had indeed been steady, the setbacks surmounted. By

1598 Shakespeare's name had appeared on the title page of three plays, and his works had been listed by Francis Meres in *Palladis Tamia, or Wits Treasury*. He had purchased New Place in Stratford and now led a double-centred existence; he was officially in residence there by February 1598. It was in December of that year that he, perhaps, helped to shiver the timbers of the Shoreditch Theatre, which were unbolted, borne through Bishopsgate and down to the wharf of the company's carpenter, Peter Street, to build the Globe, which by April was *'in occupatione Guilielme Shakespeare et aliorum'* (see above p. 142).

The Globe

Its very special financial aspects and the effects on the audience of its seating plan have been developed in an important article by Andrew Gurr.[1]

The Shoreditch Theatre when built became the property of the ground landlord, Giles Allen, although James Burbage had attempted to write in to the lease the right to remove what was 'a platform stage and a booth into a galleried amphitheatre' which had been anticipated at the Red Lion, more obviously moveable. Faced with losing his edifice, he hopefully sunk all his money in the Blackfriars enterprise, catering for the well-to-do who sat near – indeed, on the stage; whereas in Shoreditch, the closest places were the cheapest. Ready in November 1596, Blackfriars permission was refused him; and he died soon after. The company as sharers were brought in to stave off disaster. The removal of the timbers of the theatre was a desperate act and of doubtful legality; litigation followed for two years. The Globe, built in 28 weeks, was cheaply set up with thatched roof, which fed the fire that later destroyed the whole theatre. The Burbages' lack of cash and their close friendship with the troupe introduced a new system of finance; when they at last gained possession of the Blackfriars in 1608, Richard did not let it to another company, or keep it for himself, but admitted the sharers. The company straddled the arena and the hall type of acting.

Its new system of seating, which later became that of the modern theatres in general, prevailed; the charge was sixpence for a seat near the stage, contrasting with a penny at the Globe. Running two playhouses was an extravagant way of working; perhaps not a purely financial choice. But when a few years later, Beeston moved his players from the cheap Red Bull to the indoor and expensive Cockpit, some apprentices wrecked the new theatre. The two houses gave the King's Men good relations with a wider audience. In other theatres, any wealthy actors might be sharers, but only here the resident players become the share holders. They achieved transition to a 'private' enclosed theatre whilst also they kept the traditional structure of the Globe; the effect on acting, whether in fights or soliloquies, must have called for adaptation of the courtly kind. With two theatres must have emerged control and adjustment in style.

Hamlet and the Players

The reflection of the struggle appears in the play scenes of *Hamlet*, which were printed only in the Folio of 1623, showing all the conflict with the 'little eyasses' and the players driven out of town. *Hamlet* was, of course, a success at the Globe and the actual triumph alone would justify the ironic humour here. Burbage, playing Hamlet, was confronted by a player who was his mirror image. This scene does not include its full extent of the story in the Quarto of 1604, where the players are driven off 'by the late innovation' – and Hamlet welcomes them as giving old fashioned foil and target plays, but also asks for a very refined act.

He enquired about the boys 'How are they escoted', that is, 'Who pays the rent?' Whoever paid it in London, Richard Burbage received it! The choristers were back on the scene in Blackfriars, where they had played for Lyly – who had been quite unable to leap the gap between the hall and arena in *The Woman in the Moon*, his last play, written for public players.

The open debate, the self-knowledge and the clarification that led to the next decade are epitomised in *Hamlet*. The hack work of collaborative writers in other theatres was replaced by Shakespeare's collaboration with his actors, especially Burbage. It is noticeable that in the troupe at Elsinore was no clown; and a rebuke to the dominating clown is given to Hamlet himself in his speech to the actors.

His group had provided Shakespeare with the instrument which he could refine from the strict patterns of *King Richard III*, in four years from the duets of *The Two Gentlemen of Verona*, to those of *Romeo and Juliet*. The deep collaboration (and not only with the actors) grew from generative powers both collaborative and individual; 'I am not only witty, but the cause of wit in other men' declared Falstaff, who produced scenarios for his master. The relative isolation of earlier separate parts can be seen in *Tancred and Gismond* (revised 1591) where the star-crossed lovers never appear together; only laments and curses from Gismond and from her tyrant parent are heard, with messengers' speeches of oration. There is nothing of the tender banter of Romeo and Juliet, played perhaps by Burbage and his own apprentice. In *Hamlet* Rosencrantz's smile may be commented on by the prince who especially denounces the ranting style when 'nature's journeymen' played one of their works – presumably the earlier *Hamlet* itself – in this way. The choristers' placing is given to Rosencrantz with a lightness and cool nonchalance that disposes of pretensions really below Hamlet's courtly attention. Hamlet is more serious about the art of acting, and whilst dismissing rant, he admires the style of Marlovian tragedy in 'Aeneas' tale to Dido'. The Bad Quarto, as an actors' version of this scene, complains here that

> Novelty carries it away,
> For the principal public audience that
> Came to them, are turned to private plays
> And to the humour of children.

(Sig. E. 3)

The part Shakespeare played by tradition is the Ghost, whose first scene suits the big open stage, his second the indoor 'private' style. Jonson's Inductions, commentaries, and caricature give the background here and deserve to be printed with *Hamlet*. His *Apologetical Dialogue,* appended to *Poetaster* was suppressed and appeared only in his own folio of 1616. Jonson's fireworks were really for print; he is pleading for drama as literature. As Anne Barton observed, his first satire 'Comes close to being crushed by the insupportable weight of its own commentary'[2] but Tucca and Histrio offer burlesque:

Tucca: I would fain come with my cockatrice one day and see a play, if I knew where there were a good bawdy one; but they say you have nothing but Humours, Revels and Satires, that gird and fart at the time, you slave.

Histrio: No, I assure you, Captain, not we. They are on the other side of Tiber; we have as much ribaldry in our plays as can be, as you would wish, Captain; all the sinners in the surburbs come and applaud our actions daily.

Tucca: I hear you'll bring me o' the stage there; you'll play me, they say I shall be presented by a sort of copperlaced scoundrels of you; life of Pluto an you stage me, stinkard, your mansions shall sweat for't, your tabernacles, varlets, your Globes and your Triumps.

(III.i.187–201)

'Humours' do not intermesh, but cannon off each other, like billiard balls.

Sixty years ago T.W. Baldwin made a gallant attempt to stake out
the parts played by different actors; but not being a theatre man, he
gave little heed to the practical needs of the stage and worked back
from the stronger typecasting of later Jacobean times.[3] More recently the practice of doubling has been studied in greater detail, to
work out the possible roles for the chief players. G.E. Bentley again
depended heavily on the practice of the later Jacobean and Caroline
stages, but made very plain the unique success of Shakespeare's
company.[4] It is not possible to guess the felicity built into his fluent
script for his particular friends, because we do not know enough
about them. In such a company parts must also be adaptable; cuts
were made or additions, by request, implanted; the whole performance must be cut down for touring, with more doubling of minor
roles. Shakespeare must have heard what happened to Marlowe's
texts at the other theatres, and his own were not treated like
Marlowe's, but they can hardly have been spoken with the pristine
clarity that the boys' companions achieved.

Two actors who influenced him deeply were Richard Burbage
and, later, Robert Armin, who played Touchstone, Feste and the
Fool in *King Lear*. Audiences came to the lure of a star actor; he loses
himself in his part, and it was reputed Burbage 'never put it off, so
much as in the tiring house'. Burbage also built a reputation as a
painter, and on the King's accession day, March 1613, the Earl of
Rutland bore an *impresa* devised by Shakespeare and painted and
executed by Burbage. Burbage also made the *impresa* Rutland bore
in March 1616 just before Shakespeare's death. His portrait at
Dulwich is reputedly of his own composition. Perhaps the discussion
of poet and painter in *Timon of Athens* represents a wit combat
between Shakespeare and Burbage. Armin, who joined the group
when Shakespeare and Burbage had intermeshed it, integrated the
fool's role more closely with the others, though he never dominated
as did some.

The Hero's Role (see above Chapter III)

Burbage's roles showed a dynamic power of development within
themselves, as distinct from sudden transformations, moving from
the supernatural towards the natural, from hubris towards mortal-
ity. This had provided the movement in Tamburlaine, but in the last
speech of Faustus, the new mathematical time ticked inexorably
within the movement of the starry cosmos. A second pattern, of man
transposed into demon, is shown in Revenge plays. Hieronymo, the

one just man in an unjust society, entertains revenge, springing from the natural impulse to return a blow for a blow, as surely as did Orestes in the play of 1567, *Horestes*, when revenge was presented by another actor. Demonic possession, a fearful possibility and an accepted one, led to horrific tales told of some stage performances, when a new and unknown actor materialised in *Dr Faustus*.

Richard III, the first great collaborative role, shows the hero demonically renouncing his humanity; the stories of his monstrous birth suggest that a demonic power had inhabited him always. Richard's wit and repartee, twisting all his opponent's acts and words against them till finally he is confronted by the chorus of ghosts, their faces whitened, their choric refrain 'Despair and die!' beckons him to 'the kingdom of eternal night'. He ends as man, shaken by the vision which he shares with Richmond, his antagonist. Act V, when the devil is reborn as man, was Garrick's supreme moment, but in the 1985 Royal Shakespeare Company production Antony Sher found it impossible to modify the fiendish exuberance and boundless resource of his spiderlike cripple.

Burbage's most famous line was 'A horse! a horse! my kingdom for a horse!' – a perfectly built combination of the panting of a battle-weary man with the defiance that sets fighting at a higher price than rule.

In the pattern of *Titus Andronicus*, and, presumably, of the lost *Ur-Hamlet*, the tragic revenger reveals both mask and face. On the late Elizabethan and Jacobean stage, supernatural beings might wear 'vizards' – either devil masks or the golden vizards of angels, who in Shakespeare's latest play visit the dying Queen, Katherine of Aragon. But antics, or 'momes', with animal heads also appeared at revels; a humble example is Bottom with the ass's head.

The inner force released in Shakespeare's roles makes the parts protean. The relation of the hero to his mask can be traced within the tragic plays from *King Richard II* to *Coriolanus*, the latest written solely for the Globe. When in autumn 1608, his company acquired use of Blackfriars, Shakespeare returned for material to the romances of his youth, such as *Clyamon and Clamydes*, linking them with elements of the court masque in dreamlike transformations when situations do not so much unfold as explode. The indoor theatre modifies the tragic conception.

Audience and Actors

The most difficult task of the dramatic poet was to create the network of relations between all the characters, a network that developed each role as individualised yet part of the whole action – that is to say, not merely part of the unfolding events but as in a macrocosm: as in the richest example, *A Midsummer Night's Dream*. Theatrical spaciousness is at the heart of the woodland, in the icon of the flying Cupid and the Virgin Queen. Although part of a narrative, not presented, this image carries the quality of a masque-spectacle, the play perhaps being for such an occasion itself.

> That very time I saw (but thou couldst not)
> Flying between the cold moon and the earth
> Cupid all arm'd; a certain aim he took
> At a fair vestal throned by the west . . .
>
>   (II.i.155–58)

The fair vestal enthroned would hold an orb; the round world with its cold moon dominated by the armed but naked little god suggests the lofty space which it is the art of the stage to fill. Although imaginary, Cupid probably flew on the creaking winches of a degrading drum, as he had done long before in *Gismond of Salerne* (1567). The echoing sound itself lifts the imagination of the hearers toward the region invoked a few years later in the Prologue to *King Henry V*, when Shakespeare calls on his audience to let the players: 'On your imaginary forces, work' and to 'Piece out our imperfections with your thoughts'.

> O for a Muse of fire, that would ascend
> The brightest heaven of invention:
> A kingdom for a stage, princes to act
> And monarchs to behold the swelling scene.
>
>   (I.i.1–4)

A deepening sense of the relations with the audience as well as the actors can be traced in the plays within the plays. The true hero of *A Midsummer Night's Dream* is Bottom the weaver; while outside the walls of Athens lie the woods of Warwickshire. The clown's solo acts were integrated into the whole, in spite of his desire for personal display (still, for Hamlet, the subject of admonition). Clowns, the delight of the groundlings, were essential for travelling companies. Rebelliousness is magnificently contained in the figure of Dogberry, but with the advent of Robert Armin, round 1599, Shakespeare discovered the clown's tragic potential, which he explored up to his latest plays.

It may have been a coincidence that at the time when he lost his only son, Shakespeare developed also the delicious parts for apprentices which dominate the middle comedies. These boys lived with their masters; in the Henslowe Papers a charming letter of banter is sent home from Alleyn's prentice, John Pyk, then on tour:

> Mistress, your honest ancient servant Pig hath his humble commendations
> to you and to my good master hinsely and to my mistress' sister Bess for all
> her hard dealings with me . . . and to my neighbour Doll for calling me up
> in a morning and to my wife Sarah for cleaning my shoes and to that old
> gentleman Monsieur Pearl that ever fought with me for the block in the
> chimney corner . . .

Written in the left hand margin: 'Mistress, I pray you keep this that
my maister may see it'. The letter is in Edward Alleyn's own hand.[5]

Heminges's two boys, Alexander Cooke and John Rice, became
famous actors; Burbage's Nicholas Tooley, talented, died young, but
Richard Robinson married Burbage's widow, time-honoured culmination for an apprentice!

To the end of his writing Shakespeare remained sensitively respon-
sive to the shape of his company; younger poets imitated and reacted
to him. Fletcher's *Philaster* (1608–10) is even more closely endebted
to *Hamlet* than to *Cymbeline*. The 'second wave' of Revenge plays
all shew his impress, from Marston to Webster. That very freedom
with which Shakespeare provokes adaptation is a proof of the
dramatist's elasticity and his continuing magnetism. We all become
members of his company and 'offer to put in with our experience' (as
the prompter says in the Induction to *Bartholomew Fair*).

When, seven years after Shakespeare's death, Heminges and Condell offered the plays to the Lord Chamberlain, the Earl of Pembroke, and his brother, their attitude was that of members of a family
– affectionate:

> We have but collected them and done to an office to the dead to procure
> his orphans, guardians; without ambition either of self profit or fame:
> only to keep the memory of so worthy a Friend, and Fellow, alive as was
> our Shakespeare . . .

It was the height of their care, they continued, to make the present
worthy by perfection.

> But there, we must also crave our abilities to be considered, my Lords. We
> cannot go beyond our own powers.

They claim that these are the best versions they can offer, but do not
claim anything more for the kind of work that Sir Thomas Bodley
was to term 'baggage books'.

The prestige of print, which the lawyer-dramatists and Ben Jonson
had sought, is also claimed by them for Shakespeare; Jonson's verses,

with their generous warmth ('Soul of the age!') bear out his testimony to Drummond of Hawthornden:

> I loved the man and do honour his memory as much as any, this side idolatry.

The superiority of the King's Men, established by that title in 1603, was so overwhelming by the end of the reign of James, their growing scale of numbers and operations so manifest, that the work of the other companies did not dispute their field. They exploited alternatives – some very successfully – both in London and overseas.

Modern Reconstruction

Modern interest in the performing arts of Shakespeare's day has come within the last half century to dominate Shakespearean criticism. From the editors who attempt to present authentic scripts fleshed out with details of performance, to the several attempts physically to rebuild these playhouses (the most serious of which is the project of the Globe on Bankside), the poet has been put back into his context. The theatrical structures, which have been investigated by new techniques from surviving illustrations and remaining contracts, can now be reconstructed with tolerable exactitude as far as dimensions of the auditorium go; but large areas of conjecture remain. The human element of actors and audience must stay more difficult to assess, but very careful accumulation of fragmentary evidence can put the detailed knowledge of popular literature to new uses. Heightened general awareness of theatrical communication, springing from new developments in media, puts a spotlight on the play in action.

The diameter of the Globe at 100 feet is securely established, but since modern Englishmen are larger than their ancestors, choice must be made between a true dimension or an audience on the original scale. Nothing is known of the backstage area and in the modern Globe the dressing rooms will be underground. Nothing is directly known of the working of the traps, the hoist, the number of doors to the stage, but after prolonged academic discussion, decisions were taken, e.g. to build the turret (for the hoist) over the stage roof on the model of John Norden's illustration, in the small inset in his panoramic *Civitas Londini* (1600), although the general dimensions are calculated from Wenceslas Holler's panorama which includes the Second Globe. John Orrell set out the basis for calculation;[6] and numerous meetings have been held about the finer details. Digging began in the summer of 1988.

Norden or Holler used a simple surveying instrument, the topographical glass which was put in the tower of St Saviour's Southwark. Norden was a Londoner and familiar with the district; neither was concerned to make a photographic likeness, but combined surveyors' exactitude with artistic composition; their work needs careful interpretation. Orrell discovered a seating plan for a royal entertainment at Oxford, which gave the dimensions for gallery seating; and his detective work is completed by his discovery that the Globe 'did, more or less accurately, face the midsummer sunrise'.

Other buildings supply analogies for the brightly coloured painting of the interior and the 'heavens', or roof, over the stage. The model cannot be totally accurate but it will represent something that Shakespeare's troupe would have recognised as a playhouse. Inigo Jones's plan for an indoor theatre will provide the Bankside's basis for the Cockpit; both theatres will be used for live performance by professionals and visiting groups, as well as for other educational work. The Bankside area will also house scale models of eight other Elizabethan theatres.

Risks are obvious and objections have been recorded. Some actors have rejected the cramping of their art into what they insist is a museum. The perils of colonial Williamsburg, Yorvik, and the commercial exploitations at Bancroft of Stratford-upon-Avon are palpable. Yet the advantages of playing Renaissance music upon period instruments has long been understood, and the new theatre at Stratford, the Swan, has stimulated actors by giving them a different kind of acting space and a different relation to their audience. This, without any particular adaptation of the plays.

The London Globe will be much stricter in its conformity with what is known than either the projected Globe in Detroit or that opened in April 1988 in Tokyo. A number of theatres of the Elizabethan type already exist in La Jolla, California; in Portland, Oregon; in Stratford, Ontario and in Minneapolis. In London, the oak frame, the open-air site, the standing room for groundlings will, of course, be supported by modern hygiene and conform to modern safety regulations. During the seventeen years that the plan has been maturing, much intensive work has been stimulated. It parallels such other recreations of the past as the building of a Greek trireme if not the raising of the *Mary Rose*.

Creating the strange and unfamiliar nature of the original gives something to start from, not something to be imposed. The comprehension of alien systems is a part of every educational study, and recognition of what is not of an age but for all time depends on some respect for its differentiation. By submission, new insights may emerge more generally of concern to all modern theatres. Other actors and audiences may learn; this, of course, is an alternative to the 'alternative Shakespeare' of the do-it-yourself school.

It is as a context for Shakespeare's drama that his theatre is of concern today. The variety of other theatres in his time and the other forms of dramatic entertainment also provided a context and these other popular theatres, and the troupes that used them, should be seen in this aspect.

Notes

Many studies might be related here; among the obvious are: Herbert Berry (ed.), *The First Public Playhouse: the Theatre in Shoreditch* (Montreal, McGill and Queen's University Presses, 1979); Richard Hosley, 'The Playhouses', *The Revels History of Drama in English*, vol III (London, Methuen, 1975); Andrew Gurr, *Playgoing in Shakespeare's London* (Cambridge, Cambridge University Press, 1987); Peter Thomson *Shakespeare's London* (London, Routledge & Kegan Paul, 1983) and a companion volume, Michael Hattaway, *Elizabethan Popular Theatre* (London, Routledge & Kegan Paul, 1982); G.E. Bentley *The Profession of Player in Shakespeare's Time* (Princeton, Princeton University Press, 1984) summarises his earlier work.

Philip Edwards, in *Hamlet* (Cambridge, Cambridge University Press, 1985) summarises relations to Marston (pp. 4–8), dissenting from Harold Jenkins in *Hamlet* (London, New Arden, 1982). The best account of the theatre war is Cyrus Hoy, in notes to *Satiromastix* (*The Dramatic Works of Thomas Dekker*, F.R. Bowers (ed.), Cambridge, Cambridge University Press, 1980) pp. 179–98). John Orrell, *The Quest for Shakespeare's Globe* (Cambridge, Cambridge University Press, 1983) forms the basis of the plans for the Bankside Globe; he also discusses Blackfriars. Reavley Gair, *The Children of Paul's* (Cambridge, Cambridge University Press, 1982) discusses new material about the theatre of Paul's and the boy actors.

1 'Money and audience; the impact of Shakespeare's Globe' *Theatre Notebook*, vol. xliii, No. 1, 1988.
2 Anne Barton, *Ben Jonson Dramatist* (Cambridge, Cambridge University Press, 1984) p. 68.
3 T.W. Baldwin, *The Organization and Personnel of the Shakespearean Company* (Princeton, Princeton University Press, 1927).
4 G.E. Bentley, *Op. cit.*
5 R.A. Foakes and R.T. Rickert (eds), *Henslowe's Diary* (Cambridge, Cambridge University Press, 1961), p. 282.
6 See John Orrell, *Op. cit.* John Orrell's latest book, *The Human Stage* (Cambridge, Cambridge University Press, 1988), dealing with all London theatres 1567–1642, support my accounts, but appeared only when this volume was on press.

Epilogue – Two Moderns and *King Lear*; Dover Cliff; Earth and Cosmos

XIII.

Guy Butler; South African Scene

Guy Butler, president of the Shakespeare Association of Southern Africa, writing from Drake's 'fairest Cape', has produced plays — Shakespeare's and others' including his own — has written poems, of which the latest is the tormented *Pilgrimage to Dias Cross* (1988), and has been working for years on *King Lear*, so that its influence is suffused through his own writings.

Guy Butler's lyric is distinguished by two virtues rarely found in conjunction elsewhere. The first is an exact and sensitive adaptation to whatever he is looking at, either great or small. This is the prime virtue of attentiveness; it means an outward turning, a readiness to ponder well, to absorb. The second, counterbalancing this, is serenity, a power to inhibit personal emotions which might distort the fidelity of his art. Alertness and repose, keenness and stillness (one of his keywords) complement each other; contraries, not opposites.

In many poems, a delicate blend of scene painting and mood come together to make a statement that is more than the sum of its parts. The poet Edwin Muir once dreamt something that seemed to him to convey the deepest truth about writing. The dream was very simple; it consisted of a semicolon. The poet never knows all he is writing and he writes as far as the semicolon; beyond his statement lies something more that completes his meaning.

Near Hout Bay begins casually, in a tone of easy speech:

> Stopping the car, our childhood friends, now hosts,
> suggested we stroll to the fabulous view.

The climb, with its unfolding glimpses, brings the gradual fading away of speech, for talk

> only exposed the gaps, unbandaged sentence by sentence
> the gashes and wounds of time, great spaces and falls
> between us all

which appeared mirrored in the revealed expanse before them, reaching

> out, out into the distance, finding nothing to cling to –
> the next land Buenos Aires.

Speech fails, but motion is also halted 'before the sufficiently epic view'. Safeguarded by such irony, the lyric can move to its central statement:

> Silence took charge, a blessed burial of words . . .
> We stood a long time, still just listening:

listening to the cicadas, the doves, the pine woods, and the

> . . . grumbling,
> perpetual, unpitied,
> crumbling of the surf.

Unpitied? That just word allows the poem to end with renewed talk, now recognised as achieving nothing:

> We accepted separation
> as the ear those ignorant sounds
> that filled that primitive silence
> with sadness and with praise:
> cicadas; doves; wind; surf.

The cunning drop to a final monosyllable depends on no fewer than three semicolons, to enact how 'words, beyond speech, reach into the silence'.

A view of such emptiness that it might be infinity gives a wedding of the near and the far, of outer and inner landscape; but Guy Butler has eschewed description of the 'sufficiently epic view'. That is left, as his share of the poem, to be filled in by the reader or auditor. The gap left here channels movement, through rhythm and sound, from the deflationary phrase to that point where the 'ignorant' sounds become 'praise' as well as sadness. Hout Bay is a sacred place, a holy place; everyone has his own sacred places. Transformation by the sacred is more commonly a solitary experience, like that of Wordsworth in crossing the Alps, and that of Eliot beside the empty pool that suddenly filled with sunlight (though he also used such a moment in *The Waste Land* to bridge a gulf 'looking into the heart of light, the silence.').

The moment of transformation is familiar enough to be invoked very crudely, as Sir Arthur Sullivan evoked it with his celebrated song *The Lost Chord*, calling fluently upon the highest sentiments. The discretion and reticence of *Near Hout Bay* safeguard the central gap in the poem by surrounding it with lesser gaps. 'Great spaces and falls between us all' applies alike to the view and to the relationship between friends. Equal attentiveness to the scene and the dialogue is balanced from a point beyond both; the point which allows sadness and praise to be heard together in the last line. More than a hundred years before, Matthew Arnold had imagined (in *To Marguerite*) such a scene and such a dialogue, but arrived at an opposite and unconsoling end:

> A god, a god their severance ruled:
> And bade betwixt their shores to be
> The unplumb'd, salt, estranging sea.

But Arnold dips a loaded brush; the confidence behind his despair is positively Byronic. He is exploring not friendship but romantic love; Guy Butler very rarely touches these extremes or directly invokes God.

At about the same time that Arnold wrote his poem, Livingstone was crossing Africa; Butler, in his poem of that title, describes how Livingstone turned his back upon the sea and the ship bound for home, retracing his way to gather, at the cost of 'great deaths', new facts today 'grown trite among our daily speech':

> The cold and noting eyes can see, can see
> Not leap the gap which isolates us all.

The balance sheet is different for each generation. As one modernist said of the older poets, 'We know so much more than they did', to which T.S. Eliot responded, 'Precisely; and they are that which we know.' Guy Butler is a learned poet, not only because learning about poetry is his trade, but because he is constantly calling upon the past to interpret the future, using traditional forms in new combinations. Livingstone gives him his clue; 'go back', for 'deeds of the great possess the power of myth'.

Elegy and satire would seem incompatible, but they meet in a lighter and more fluent sketch, a favourite for anthologies, *Cape Coloured Batman*. Set in Italy during the Second World War, it outlines speedily, with words and rhythms which sometimes echo Kipling, the pathos of the drunk soldier and banjo player asleep under the Tuscan trees. The movement dances in triplets in the centre of the poem, as the watcher ponders on the mixed inheritance from all the traders who put in at the 'Tavern of the Seas' and who contributed to the batman's making.

> No doubt a pirate Javanese
> From Malacca Straits or Sunda Seas
> Shapes those almond eyes of his;
>
> A Negress from the Cameroons –

> Bought for brandy, sold for doubloons —
> Gave him a voice that wails and croons;
>
> An eagle Arab trading far
> From Hadramaut to Zanzibar
> Left him a nose like a scimitar;

a Bushgirl gave him his birdlike hands, while English, Dutch and Portuguese seamen

> Drank red Cape brandy, and got tight —
> And left him a skin that's almost white.

But they also left him 'without hope in History's shade'; he is 'Shouldered aside into any old place'. The routine army epithet, 'bastard', has come painfully to life. As an earlier war poet said, 'the Poetry is in the pity'; the sound of Nelson's banjo (as he lies in drunken sleep, as drunk as the men who got him) is revived by a gentle wind that touches the strings.

Sardonic as well as tender, the humour of these verses (given their military setting, the drunken batman's khaki legs splayed in a V, the sorrow of the seven seas) distances Kipling and the earlier men that founded South Africa, even in the act of recalling them. Irony, the signature of detachment and of isolation from a group response, marks the contemporary, self-examining, privileged, and remorseful white. Being so firmly rooted in the Eastern Cape, and attached to its places and seasons and its interwoven patterns and strands of culture, Guy Butler is able to preserve both his warmth and his coolness, his devotion and his analysis, free from any desire to argue, to descend into rhetoric or polemic.

Another anthologised piece, describing a ritual bullkilling, is ironically entitled *Tourist Insight into Things*. The initial tone is chatty:

. . . you'll find our big black brother has much, so much to teach you —

Then we slide into the story of 'a ritual, a ceremony' in which 'twelve of the best and glossiest young braves' wrestle the bull down and the best of the twelve slits the midriff and kills the bull by reaching in and clutching its heart until it bursts. (In ancient Crete, as shown on Minoan vases, the killer climbed into a tree, to drop on the bull's back as he charged underneath. The effect of the ritual must have been much the same.) As the bull's life blood ceases to flow, another tide rises, and in response to his last bellowings

> the laughing-singing-clapping wave
> tumbles, sparkles, spreads in bubbles and spume
> through the veins and the brains,

> the nerves and the bloods of all that is African
> on both sides of the grave.

The ancestors, the shades, have been drawn into the killing. Quickening blood and quickening sounds are syncopated; then comes the deflation:

> White settlers, of course, don't like this way of killing,
> cattle not being sacred to them.

This insight is only that of the enlightened tourist who has read a little anthropology. The brilliant picture remains, a snapshot for the tourist's collection. Exciting and perfectly clear, the central act is sharpened and isolated until the final effect is neither nostalgic nor ironic. This is not poetry of ideas, since the two ideologies cancel each other out; the white settler and the tourist stand on either side of a carefully wrought account, itself as skilful as the braves it celebrates. The clipped, isolated speech of the spectator from outside is set against the communal, submerging tribal emotions, until the Ovidian metamorphosis emerges.

Guy Butler has composed one poem of 'praises' in the traditional form, *Isibongo of Matiwane*. It is the form used by the Xhosa A. G. Ngani to praise King George VI. Being of the generation that he is, Guy Butler took to the so-called 'free verse' at first. But it has been said that no verse is free for the man who knows his job. The tone of these earlier poems tends to the conversational, but with the conversation at many different levels. If his tone and technique are compared with those of other traditions from English-speaking regions of the southern hemisphere, it will be felt that he combines the reticence, irony and taut questioning characteristic of New Zealand with, later, the singing rhythm of Australia.

South Africa has produced poets of wit and ironic control, such as Anthony Delius and Douglas Livingstone, and has thrown up compulsively rhythmic satire (*Ag Pleez Deddy*). Guy Butler moves over the whole range; under his taut line there may be felt a pulse, rarest and most elusive sign of a poem lived from below, as distinct from a poem that is 'made'. The 'laughing-singing-clapping wave' finds an individual voice in which the conscious and subconscious are united, as Yeats declared they must be. In a collection issued in 1978, Guy Butler wrote in the preface:

> I sometimes wake up remembering that words have been moving to a distinct rhythm and mood through my sleep. The words are forgotten but the rhythm remains. Sometimes I sit down and try to find the words.

Eliot made a similar confession; Vernon Watkins and Kathleen

Raine are others who recorded that 'rhythm' or cadence precedes
words.

Some of Butler's later verses carry behind them actual tunes, or
perhaps a memory of a cadence from Zulu, as here:

> Before we troubled
> The Cape of Storms
> Or shook the Highveld
> With horses and arms,
> Before the births
> Of Shaka, Retief.
> Old Zulus were chanting
> This joy-in-grief:
> 'Body grows old,
> Heart stays young.'
> Such was the heartsease
> In their song

A form based on the Japanese *haiku* follows the strict syllabic
numbering of seventeen syllables in triplets running 5–7–5. It con-
centrates upon sensuous evocation, leaving the reader, thus roused,
to fill out deliberate gaps. *Homeland haiku* is a lament for barren-
ness, constriction, starvation; the unheard cries fill the brevity out:

> Thin cattle lowing
> Over thorn, kraals, chieftain's graves.
> A herd's voice quavers . . .

> White men's aeroplanes
> bring bread money from fathers,
> black moles underground . . .

> Her withered fingers
> Shake but she sets flame to dry
> cowdung under pots

In *Thomas Philipp's Picnic, 1821* there twangs a refrain of the tune

> Of the crickets, and yes, of the moon,
> And the sharp strange stars in their courses.

This is echoed faintly by the wondering young tribesmen who eye the
settlers' dancing from across the river and identify the circling figures
as

> Abafaz', the belles, amadod', the beaux,
> Amadod' abafaz', the beaux and the belles.

The history of his native region, told partly in his autobiography of
childhood and youth *Karoo Morning*, is now appearing more de-
finitely in Butler's verses, as his own life turns for him into history.

Some of his best earlier sketches, such as *Sweet-water*, *Farmer*, or *Servant Girl*, condense general history in the manner of *Cape Coloured Batman*. In *Cradock Mountain* the scenes of his boyhood remain as mythic powers presiding over his whole life, the ancestors, the shades; in this poem the final section, recording how he's shot 'a dassie, old, male', looks forward to his own death. More recently, in the verses whose rhythm came in a dream, *The Old Man's Fiddle*, Butler plays more lightly and poignantly upon history and death. The theme is not unlike that of Hardy's verses on Mellstock churchyard. The family of an early settler, who had landed in hope, die one by one and are buried; until the last survivor, the son, breaks his father's fiddle, the instrument that had sounded their hopes. But the tune goes on and on, until it resounds from the churchyard where the family are reuniting. The refrain which begins, 'My mother, John, Sarah and me'; ends, 'Your mother, John, Sarah and me', as the dead father speaks to the living. But will the tune go on, will there be a new fiddle? Here is where we meet the semicolon once again; tribal music comes from the ancestors.

A collective relationship is natural enough in poetry of protest, but in *The Divine Underground* it is not simply the obvious opponents who must be cast off, but a certain quality of living, a life that attracts publicity:

> Souls *in flagrante delicto* or *in extremis*,
> stretched on the rack or Cleopatra's bed,
> you have no news for me, not fit to tread
> where hawk-sure men of the media
> zoom lenses down on your limbs in spasm
> or claw at your grunts or ululations
> with glittering microphones.
>
> No, I go hungrily slumming for those who wear
> a habit of discipline on every gesture, armed
> in still affection, steel-bright after years.

That habit of discipline is seen in his own composure; it prevents sharp observation or clear-cut detail from turning into material for the media, and prevents his poetry from turning into versified prose:

> they know what they have lost,
> they guess at what they've gained;
> divining an innocent justice, they endure
> our grand and murderous razzmatazz
> as if they were God's spies.

This last line, a quotation from *King Lear* as Lear goes to prison, is an invocation to close the scene in terms of that very grandeur that is repudiated (for King Lear is at least Cleopatra's equal). The line still

imposes 'a dome of many-coloured glass' between the momentary
revelation and the 'white radiance of Eternity'.

In *A Prayer for All My Countrymen* the water-diviner, seeking
hidden springs in 'this tragic time's complexities' seeks the image of
an always hidden God, *deus absconditus*, but finds that

> here and there
> a heart stayed warm,
> a head grew clear.

In *Mountain*, 'fearful of further falling in a fallen world', the poet
seeks guidance of his hidden God:

> You alone can know if my hunger for poise is just,
> know I am held from falling
> by a tension of forces I can't pretend to know.

There is no overt response, outward or inward; but on the mountain
'with no effort I shed becoming' and entered Being. The problems of
history 'slid like a leaden cope from my shoulders', like Christian's
burden in Bunyan. In the high and sacred place the answer is given
that there is no answer. The moment that refused to be a turning
point is on the point round which his life should turn; the moment
when he simply was 'on the rocks in the sun'.

For even here the many-coloured glass does not shatter, though
the white radiance filters through more clearly. Wit and irony break
in once more, directed against the seeker:

> I came down from the mountain, unweighted
> by tablets of law . . .

In its context, the effect of this mockery is not defensive; it records an
instinctive shift of perspective, appropriate to the lower slopes. One
of Guy Butler's Shakespeareanisms is the metaphor of man as a little
kingdom. In *Livingstone Crosses Africa* his own bearers are his
'blood and bones', his 'tribal flesh' which is lazy and tells him lies. In
Home Thoughts, Butler again turns back from Europe with all five
senses:

> I must go back with my five simple slaves
> To soil still savage, in a sense still pure:
> My loveless, shallow land of artless shapes
> Where no ghosts glamorize the recent graves
> And every thing in Space and Time just is:

Simply 'to be' was to become the sole condition for achieving
beatitude in the later poem *Mountain*. Blake sees the kingdom of the
five senses as an enclosure shutting out 'worlds of delight', or other
senses not known to man. But it is within the kingdom of his five

simple slaves that Guy Butler chooses to remain, for all his agile wit and troubled questioning.

He turns back, in *Interrupted Letter, from Hospital*, from the grand certitudes of affirmation, Byronic, Shelleyan, or Mosaic:

> . . . in the craft and mystery of words
> most speech is mere noise countering noise,
> while song assumes an absolute stillness;
> for or against nothing at all,
> is needed by no one except the singer
> who may, sometimes, be overheard.

The ultimate stillness is implied in the title, for the imagined speaker is preparing for surgery; the 'semi-colon' is death.

Stillness learnt on the mountain or at Hout Bay by the attentive heart may be attained even in cities; the depth of composure is never lost, once known. The twin virtues of attentiveness and serenity which characterise Guy Butler's poetry are perhaps inherited from the family who in 1892 gave articulate voice to their region when the first issue of *The Midland News and Karroo Farmer* rolled off the presses of Butler Bros. in Cradock. For this family had also known the stillness of the Quaker meeting.

The Karoo, the 'Fairest of Capes', the 1820 Settlers' Memorial at Grahamstown, with its inscription 'We must take root and grow or die where we stand', supply the beauty and tradition which consoles, the history which presses like a leaden cope; and perhaps in this history other regions may see a mirror of the future. Uganda and the Caribbean set down in London; Indian women in bright saris shopping at supermarkets in the snows of Montreal (not to mention tourist insights in Bali) have created a larger landscape with a sufficiently epic view, a melting pot for races bubbling even more fiercely than in the Tavern of the Seas. Fidelity to what is known in one place brings larger reverberations.

XIV.

Sir William Empson (1906–84)

From the rosy brick of the small first court at Magdalene College, Cambridge, a door surmounted with the arms of the founder and the motto *Garde Ta Foy* leads to the cloisters where Empson once slept out; they form an arcade below the library of Mr Samuel Pepys.

In this very small but exclusive society, formed by a Tudor peer out of a friary, Empson spent his Cambridge years of 1925–1931; first reading mathematics; graduating; Senior Optime (Second Class Honours). He switched to English under the young Ivor Richards, who has recorded that the first 30,000 words of *Seven Types of Ambiguity* appeared in the autumn of 1928 after a fortnight's intense activity. Empson thought, lived, worked with speed and intensity beyond all parallel.

Cambridge still feels small, but a good place from which to survey the galaxies – the radio telescope at Gamlingay was built immediately after World War II by volunteer student labour. Cosmic and local scenes interact in *Sleeping Out in College Cloister*:

> Stevenson says they wake at two o'clock
> Who lie with Earth, when the birds wake, and sigh;
> Turn over, as does she, once in the night . . .
> But it's about then one stamped on someone
> And chose an animate basis for one's mattress,
> It must be later you look round and notice
> The ground plan has been narrowed and moved up;
> How much more foliage appears by star-light;
> That Hall shelters at night under the trees.
>
> Earth at a decent distance is the Globe
> (One has seen them smaller); within a hundred miles
> She's *terra firma*, you look down to her.

This appeared in the decade of the first hazardous flights across the

Atlantic. Another poem, *Earth has Shrunk in the Wash*, compares the future state of a dead and airless Globe with 'civilised refinement cutting one off from other people and scientific discovery making a strange world in which man has dangerous powers' (note). Should man survive on another planet, he would face hazards created by his own dominance.

> They pass too fast. Ships, and there's time for sighing;
> Express and motor, Doug can jump between.
> Only dry earth now asteroid her flying
> Mates, if they miss her, must flick past unseen . . .

Victorian 'ships that pass in the night', the early exploits of Fairbanks contrast with astronautic views now familiar, but which at that date remained below the horizon for most visionaries. Anxiety about human relationsihps sprang from the philosophic puzzle of relations between unknown objects 'out there' and internal recording – Empson once remarked 'One of the damned things is ample'. Another poem on the outdoor begins:

> And now she cleans her teeth into the lake:
> Gives it (God's grace) for her own bounty's sake
> What morning's pale and the crisp mist debars . . .
> Milks between rocks a straddled sky of stars.

Bliss was it in that Cambridge dawn to be alive: as in the Old Cavendish Laboratory Rutherford prepared to split the atom, while in Trinity, a few hundréd yards south of Magdalene, Wittgenstein darkly expounded; he heard Empsom's poems from Leavis and furnished an ironic joke for *'This Last Pain'*. The poet Kathleen Raine has described a lunch party in Empson's rooms, the meal parked on his windowsill.

> . . . the impression of a perpetual self-consuming, self-generating intensity that produced a kind of shock; through no intention or will to impress, for William was simply himself at all times . . . Never I think had he any wish to excel, lead, dominate, involve or otherwise exert power.[1]

Another poet, George Fraser, celebrating Empson's fiftieth birthday, was later to acknowledge:

> He is an electric eel
> From whom our soft flat flounder thoughts rebound.
> He stirs up in his own air his own sea
> Of lithe prehensile ambiguity . . .
> He taught us thinking is a kind of feel . . .

Empson discarded his own views as easily as he accepted paradox, with the lightness of one conceding points in a game, as in the second

edition of *Seven Types of Ambiguity*: 'It seems no good trying now to
improve this paragraph but I still think the last sentence summing it
up is sufficiently true' (p. 21), or 'I now think this example a mare's
nest' (p 171). A *sprezzatura* like Philip Sidney's blows through
criticism and poems, for Empson was writing for his friends, and all
flowed from good talk in little college courts, where new ideas were
seeded. The startling alteration of scale continues in *Legal Fiction*,
and *Letter I*:

> You were amused to find you too could fear
> 'The eternal silence of the infinite spaces' . . .
> I approve, myself, dark spaces between stars. . . .

Some anxieties from World War I still shuddered and refracted in the
talk. The two brightest stars of the English Faculty, Ivor Richards
and Manny Forbes, like our great exemplar T.S. Eliot, had been
rejected for military service, had stood by to see a generation
slaughtered. All three in 1920 suffered nervous breakdowns from
which creative work eventually came. Empson, like Isherwood and
others of our generation, felt they had missed this initiation (Charles
Empson, William's elder brother by eight years, had served in the
Middle East and was now in the Foreign Service); but William's
views were fiercely antimilitarist, if not antimilitary. He wrote a
squib for the comic magazine *Granta* – of which he was editor – as
well as editing, with others, the avant-garde *Experiment*, where his
poems and extracts from *Seven Types* appeared. In this squib, the
Saint Vitus School Contingent of the Officers' Training Corps is
addressed by a general: 'Well, you young fellows, this has been a very
decent show' and – noting dust on their boots – 'Can't expect you all
to take taxis (Ha!) but if you'd just spat on them and wiped them up
with your sleeve at the last minute . . .'
He goes on to warn them of their responsibilities in the next war
('and mind you, it's going to come very soon'); all those 'who have
taken Certificate A' will be given charge of thirty men.

> Now that's a very great honour and privilege. And I'll tell you why: it's
> true the actual cost of a man to this country, the cost of training him and
> throwing him into the field, that's not very much, it may not come to more
> than thirty pounds, all told; and you may set that against the cost of a
> machine gun, which may be a hundred pounds . . . But what you've got to
> remember, is the question of reserves. It takes twenty years to grow a man
> to fight for his country and they can turn out a machine gun in a week. It
> won't be a question of money, when this country's in a life and death
> struggle; it'll be a question of manpower. You'll find you come to the end
> of the men long before you come to the end of the machine guns . . . we're
> putting on you a great trust, a great responsibility. File out by the right.
> Quietly, please.

This irony, published in the week of November 2, 1928, just before the national commemoration, the two minutes' silence on November 11, 1928, seemed to me something to produce for Empson's own commemoration if given with an innocent Irish brogue.

What was bred in the bone supported and permitted the footloose intellectual gyrations, the speculative games by which Empson dazzled us in his Cambridge years. Anthony Blunt was recruiting his celebrated spy ring at King's and Trinity, through the 'Apostles' in part. Empson was president of the 'Heretics', whose title marked its claims to be antiEstablishment; yet *Garde Ta Foy* might have served for Empson's motto – as might his school's motto: *Manners makyth man*. His deeply secure roots in East Yorkshire at the family home, Yokefleet Hall, gained their place in his verses *'To an Old Lady'*; his mother, his original, thought he was writing about his grandmother! A film about Empson made in the early 1970s by the BBC was shot at Yokefleet.

In the late summer of 1931, the withdrawal of his bye-fellowship – an act tantamount to ejection – took him as far as Tokyo. On this, Ronald Bottrall commented:

> Betrayed by the head porter, ostracised by dons,
> Lacking the pros, he was sentenced by the cons,
> A lamentable case of academic *mores*,
> Promoted by Puritan envy and trumped-up stories.

Ivor Richards was far away, in China; another friend tried to place Empson at Birmingham, but he wrecked his chances by airily citing some recent iconoclastic work to an influential person.

Those who knew said Empson's relations with women went wrong all the time, but as a junior fellow at Magdalene, he suffered under an unusually authoritarian constitution and a Master who was Nonconformist, of a joylessness that offered a very ready target for the barbed wit of Queenie Leavis and others. When, a few years earlier, Empson's friend J.B.S. Haldane was asked to resign his university post on appearing as co-respondent on a divorce case, he successfully brought an action in the civil courts.

Empson arrived in Japan in time for the 'Manchuria incident', the start of Japanese campaigns on the mainland, and was received in the Bunrika Daigaku with enthusiasm:

> The garden house being in the western part of Tokyo, it was a long journey for Mr Empson to come from there to the University; it was Empson's good idea that he got a motor bike by which he was free to run about the big city; and I am glad there occurred no accident even if Tokyo forty years ago may have been a little less crowded in the streets. We sent an applause every time when the explosive sound of the full speed wheels told us that the poet was come to his classes.[2]

On his return to England, after publishing his first book of poems and *Some Versions of Pastoral*, he took a yet longer journey to teach exiled Chinese university students in a long march through the interior. Lecturing from memory, he relied heavily on Housman and Shakespeare. The darkening political scene brought Lord Rochester's line to serve as epigraph to new verses, 'But wretched man is still in arms for fear'. The refrain of another poem was 'The heart of standing is you cannot fly', which catches an idea from Dryden: 'Charge, charge, 'tis too late to retreat'.

> . . . entirely rousing and single-hearted. Evidently the thought that it is no good running away is an important ingredient in military enthusiasm . . . Horses in a way very like this display mettle by a continual expression of timidity.[3]

In *Flighting for Duck*, set in his own Yorkshire countryside, Empson used the blandness of eighteenth-century pastiche to reinforce the joining of political menace with a familiar landscape; by contrast, in *Just a Smack at Auden* he came skimming down from a great height, like the practised skier he was, to meet the fashionable and self-righteous gloom of the left-wing poets with a practised brushoff, to be justified by the event.

The poems, eventually collected in *The Gathering Storm* (1940), showed Empson truly engaged, but with a cool sardonic wit, of the kind that fighting men develop in the face of the enemy.

> It is more hopeful on the spot.
> The 'News', the conferences that leer,
> The creeping fog, the civil traps,
> These are what force you into fear.

His accents vary from the Wykehamist 'Hark at these Germans, hopeful chaps' into Yorkshire dialect and back again:

> Besides, you aren't quite good for nowt
> Or clinging wholly as a burr
> Replacing men who must get out
> Nor is it shameful to aver
> A vague desire to be about
> Where important things occur.
>   (*'Autumn on Nan Yueh'*)

So he made a beeline for London, working in the Eastern section of the BBC to such effect that one of the top German propagandists (to his gratification) termed him 'a curly-headed Jew'. One may transpose for England what he said on China, 'I felt that while I was trying to help China I need not be solemn about her'.

During World War II Empson had said in a broadcast:

What the Japanese cannot stand is surprises. The Chinese guerillas are extremely powerful against the Japanese mind, because they continually give the Japanese subordinate a problem which his superiors have not seen. So what we must plan to give them is surprises.[4]

It might be retorted that Pearl Harbour and the fall of Singapore had shown the Japanese not devoid of this primary military equipment, but the surprise given at Hiroshima on August 6, 1945, left Empson, the 'pygmy', with no more to say on military topics. Underlying his antimilitarist campaigns of early days was an assumption that he was tilting against a secure and established order. There would always be an army; therefore, it was a legitimate target. The argument, though passionate, could use ironically the accents of the opponent – which by training were part of Empson's makeup, as his own actions demonstrated. "Double irony', he said later, needs 'a show of lightness and carelessness'; some Americans think every upper-class English voice does this, however unintentionally: Empson thinks every tough American voice does it too.[5]

In 1941 he married Hester Henrietta Crouse (Hetta), a handsome South African whose affiliations were of the extreme left and whose life style was Bohemian. This was probably more of a shock to the elder members of his family than the loss of his fellowship. A son was named Mogador, because when he was born that Moroccan city was in the news; another son received the Biblical name Jacob. After the war, Empson briefly returned to Peking, but regularly visited Kenyon College, where he felt very much at home. Robert Lowell wrote a parody of his verse. Soon after he had published *The Structure of Complex Words*, in 1951, he was elected to a Chair of English at Sheffield in his native county. He commuted, while Hetta remained in London. Empson never became a really committed academic, but he found universities agreeable places to be. Moreover, his sons were now of an age to be educated. He faithfully tried to conform to academic 'mores', engaging with contemporary figures – E.E. Stoll, Hugh Kenner, or W.K. Wimsatt – but he talked as if in a club and did not bother to give clues for the eavesdropping reader. The mathematician in him led to close examination of minutiae, when he would run rings round his opponent in the most good-natured and even respectful way. Great politeness or great plainness were equally at his command, as they had been at the command of I.A. Richards. I remember a scene in the 1930s at Cambridge where Empson was being subjected to interruption about some passages in his book on pastoral. He endured with exemplary courtesy, but Richards lost patience and, turning around, hurled at the interrupter 'And if a sunstroke hit you on the back of the neck you'd be dead!'

This variation on a familiar wish was uttered with such force that it
proved a knockout.

Empson could be generous in concessions – 'Oh, to be sure, to be
sure! Now that you mention it . . .' while equally ready to give the
brushoff. He was exactly on Eliot's wavelength here, but found
Leavis's mode of 'insisting' repugnant. When moving against any
form of pretentiousness and especially when defending an impossible position, he relied much on that Chinese aspect of meaning
which Richards had imparted as 'tone'. (Chinese tones mark attitudes of authority or deference; mock deference in English suggests
authority.) Writing on Richards in a celebratory volume, he declared
that the English language, being so complex

> positively likes to purge itself and act simple. If you heard Charles II
> talking to a Bishop, you felt not merely that he showed the man up as a
> fool and a pedant but that this was the right man to be king because he
> spoke in such an absolutely plain man way. If you felt so you were
> deluded, and I do not say that the political effects were good, only that the
> effects on the language were.[6]

With this anticipation of 'The Great Communicator' on television,
we reach the new target which for Empson replaced the military – the
'Neo-Christians'. These ranged from Rosemond Tuve and Hugh
Kenner to C.S. Lewis and Dorothy Sayers. Empson, who, as Christopher Ricks said in his memorial notice,[7] found his energy not in
repudiation but in welcome, turned to Charles II's subjugated
enemy, and in *Milton's God* (1961), elegantly, with an air of
innocent unpretentiousness (though well informed), he released the
heroic poet, who finally mastered the horrible God he had created.
The existence of God is as firmly assumed as the persistence of the
British Army had been earlier; only He turns out to be the Devil. In
Milton's fictions, the Father and the Son are human figures enlarged;
the Atonement in its legal and substitutionary form is the evil
Empson gets his teeth into. An angry judge demanding human
sacrifice, and the ejection from Paradise for a noble motive were
monstrous! What preachers term 'the Application' is not omitted,
'No one when I was at school believed this stuff'. In its Voltairean
tone, *Milton's God* can be lighthearted and very funny:

> When composing, he felt like a defending Counsel . . . he does not feel
> personally disgraced if his client still loses after he has gone as far as he
> can. Adding a little human interest to the admittedly tricky client God, by
> emphasising his care to recover the reputation of his son, and giving a
> glimpse of the deeper side of his nature which makes him prepare for his
> latter end [i.e., his demise, or transformation to the Absolute] is about all

that can be done to swing the jury when the facts of the case are so little in dispute.

(p. 209)

A chapter defending Delilah opens 'Her case is easier even to defend than Adam's – it is a pushover' (p. 211) although 'This picture of her as a hospital nurse will no doubt be resisted' (p. 224). The final chapter 'On Christianity', however, rises to a scream that this religion worships torture, the doctrine of the Trinity is evil double talk by which Christians hide from themselves the wickedness of their God (p. 245). After touching on such modern issues as abortion, tolerance of homosexuality, the infamous habits of the police, by way of confession of faith it ends with the theory of Bentham, 'which was in favour when I was a student at Cambridge' (p. 259) but not before the squire's son has surfaced to tell how father warned the local parson he would walk out if asked to recite the Athanasian creed, but failed to do so because he had fallen asleep!

This book is dedicated to Hetta. The next twenty years saw a series of biographical studies of poets and novelists, every one treating some contemporary issue. A posthumously published collection, *Using Biography* (1984), explains that the uses of biography are to combat 'Wimsatt's Law'.[8] A student of literature ought to be trying all the time to empathise with his author (and of course the assumptions and conventions by which the author felt himself bound)' (p. viii). Inverting this, the uses of biography are seen to be obliquely autobiographical. Empson's traumas dominate his later criticism as they had formerly shaped his poetry, of which he said 'No grit; no pearl!'

Empson told Ricks he hoped to write more poetry when he retired but thought with most poets 'the middle bit is frightfully bad!' I would gladly exchange *Milton's God*, entertaining as its Voltairean wit may be, for *The Faces of the Buddha*, which Empson thought his best book. He sent the manuscript home from the Far East; John Davenport lost it. Kathleen Raine, who had read it, reports:

One of the contrasts made between the figures of the Christ and those of the Buddha was that, whereas it demanded supreme artistry to capture the Christlike aspect, the Buddha's face itself (not some symbol comparable to the Cross) was the Icon of the Buddhist world; an aspect capturable in its mysterious vacancy even by some ignorant village woodcarver. That expression, written upon the void itself, exerted its power upon the poet of the new void of our world of photons. The sense of the relative, the impermanence, the unreality of the appearances, opened by the scientific universe, was old in Buddhism before our civilization was born.[9]

Here, it seems, was an important bridge from the poetry to the prose. The indirect autobiography of *Using Biography,* inimitably Empsonian in its darting intelligence, its arresting ironic phrasing, and its high eccentricity – the important remarks come in asides or subordinate clauses – offers as its most generous and most useful piece the earliest, the essay on 'Tom Jones' from *The Kenyon Review.*[10] Empson asserts that Fielding set out with high moral intent, putting forward his story with double irony, conceding so much to the object of admonition that both moralists and dissidents are satisfied. Tom, who is good but always being rebuked, is 'a better Adam'. His generosity to the gamekeeper, to the highwayman and to Nightingale not only refutes Hobbes on the inevitability of egoism, it also matches Empson's own doctrine of empathy exposed in *Using Biography*:

> The novel is glowing with the noble beauty of its gospel . . . when Fielding goes really high in *Tom Jones,* his prose is like an archangel brooding over mankind and I suppose is actually imitating similar effects in Handel . . . If good by nature, you can imagine other people's feelings so directly that you have an impulse to act on them as if they were your own; and this is the source of your greatest pleasures as well as of your only genuinely unselfish actions.
>
> (pp. 135–37)

Fielding, who sympathetically understands rival moral codes, believes in humanism, liberalism, materialism and happiness on earth (p. 134): the sense of alternative points of view does not preclude judgement but confers insight. Empson accepts his aristocratic view that 'Well-brought up persons do not need to keep prying into their motives as these Nonconformist types do'; however, 'The outstanding moral of *Tom Jones* is that when a young man leaves home, he is much more in a goldfish bowl than he thinks' (pp. 136, 144).

Using Biography presents three writers from the Restoration and Augustan times (Marvell, Dryden, and Fielding) with three Modernists (Eliot, Yeats and Joyce); each permits a bash or two at God. 'Yeats probably set off from the Christian horrors but drove them steadily into the background of his world picture' (p. 137). There is a continual concern with the minutiae of *Byzantium*: he thought Yeats, when a boy, must have seen a toy golden bird, as Empson himself had done. 'The poem feels much better if one takes a waking interest in its story' (p. 186). One essay on Marvell (among the last to be written) offers the substance of Empson's Clark Lecture at Cambridge in the late 1970s, on 'Marvell's Marriage'. We saw him mount the rostrum at Mill Lane, and then with a cry of 'The wrong spectacles!' dash off again. We thought it might be a ruse to get away, but, no, he was back again, pulling many small pieces of paper out of his pockets, helping himself liberally to the erudition of Elsie Duncan-Jones, whose name he had forgotten – she was sitting in the audience.

I did not hear 'Natural Magic and Popularism' given at Hull in 1978, but Ray Brett told me that when he asked for the script, he was told there was no script. After many proddings, Empson produced that which, with a postscript of 'Other people's views', is reprinted in *Using Biography*. It tells that Marvell was employed as a London agent by various Hull merchants, who paid well; he refused to join his brother-in-law's wine firm. His career had been determined by the marriages of his elder sisters in Hull. His own London marriage was kept secret, but leaked out. He died as a result of his last visit to Hull, where he had quarrelled with the burgesses about the forthcoming Titus Oates Plot, of which he had early warning – and then walked about the marshes all night, catching malaria, which killed him soon after he returned to London. Empson goes on expanding this story of his own invention, as he does also with Dryden. Marvell's *sprezzatura* gave models to Empson as poet, but now it is the Yorkshire MP that interests him. The Yorkshire countryside, Cambridge, and the Far East were Empson's sources of power. London, Eliot's theme in *The Waste Land*, he thinks 'has just escaped from the First World War, but it is certain to be destroyed by the next one, because it is in the hands of international financiers' (p. 191). Empson ends with *The Confidential Clerk* and 'just a smack' at Eliot's Christian worship of torture. But he was always courteous personally, as when he discussed points in Marvell's poetry with me. For the Founder of Christianity he revered: 'Jesus, yes; the Church, no' is not at all uncommon today. The Voltairean Empson may be used by Jonathan Culler in *The Times Literary Supplement*[11] or by the dour Christopher Norris in *Essays in Criticism* to have a bash at some of their own Christian enemies, but the Empson they make use of was twinned with another, whose loyalties were unwavering and unexamined.

When the Queen visited Sheffield, Empson wrote a masque, *The Birth of Steel*, which attributed to her personally the entire invention of processing the metal, and he was pleased when she asked, 'Mr Empson, why don't they laugh?' He celebrated his dubbing as a knight, but one of his last recorded remarks was a disrespectful adaptation of a text; 'Isn't it *awful* about ———'s knighthood! It takes the point out of mine. Ah, well; "put not your trust in princes!" ' (His brother Charles, a former ambassador, took precedence as Knight Commander of the Order of Saint Michael and Saint George.)

For the occasion of his honorary degree at Cambridge, Empson appeared as a country gentleman, a reformed Tom Jones in a canary yellow sporting waistcoat. The proctors would have removed it from anyone taking a degree by examination, and fined the presenter, in this case the Public Orator, a bottle of port; but they could no more object to this sartorial impropriety than to the Queen Mother's hatpin, with which she firmly skewered her doctoral bonnet in place. Empson's introduction to *Using Biography* returns to his early preoccupation with Lord Rochester who 'wrote smart poems in favour of drunkenness and promiscuity; they are often exquisitely graceful, though one may reflect that his ladies were probably disagreeable'.

> But in his surviving letters and a few late poems, it becomes clear that he remained deeply in love with his wife, with whom he had eloped and hated his iron duties at court as a leader of fashion, which were plainly dragging him down to an early death. He had some conversations, with Bishop Burnet shortly before he died, which were interpreted as a complete betrayal of his previous enlightened views, in the hope of escaping from Hell; but in fact they were reasonable, responsible, and unafraid. He need not be claimed as a profound thinker, but his apparently careless verses undoubtedly proceeded from an inner conflict. Whether his life and work are tragic or ridiculous or positively good after all, only the individual reader can decide.
>
> (p. viii)

Empson too is elusive, a quicksilver Quixote always ready to couch a lance, whether at dragons or windmills. Or – not too distant in time from Quixote and his servant – there appeared King Lear and the Fool to present Empson with the opportunity to make his first and best exploration of ambiguity in Shakespeare, which is also an exploration of the two sides of Empson himself. In the dialogue of these two, it feels 'as if the Fool's talk were probably his own hallucination . . . the Fool acts as a divided personality externalised from the King'.[12]

Notes

1 Roma Gill (ed.), *William Empson* (London, Routledge, 1974) p. 15.
2 R. Fukuhara in Roma Gill (ed.) *Op. cit.*, p. 22.
3 *Seven Types of Ambiguity* (London, Chatto & Windus, 1930) p. 252.
4 Roma Gill (ed.), *Op. cit.*, p. 45.
5 *Using Biography* (London, Chatto & Windus, Hogarth Press, 1984) p. 132.

6 'The Hammer's Ring' in Reuben Brower et al. (eds), *I.A. Richards* (London, Oxford University Press, 1973) p. 79.

7 *The Sunday Times,* April 22, 1984.

8 'Wimsatt's Law' was Empson's term for 'The Intentional Fallacy'. W.K. Wimsatt's well-known article with this title was printed in his book *The Verbal Icon* in 1952.

9 Roma Gill (ed.), *Op. cit.* pp. 16–17.

10 vol XX, No. 2, Spring 1958.

11 November 23, 1984.

12 *Seven Types of Ambiguity,* p. 60. His posthumous *Essays on Shakespeare,* David B. Pirie (ed.) (Cambridge, Cambridge University Press, 1986), contains some brilliance, especially on *Hamlet,* and some nonsense.

Acknowledgements

Some of the chapters in this book started out as papers I delivered in various parts of the world, others were articles or contributions originally published elsewhere. I am grateful for permission to include them in this collection and should like to express thanks to all concerned.

Chapter I, What is 'Shakespeare'?, The editorial board of *Poetica*, vols xv–xvi, ed. Michio Masui, Tokyo, Shibun International Co. Ltd. Reprinted by permission.

Chapter III, The Building of Tragic Character in Shakespeare, and Chapter VI, *Romeo and Juliet* in Performance, first appeared in *En Torno a Shakespeare*, Fundación Instituto Shakespeare, Valencia. Reprinted by permission.

Chapter XIII, Guy Butler; South African Scene appeared as ' "A dome of many-coloured Glass", a tribute to the president of the Shakespeare Association of Southern Africa' in *Olive Schreiner and After* (Cape Town, David Philip Publisher Ltd, 1983). Reprinted by permission.

Chapter XIV, Sir William Empson (1906–84) was first published as 'Sir William Empson (1906–1984): A Memoir' in *The Kenyon Review*, New Series, Fall 1985, vol. VII, No. 4. © 1985 Kenyon College. Reprinted by permission.

Chapter IX, Publication and Performance in Blackfriars' Drama, was first published as 'Publication and Performance in Early Stuart Drama: Jonson, Webster, Heywood' in J.C. Gray (ed.), *Mirror up to Shakespeare: Essays in Honour of G.R. Hibbard* (Toronto, University of Toronto Press, 1984). Reprinted by permission.

The following works are reprinted (copyright of the author):

Chapter II 'The Cause of Wit in Other Men' *Shakespeare in Southern Africa, Journal of the Shakespeare Society of Southern Africa*, vol. I, 1987.

Chapter V, Love and Courtesy in *The Two Gentlemen of Verona, Atti e Memorie della Academia di Agricoltura Scienze e Lettere di Verona*, Serie VI, vol. XXXVII.

Chapter IV, Social Nuances in Shakespeare's Early Comedies, in Peter Bilton et al. (eds), *Essays in Honour of Kristian Smidt* (Oslo, University of Oslo, Institute of English Studies, 1986).

Chapter VIII, The Politics of Pageantry, was first published in Antony Coleman and Antony Hammond (eds), *Poetry and Drama 1570–1700: Essays in Honour of Harold F. Brooks* (London, Methuen, 1981).

Other works appear for the first time.

I wish warmly to thank Jackie Jones of Harvester Wheatsheaf and Serena Jones of Woodhead-Faulkner for their help towards this work, as well as Julia Allen for checking the manuscript most meticulously. The remaining mistakes are my own.

Books and Essays by Muriel C. Bradbrook 1978–88

An earlier list was compiled by Patricia Rignold in Marie Axton and Raymond Williams (eds) *English Drama, Forms and Developments* (Cambridge, Cambridge University Press, 1977).

1978   *Shakespeare, the Poet and his World* (London, Weidenfeld, New York, Columbia University Press); *George Chapman* (London, Longman for the British Council).

'Marvell and the Masque' in K. Friedenreich (ed.), *Tercentenary Essays in Honor of Andrew Marvell* (New York, Archon Books).

'Intention and Design in *October Ferry to Gabriola*' in Anne Smith (ed.), *The Art of Malcolm Lowry* (London, The Vision Press).

1979   *A History of Elizabethan Drama* (Cambridge, Cambridge University Press), six volumes previously published.

'Marvell our contemporary' in R.L. Brett (ed.), *Andrew Marvell* (Oxford/Hull University Presses).

'Shakespeare and the Multiple Theatres of Jacobean London' in G.R. Hibbard (ed.), *Elizabethan Theatre VI* (Toronto, Macmillan of Canada).

1980   *John Webster Citizen and Dramatist* (London, Weidenfeld, New York, Columbia University Press).

'Shakespeare's Recollections of Marlowe' in Ewbank, Edwards and Hunter (eds), *Shakespeare Styles* (Cambridge, Cambridge University Press).

'*Measure for Measure*' in *Poetry and Drama in the English Renaissance: in Honour of Jero Ozu* (Tokyo, Kino Kuniya Bookstore Co.).

1981   'Herbert's Ground' in Anne Barton (ed.), *Essays and Studies 1981* (London, John Murray).

'Doing Literature on Dover Beach' in John Agresto and Peter Reisenberg (eds), *The Humanist as Citizen* (Chapel Hill, University of North Carolina Press).

'The Politics of Pageantry' in Antony Coleman and Antony Hammond (eds), *Poetry and Drama 1550–1700: Essays in Honour of Harold Brooks* (London, Methuen).

Collected Papers Vol I: Artist and Society in Shakespeare's England, Vol II: Women and Literature (Brighton, Harvester Press and Totowa NJ, Barnes & Noble).

Thomas Heywood *Essays in Theatre I* (Guelph Ontario, University of Guelph), reprinted in *Collected Papers*, vol. III.

'Queenie Leavis, the Dynamics of Rejection' *Cambridge Review*, vol. ciii, No. 2265, Reprinted in *Collected Papers*, vol. II.

1983 *Collected Papers Vol III: Aspects of Dramatic Form in the English and Irish Renaissance* (Brighton, Harvester Press and Totowa NJ, Barnes & Noble).

'A dome of many-coloured Glass' in Van Wyk Smith and Maclennan (eds), *Olive Schreiner and after* (Cape Town, David Philip Publisher Ltd).

1984 *Muriel Bradbrook on Shakespeare* (Brighton, Harvester Press)
'Publication and Performance in Early Stuart Drama' in J.C. Gray (ed.), *Mirror up to Shakespeare* (Toronto, University of Toronto Press).

'Vacláv Havel's Second Wind', *Modern Drama*, vol. XXVII, no. 1.
'Nor shall my Sword . . .' in Denys Thompson (ed.), *The Leavises* (Cambridge, Cambridge University Press).

'Ut Pictura Poesis and the Shakespearean Theatre' in Scattergood (ed.), *Literature and Learning: Essays in Honour of Fitzroy Pyle* (Dublin, Irish University Press).

1985 'London Pageants and Lawyers' Theatre' in Erickson and Kahn (eds), *Shakespeare's Rough Magic: Essays in Honour of C.L. Barber* (Newark, Delaware University Press).

'Sir William Empson (1906–1984): A Memoir', *The Kenyon Review*, New Series, vol. VII, No. 4;

'The Cause of Wit in Other Men' (Grahamstown, Shakespeare Society of South Africa, published 1987).

'Shakespeare and his Contemporaries' in John F. Andrews (ed.), *Shakespeare, his World, his Work, his Influence* (New York, Scribner's Sons), three vols.

1986 'What is "Shakespeare"?' *Poetica*, vols xxv–xxvi, ed. Michio Masui (Tokyo, Shibun International Co. Ltd).

The Tempest, Bunraku (Tokyo, Tokyo University), in Japanese.

'Social Nuances in Shakespeare's early Comedies' in Peter Bilton *et al.* (eds), *Essays in Honour of Kristian Smidt* (Oslo, Oslo University Press).

1987 'When Everyone is Somebody' in P. Edwards (ed.), *K.M. 80: Essays in Honour of K. Muir* (Liverpool, Liverpool University Press).

'Love and Courtesy in *Two Gentlemen of Verona*' *Atti e Memorie della Academia di Agricoltura Scienze e Lettere di Verona*, Serie VI, vol. xxxvii.

'The Building of Shakespeare's Tragic Character' in M.A. Conajero (ed.), *En Torno a Shakespeare* (Valencia, Fundación Instituto Shakespeare).

Reviews in *The Guardian, The Listener, Shakespeare Quarterly.*

Forthcoming:
'Lowry in Cambridge' in Sue Vice (ed.) *Lowry 80 years on* (London, Methuen).

'Castiglione, Lyly and Shakespeare's *Two Gentlemen of Verona*' in R. Mulryne and M. Shewring (eds), *English and Italian Theatre of the Renaissance* (London, Macmillan).